Jacksonian Democracy

in New Hampshire

Donald B. Cole

Jacksonian Democracy in New Hampshire, 1800-1851

Harvard University Press

Cambridge, Massachusetts

1970

For Henry and Phil

Preface

My interest in Jacksonian Democracy goes back to my college days when I listened to Professor Frederick Merk discuss the New Hampshire Democrats. A short time later my interest was renewed when I read Arthur Schlesinger's *Age of Jackson* aboard ship in the Pacific. Since then I have considered Isaac Hill and his followers in many contexts but have always remembered the geographic and economic insights of professors Merk and Schlesinger.

Many persons helped me gather material for this book. I am grateful to the following for permission to quote from manuscript collections: Mr. P. Blair Lee, Mr. John P. H. Chandler, the New Hampshire Historical Society, the Houghton Library at Harvard University, the Connecticut Historical Society, the Astor, Lenox, and Tilden Foundations of the New York Public Library, the New-York Historical Society, and the Huntington Library. Librarians at the Davis Library of the Phillips Exeter Academy, at the New Hampshire Historical Society, at the New Hampshire State Library, and in the Manuscript Division of the Library of Congress were particularly helpful. I especially want to thank Mrs. Margaret P. Tate and Mrs. Norbert B. Lacy.

Other scholars shared the results of their own investigations. Herbert W. Hill answered my questions about New Hampshire politics and provided a photograph of the portrait of Isaac Hill.

Mark D. Kaplanoff tempered my thinking on the political structure of Federalist and Republican New Hampshire. Vincent J. Capowski offered many clues to the early career of Levi Woodbury. Nobel Peterson confirmed my hunches about soil conditions in the Granite State. Edward Pessen and William Greenleaf disciplined my treatment of the locofoco movement. Robert V. Remini and Richard H. Sewell read the next-to-last draft and made valuable suggestions. I am particularly grateful to Frank Otto Gatell, who let me read his notes on banking in New Hampshire and who subjected my first six chapters to a searching examination. My colleagues Henry F. Bedford and Henry W. Bragdon analyzed the entire manuscript with painstaking care. Their judgment and encouragement contributed immeasurably to the book.

This research began in 1959 with a sabbatical leave granted by the Trustees of the Phillips Exeter Academy. Mrs. Jonathan S. Hoxie and Mrs. Edgar Savage turned messy drafts into spendidly typed copy. John C. Warren, Martin Carmichael III, and Leslie Koepplin initiated me into the world of quantification. Robert N. Richardson transformed two rough sketches and the cluttered page of an old atlas into handsome maps. John F. Page, Director of the New Hampshire Historical Society, furnished a photograph of the portrait of Levi Woodbury.

Any book is a family affair. My sons Douglas, Robert, and Daniel, and my daughter Susan have checked footnotes, improved style, and, most important, cared about the progress of the work. As always, their mother has smoothed my way, making research and writing possible. New Hampshire Jacksonians have shared our home for over a decade; my wife and children made the visitors welcome.

Donald B. Cole

Exeter, New Hampshire
May 1970

Contents

I   The Summer of 1832   1

II The Republican Origins of Jacksonian
    Democracy, 1800–1822   16

III The Rise of the Democratic Party, 1822–1829   47

IV Jacksonians in Washington, 1829–1832   82

V   The Bank War, 1829–1837   102

VI The Presidential Election of 1832   136

VII The Jacksonian Commonwealth in the 1830's   160

VIII Radical Democracy, 1836–1846   185

IX The Slavery War, 1843–1851   216

X   Presidential Politics and the Passing of
    a Generation, 1843–1851   234

    Conclusion   246

    Appendix   248

    Bibliography   257

    Index   275

Maps

1. New Hampshire c. 1829   2
2. Presidential Election of 1832   141
3. Geographic Regions of New Hampshire   143

Illustrations

Isaac Hill   7
Levi Woodbury   8

Jacksonian Democracy
in New Hampshire

The early history of the Democratic Party in New Hampshire presents an opportunity to reassess the Jacksonian scholarship of the twentieth century. As the story unfolds, it confirms a number of the well-known interpretations and suggests that there is no suitable single explanation for the national movement. Regional patterns confirm the geographical interpretation of Frederick Jackson Turner; the fight over the Bank of the United States supports the class-struggle ideas of Arthur M. Schlesinger, Jr.; and voting statistics sustain Richard P. McCormick's view that democracy in America did not begin with the election of Andrew Jackson. Isaac Hill was a bank director and railroad promoter in the entrepreneurial tradition of Bray Hammond; Democrats spoke in the rhetoric outlined by Marvin Meyers; and the symbolic image of John W. Ward's Andrew Jackson hovered constantly over the scene.

But although the story supports a synthesis, it also suggests that the older interpretations of Turner and Schlesinger are more valid in New Hampshire than the views of the recent consensus school. There was political continuity from the Jefferson party to the party of Jackson. Because the roots of Jacksonian Democracy in New Hampshire go back before the War of 1812, I begin this study with the election of 1800. Once the second party system was formed after 1825, Democrats represented a different economic group than did National Republicans and Whigs. Democrats, furthermore, disagreed with their opponents on many issues. In short, "Jacksonian Democracy" is a legitimate concept in the history of New Hampshire politics.

I

The Summer of 1832

Late in July 1832, a few weeks after he had vetoed the bill to
recharter the Bank of the United States, Andrew Jackson left
Washington on his way home to the Hermitage. The President,
who was fleeing the cholera, planned a vacation before the political campaign in the fall. At Wheeling, Virginia, where he was
taking the boat down the Ohio River, he met Senator Isaac Hill
of New Hampshire, who was on a political tour of western Pennsylvania and eastern Ohio. As the Old General shook Hill's hand
in farewell, he supposedly predicted: "Isaac, it'll be a walk [the
forthcoming election]! If our fellows didn't raise a finger from
now on, the thing would be just as well done. In fact, Isaac, it's
done now."[1]

1. The quotation is taken from a letter from Hill to Thomas Green of New
York, Oct. 8, 1832, cited in Augustus C. Buell, *History of Andrew Jackson*
(New York, 1904), II, 271. Unfortunately, I have been unable to find the
original. Since Buell is notoriously untrustworthy, the words are not necessarily
accurate. Like many of Buell's quotations, however, this one does express the
flavor of the historical scene. Claude Bowers, who is also unreliable, tells the
same story in *The Party Battles of the Jackson Period* (New York, 1922), pp.
250-251. Buell and Bowers incorrectly state that Jackson left Washington in
August. He actually left on Monday, July 24, with Governor John Breathitt of
Kentucky and reached Lexington, Kentucky, July 28. He probably saw Hill at
Wheeling on July 25 or 26. [Washington, D.C.] *Daily Globe*, July 24, 1832;
Andrew Jackson to Andrew Jackson, Jr., July 28, 1832, Aug. 10, 1832, Andrew
Jackson Papers, Library of Congress (LC). There is a reference to Hill's cam-
paigning in Harrisburg, Pennsylvania, in *Niles' Weekly Register*, 42 (July 28,
1832), 395.

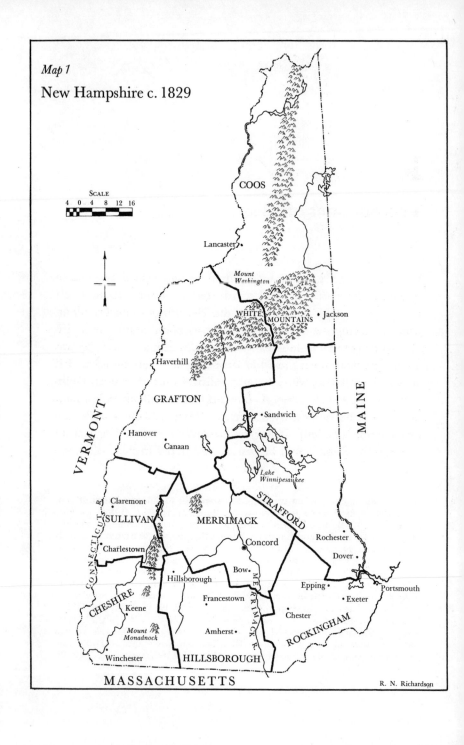

Map 1

New Hampshire c. 1829

SCALE
4 0 4 8 12 16

COOS

Lancaster

Mount Washington

WHITE MOUNTAINS

Jackson

Haverhill

GRAFTON

Sandwich

Hanover

Canaan

Lake Winnipesaukee

VERMONT

MAINE

Claremont

STRAFFORD

SULLIVAN

MERRIMACK

Concord

Rochester

Charlestown

Dover

Bow

Hillsborough

Epping

Portsmouth

CHESHIRE

Francestown

Exeter

Keene

Chester

Mount Monadnock

Amherst

ROCKINGHAM

Winchester

HILLSBOROUGH

MASSACHUSETTS

CONNECTICUT R.

MERRIMACK R.

R. N. Richardson

Back in Concord, New Hampshire, two weeks later, Hill was guest of honor at a Democratic dinner at the Eagle Hotel and Coffee House, opposite the state capitol. After dinner he launched into a heated defense of Jackson's first presidential term. He praised the veto of the bill to provide federal funds for a road from Maysville to Lexington, Kentucky, because the veto had checked a dangerous trend toward a general policy of internal improvements at federal expense. The Bank Bill veto would soon destroy a privileged monopoly. Hill described his hard fight in Washington to protect the common people. It was a lonely fight, he said, because he was the only Democratic Senator from New England. (Henry Clay called him "a still small voice from the East.") Hill concluded with a summary of his Jacksonian Democratic faith: "A limited Government, State Rights, Rotation in Office, Economy in the public expenditures, no unnecessary taxation, and universal Liberty and Equality."[2]

Isaac Hill was the eldest son in a poor family of nine children. He was born in Cambridge, Massachusetts, in 1788 and traced his ancestry back five generations to Abraham Hill, who in 1640 was a freeman of Charlestown, Massachusetts. There was a history of insanity in the family: both his father and his grandfather were intermittently insane. The burden of bringing up the large family thus rested on Isaac Hill's mother and before long on Hill himself. It was a heavy burden because, after a childhood injury, he was lame throughout his life. When he was ten, the family moved to a farm in Ashburnham, Massachusetts, near the New Hampshire border. Here Hill received a few months of formal education, but otherwise he taught himself.[3]

Poverty, deformity, and the lack of a father shaped Hill. Self-educated, forced to care for himself at an early age, he grew up believing in the values of independence, hard work, and thrift.

2. *Proceedings at the Dinner to Honorable Isaac Hill, at the Eagle Coffee House, . . . Concord, N.H., August 8, 1832* (Concord, N.H., 1832).
3. Cyrus P. Bradley, *Biography of Isaac Hill* (Concord, N.H., 1835), pp. 1–11, 153. Bradley does not describe the childhood injury that caused Hill's lameness.

Perhaps because he was small and crippled, perhaps because his father was insane, Hill was often defensive. When he was twenty-five years old, he wrote sadly that he wished he had "grown up and flourished under the benignant smiles and patronage" of a real father. Whatever the reasons, Hill was aggressive and often vindictive—all in all, a fighter—throughout his career.[4]

Since his lameness ruled out farming, in 1802 Hill at fourteen was apprenticed to Joseph Cushman, the publisher of the *Farmer's Cabinet* in the village of Amherst in southern New Hampshire. When he was an old man, he recalled those early years in Amherst: picking berries in the hot August sun, reading the Bible by a blazing fire on a December night, working at his printing craft for small wages, listening to tales of the Revolution told by old veterans, contending with other young men in the debating society.

After seven years of saving his earnings at Amherst, Hill moved north to Concord to become owner of the *New-Hampshire Patriot*. He arrived in the slush and cold of early April 1809, the day before his twenty-first birthday. In the first issue of the *Patriot* he said that he had been "educated in the simplicity of truth, early taught to revere the patriots of '75," that his "juvenile years" had been Republican, and that he had "detested tyranny." "The axioms of political morality, as expressed by" Washington, Jefferson, and Madison, were "precisely those" he would follow. He added: "In our views of parties . . . we consider the contest . . . between the friends of our own independence, of our government, and our rights—and our enemies, the friends of a foreign nation." The position never changed, for throughout his career Hill continued to call on the spirit of the Revolution, the founding fathers, and Republicanism.[5]

After 1814, when he married Susan Ayer, who came from a prosperous Concord family, he became socially prominent. He helped found the first Episcopal church in Concord; he was a

4. Hill to Woodbury, Nov. 29, 1813, Levi Woodbury Papers, LC.
5. [Concord] *New Hampshire Patriot*, April 18, 1809; Bradley, *Hill*, pp. 1–23.

founder of "The New Hampshire United Society for the more general diffusion of useful knowledge, and for the promotion of good morals." In addition he was a trustee of the New Hampshire Literary Institution, a member of the New Hampshire Historical Society, and a director of the Merrimack Agricultural Society.[6] Hill also succeeded economically. He came to Concord with little money, but he gradually accumulated property. He made a good income from his newspaper, which had a wide circulation, and which was paid by the federal government for delivering the mail and for printing the federal statutes. He also had a bookstore, which was the largest in New Hampshire. To house his newspaper, printing shop, and bookstore as well as to rent office space, Hill built a large, three-story brick block on Main Street in Concord next to the capitol. He was a director of the Concord and Union Boating Company. He had money invested in two insurance companies, several factories, one silkworm company, and two Vermont newspapers. From his "fifty acres of bottom land" near the Merrimack River in Concord he harvested in one year forty-five tons of hay, 350 bushels of oats, 150 bushels of corn, and 700 bushels of potatoes. To cap it all he was a director of the Merrimack County Bank.[7]

Despite his many business ventures, politics dominated Hill's life. He used the columns of his newspaper effectively to defend his political views and to promote the interests of the Democratic-Republican Party. By 1828 the *New-Hampshire Patriot* was one

6. Bradley, *Hill*, pp. 142–158; Francis E. Robinson, "Isaac Hill," unpublished thesis, University of New Hampshire, June 1933, p. 7; Minot Hill, "The Life of Isaac Hill," unpublished paper, Phillips Exeter Academy, 1958; Hill to Woodbury, Jan. 17, 1815, Woodbury Papers, LC; Vincent Capowski, Jr., "The Making of a Jacksonian Democrat: Levi Woodbury 1789–1831," unpublished dissertation, Fordham University, 1965, p. 57. Though he came from a long line of Yankees, Hill was not a Congregationalist and throughout his career he opposed the Congregational Church. He attended both Episcopal and Methodist churches.

7. Hill to Nathaniel Russell, Sept. 16, 1830, Hill Papers; Bradley, *Hill*, pp. 142–147; Robinson, "Hill," pp. 28, 38; Hill to General Benjamin Pierce, Nov. 4, 1837, Hill Papers, New Hampshire Historical Society (NHHS) (henceforth called Hill Papers).

in a string of Democratic newspapers that brought about the election of Andrew Jackson. After his election in 1830, Hill became a well-known Democratic Senator in Washington.[8]

In 1832 Isaac Hill's Concord was a farming town, barely fifty miles back from the northern frontier. But as the state capital with almost 4,000 people, it was a busy place, the third largest town in New Hampshire. Clothing mills, bark mills, tanneries, and the Abbot-Downing Stagecoach Company provided alternatives to farming. Woodsmen cut logs to the west, and in the spring rafts of lumber floated down the swollen Merrimack River to Lowell, Massachusetts. From Main Street, the center of Concord, the land sloped upward toward hills in the west and eastward down to the Merrimack.[9]

Concord was the transportation center of the state. Trim boats measuring sixty feet by ten feet made the round trip down the Merrimack River and the Middlesex Canal to Boston in seven to ten days. Roads fanned out of Concord north along the Merrimack, past Lake Winnipesaukee, through the mountains to the upper reaches of the Connecticut River. To the west a road passed through the village of Hillsborough on to the Connecticut River at Charlestown and Claremont. Other well-traveled roads led east to the seacoast region at Exeter, Dover, and Portsmouth. Twenty-two stages a week departed for Boston, six for Portsmouth, five for Lake Winnipesaukee, and twenty-nine more for other destinations.[10]

Concord lay in the midst of the hilly interior part of the state, midway between the southeastern seacoast region and the western Connecticut River Valley. Although the seacoast and

8. Bradley, *Hill*, pp. 28–114.

9. *Patriot*, June 27, 1815; Abial Rolfe, *Reminiscences of Concord or Personal Recollections of Seventy Years* (Penacook, N.H., 1901), pp. 46–57; Henry McFarland, *Sixty Years in Concord and Elsewhere: Personal Recollections of Henry McFarland* (Concord, N.H., 1899), pp. 12–72.

10. Rolfe, *Reminiscences*, pp. 52–57, 95; McFarland, *Sixty Years*; H. C. Carey and I. Lea, *Geographical, Statistical, and Historical Map of New Hampshire* (Philadelphia, 1822); Nathaniel Bouton, *The History of Concord from Its First Grant in 1725 to the Origins of the City Government in 1853* (Concord, N.H., 1856), pp. 398–399, 404.

Isaac Hill shortly before his death in 1851.

valley were most densely populated, many people lived in the
hills. Farmers often preferred the hills because the high land
dried more rapidly in the spring. Furthermore, hard oaks, maples,
and beeches grew on the hills, while the valleys were filled with
soft white pine. The pine was good for inside carpentry work,
but the farmers preferred the hard wood for lumber and fuel,

Levi Woodbury (1789–1851).

liked the leaves for mulch, and tapped the maple trees for syrup. The hill farmer read the Bible and disciplined his children. He was thrifty and independent. Isolated, suspicious of the prosperous communities along the seacoast and in the Connecticut Valley and hostile to Washington, D.C., he became the backbone of the Jackson party in New Hampshire.[11]

While Senator Hill received the plaudits of his Concord friends, the other leading New Hampshire Democrat, Secretary of the Navy Levi Woodbury, remained in Washington preparing for trouble with South Carolina that became the nullification crisis in November. Like Hill, Woodbury, who was born in 1789, was in his early forties in the summer of 1832 and had descended from an old American family. He could trace his ancestry back to John Woodbury, who arrived at Cape Ann, Massachusetts, in 1623. His grandfather, James Woodbury, fought at Quebec in the French and Indian War. By 1770 both of his grandfathers had settled in Amherst, New Hampshire, where in April 1776, they signed a pledge to resist Parliament. His father, Peter Woodbury, farmed a sunny ridge in the interior village of Francestown, cultivated shipping interests in Portsmouth, and served for fifteen years in the New Hampshire legislature. Levi Woodbury came from good Republican stock, for his mother was related to former Republican Governor John Langdon of Portsmouth.[12]

Woodbury's education far surpassed Hill's. At Atkinson Academy he showed both ability and early Federalist leanings with an essay calling John Langdon a "firebrand" and "a pest of society." In 1805 Woodbury went to Dartmouth College, where

11. Harold F. Wilson, *The Hill Country of Northern New England: Its Social and Economic History, 1790–1930* (New York, 1936), pp. 16, 53, 124–127; John Hayward, *A Gazeteer of New Hampshire . . .* (Boston, 1849).

12. Charles L. Woodbury, "Levi Woodbury," New England Historic Genealogical Society, *Memorial Biographies* I (1845–1852), 295–327; Capowski, "Woodbury," pp. 3–5; Woodbury to John Farmer, April 30, 1819, Mar. 5, 1826, Woodbury Papers, New Hampshire Historical Society; Philip D. Wheaton, "Levi Woodbury—Jacksonian Financier," unpublished dissertation, University of Maryland, 1955, p. ii.

he soon became a Republican and where he met Amos Kendall, who later served with him in Jackson's cabinet. After graduating in 1809, Woodbury sought out a congenial atmosphere in various law offices, first in Litchfield, Connecticut, next in Boston, then in Exeter. In 1812 he settled down to practice law back home in Francestown.[13]

Something of a Puritan, Woodbury often worked sixteen hours a day and spent time on Sunday writing "examinations of conscience." At the age of twenty-three he listed "Faults and improprieties to be corrected," including "Hawking and spitting on the floor." Born to power and position, he had none of Hill's irascibility, could afford to be "bland and kind," and was "never irritable." Yet he lacked the skill of ingratiating himself with fellow politicians. One Democrat writing to President Jackson remarked that Woodbury had "but little of the *suavitur in modo*." Cautious and slow to commit himself, Woodbury was far less aggressive than Hill.[14]

Marriage to Elizabeth Clapp in 1819 changed Woodbury's career. Asa Clapp, Elizabeth's father, was one of the richest merchants and leading Republicans in Maine. James Monroe recognized Clapp's position by staying at his home in Portland on his New England tour in 1817, and thirty years later, President Polk did likewise. Elizabeth Clapp brought a dowry of $50,000, and her father gave the couple a three-story home in Portsmouth. Socially and economically, Woodbury was now secure. Politically, the move to Portsmouth gave him a seacoast connection to go with his inland base in Francestown. His alliance with hill Republican farmers and coastal Republican

13. Woodbury's essay on Langdon, dated April 6, 1805, is in the Woodbury Papers, LC, and is quoted in Capowski, "Woodbury," p. 8. See also Capowski, "Woodbury," pp. 6–12, 18–38; William Stickney, ed., *Autobiography of Amos Kendall* (Boston, 1872), pp. 14–35.

14. Alfred Balch to Andrew Jackson, July 21, 1831, *Correspondence of Andrew Jackson*, ed. John S. Bassett (Washington, 1926–1935), IV, 314–315; Woodbury, "Woodbury"; *Dictionary of American Biography*, s.v. "Woodbury, Levi"; Woodbury, Memorandum Book, July 12, 1812, Woodbury Papers, LC.

merchants made him a powerful figure in New Hampshire and an important ally for Isaac Hill.[15]

The Woodbury-Hill alliance dominated New Hampshire politics from the War of 1812 until the 1840's. The alliance was never easy, and when tensions developed, the Republican, later the Democratic Party, went through periods of dissension. On the national scene, Woodbury and Hill became spokesmen for New England Democrats. Between 1816 and 1832 Woodbury was successively justice of the state Superior Court, governor, representative to the state lower house, United States Senator, and Secretary of the Navy.

The seacoast region, where the Woodburys lived after 1819, was a lowland area in the southeast corner of the state, including some twenty-five towns, running from the Atlantic Ocean in the east to Epping in the west and from Milton in the north to Kingston in the south. Most of the towns were watered by small streams that ran to the sea (see Maps 1 and 3). The first settled and most densely populated part of the state, it also had the most industry. The area naturally controlled the early politics of the state; from John Wentworth in 1723 to John Taylor Gilman in 1815, all governors except two lived on or near the seacoast.[16]

Portsmouth in 1832 was a city of over 8,000 people, the largest in New Hampshire, but only twenty-fifth in the nation. As Concord still had a frontier appearance, Portsmouth still retained its colonial charm. Here in the first capital of New Hampshire, royal governors had ruled and entertained. Here along Middle and State streets, merchants and ship captains had built imposing three-story, federal-style homes. Portsmouth had long been a thriving seaport. John Paul Jones lived there in 1778 while carpenters and shipwrights were building the *Ranger*. In 1828 the Portsmouth shipyard completed the eighteen-gun U.S.S. *Concord*,

15. Capowski, "Woodbury," pp. 86–94.
16. In 1840 $3.4 million of the $9 million invested in New Hampshire manufacturing was invested in the seacoast region. United States Census Office, *Sixth Census or Enumeration of the Inhabitants of the United States . . . 1840* (Washington, D.C., 1841), pp. 23–34.

and the seventy-four-gun *Alabama* and forty-four-gun *Santee* were still on the ways. Ships for China sailed from Portsmouth, arriving home two years later laden with pepper, silks, Souchong tea, Canton dishware, California leather, and Patna opium. To finance such trading Portsmouth had a half dozen banks with a combined capital of over a million dollars. In addition Portsmouth had a branch of the Second Bank of the United States.[17]

Nearby was Exeter, once the home of old Federalist governor John Taylor Gilman. With its trim white houses and elm-lined streets, Exeter was busy and neat. First its shipyards, then its textile mill had brought capital and prosperity to the town. The Phillips Exeter Academy, established in 1781 to teach its students the "great end and real business of living," had already attracted as students Lewis Cass, Daniel Webster, Jared Sparks, Edward Everett, John Gorham Palfrey, and George Bancroft.[18]

Like Concord, Portsmouth and Exeter were transportation centers; and even more than Concord the two seacoast communities were closely connected with Massachusetts. Partly because of roads and ship lanes, partly because of business and political ties, Portsmouth and Exeter looked toward the Bay State. Stages left Portsmouth Monday, Wednesday, and Saturday for Boston, while ocean-going ships carried people and cargo south. Letters reached Boston in two days. There were also ties with Concord and the north: two roads from Portsmouth through Exeter went to Concord; two more reached north from Portsmouth into the White Mountains. By 1840 two of the first three railroads from Boston to New Hampshire ran to Exeter and Portsmouth. [19]

17. *Niles' Register,* 37 (1828), 84; Charles A. Hazlett, *Portsmouth in the Year 1824* (Portsmouth, N.H., 1912). J. D. B. De Bow, *Statistical View of the United States . . . Being a Compendium of the Seventh Census . . .* (Washington, D.C., 1854), p. 192.

18. The Phillips Exeter Academy, *The Charter and Constitution of the Phillips Exeter Academy* (Exeter, N.H., 1953); Myron Williams, *The Story of Phillips Exeter* (Exeter, N.H., 1957); C. H. Bell, *History of the Town of Exeter, New Hampshire* (Exeter, N.H., 1888).

19. Hazlett, *Portsmouth.*

By 1832 Hill in Concord, Woodbury in Portsmouth, and the other New Hampshire Jacksonians had become masters of the state's political system. Politics began in March with town meeting, when voters elected Congressmen and state and local officials. All adult males could vote, but only Protestants and property owners could serve in the Senate or House of Representatives. The legislature did not meet until the first week of June because until then the roads were too muddy and farmers were too busy with spring planting. On Thursday morning—called election day—the new governor gave his inaugural address, after which politicians paraded from the state house to the Old North Church to hear the election day sermon. Work began on Friday. If a United States Senator's term was about to end, the legislature selected a new one, and every two years the parties nominated Congressmen. The legislature then settled down to about three weeks of debating and passing bills.[20]

New Hampshire crammed its official business into a week in March and three weeks in June, but politics went on all year. Besides the regular meetings there were frequent party gatherings to set up platforms, to select delegates, and to nominate candidates. Once every four years, the state legislature reconvened after the presidential election to apportion the state tax load. Politics in New Hampshire provided diversion from the unremitting chores of farming. Town meeting came before spring planting; the state legislature met before haying; the federal election and tax session followed the fall harvest.

Economically and socially, New Hampshire was similar to many other northern states in 1832. It was still predominantly white and Protestant, agricultural and rural; yet like the other

20. New Hampshire had a twelve-man Senate, whose members had to be Protestant and own a freehold estate worth at least £200, and a House of Representatives of slightly over 200 members, all Protestants and owning estates worth at least £100. New Hampshire Constitution of 1784. The constitution is conveniently found in Everett S. Stackpole, *History of New Hampshire* (New York, 1917), III, 355–369. See also Thorsten Kalijarvi and William C. Chamberlin, *The Government of New Hampshire* (Durham, N.H., 1939), pp. 60–63; Rolfe, *Reminiscences*, p. 30.

states it was changing. The industrial growth of the 1820's had brought the percentage of nonfarm workers up to about 20 percent. About 14 percent of the people lived in towns of over 2,500. Although New Hampshire people consumed much of what they produced, such as corn, rye, beef, fish, cloth, and lumber, they were beginning to export textiles, ashes, and a variety of agricultural products. With forty cotton mills in 1831, the state ranked seventh in the nation, and it was third in yards of cotton cloth produced. Ten state banks in 1820 had become twenty-one in 1832. In short, New Hampshire was beginning to industrialize.[21]

In the summer of 1832 the political and economic systems of New Hampshire were working the way Democrats wanted them to work. The Democratic machine had carried the state by almost 10,000 votes in March and would continue to dominate the state until 1855. The state was prosperous. Democratic farmers, mechanics, businessmen, and bankers were taking advantage of rapid economic growth. In Washington, Isaac Hill and Levi Woodbury were strongly entrenched in the federal government. Jacksonian Democracy in New Hampshire was thriving.

21. New Hampshire in 1830 had a total population of 269,328, of which all but 607 were white. The population in towns over 2,500 was 37,840, or 14 percent of the total; only Portsmouth with 8,082 had over 8,000 in population. *Manual for the General Court, 1957* (Concord, N.H., 1957), pp. 269–271; *Patriot*, April 11, 1831; United States Census Office, *Abstract of the Returns of the Fifth Census Showing the Number of Free People, the Number of Slaves* . . ., House Document 263, 22nd Congress, 1st Session (Washington, D.C., 1832), pp. 4, 48. The United States as a whole had 9 percent of its population living in towns over 8,000, compared to only 3 percent in New Hampshire (all in Portsmouth). *The Statistical History of the United States from Colonial Times to the Present* (Stamford, Conn., 1965), p. 9. In 1820 nonfarm workers in New Hampshire totaled 9,767 (16 percent) out of a work force of 62,151. In 1840 the nonfarm workers in the state were 21,508 (22 percent) in a work force of 99,447. John Farmer and Jacob B. Moore, *A Gazeteer of the State of New Hampshire 1823* (Concord, N.H., 1823), pp. 40, 64; United States Census Office, *Compendium of the Enumeration of the Inhabitants and Statistics as Obtained at the Department of State, from the Returns of the Sixth Census* . . . (Washington, D.C., 1841), p. 7. In the United States there were 1.2 million nonfarm

workers in 1830 out of a total of 3.9 million, or 31 percent. *Statistical History*, p. 72. Cotton manufacturing statistics were as follows in 1831:

	Spindles	Mills	Males Employed	Females Employed
United States	1,246,703	801	18,590	38,927
New Hampshire	113,776	40	875	4,090

Guy S. Callender, *Selections from the Economic History of the United States, 1765–1860* (Boston, 1909), p. 469. For other data see John Farmer, *The New Hampshire Annual Register and United States Calendar, 1829* (Concord, N.H., 1829), and John Farmer, *The New Hampshire Annual Register and U.S. Calendar, 1838* (Concord, N.H., 1838). There is an excellent survey of economic conditions in early nineteenth century New Hampshire in Norman W. Smith, "A History of Commercial Banking in New Hampshire 1792–1843," unpublished dissertation, University of Wisconsin, 1967. See also *Laws of New Hampshire*, June 1821, appendix, p. 30; John Reid, "Doe's World," manuscript, University of New Hampshire Library, n.d.; John Reid, *Chief Justice: The Judicial World of Charles Doe* (Cambridge, Mass., 1967).

II

The Republican Origins of
Jacksonian Democracy, 1800-1822

The roots of Jacksonian Democracy in New Hampshire went back to 1800. In recent years historians have denied that there was continuity from the first two-party system at the turn of the century to the second a quarter century later. Richard McCormick, for example, wrote that the second system did not "represent merely the revival in new form of pre-existing party alignments." It was, he added, "distinctive . . . differing in the circumstances of its origins and in many general characteristics from earlier and later party systems." In New Hampshire, however, the evidence suggests that there was great continuity between the party battles of the Jefferson and Jackson years.[1]

The first two-party system was fully developed by 1801 when the election of Thomas Jefferson ended twelve years of Federalist administration. Federalists everywhere were alarmed at their loss of power. Fisher Ames of Massachusetts feared that Jefferson's election endangered "order at home"; "rights" and "property," he wrote, were "subject to the vice and folly and poverty of the society." In New Hampshire, where Federalists were espe-

---

1. Richard McCormick, *The Second American Party System: Party Formation in the Jacksonian Era* (Chapel Hill, N.C., 1966), pp. 13–14. For a brief summary of party formation in New Hampshire see *ibid.*, pp. 54–62.

cially upset, Congregational ministers described the disaster that would follow. Federalist lawyer George Sullivan of Exeter warned of the dangers in Republicanism: "Our country nourishes in her bosom a faction," he said, "devoted to the interests of France, which plots the destruction of our national government, and . . . veils its hostile design beneath the garb of patriotism."[2]

Sullivan was frightened because in the spring of 1800 the Republicans for the first time seriously challenged Federalists for the governor's seat. During the 1790's New Hampshire was a one-party state in which John Taylor Gilman and the Federalists seemed to rule by divine right. Gilman's percentage of the popular vote for governor was never less than seventy, and the remaining votes were often scattered among as many as ten men. In 1800, though, Republicans gave Gilman a scare in an exciting election.

The most important reason for the strong Republican showing in 1800 was financial. Until 1799 the only bank in the state was the Federalist-dominated New Hampshire Bank, in which Governor Gilman had a substantial investment. When Portsmouth Republicans, led by John Langdon, organized a rival bank, it pleased merchants in Portsmouth and farmers in the country districts by making small loans on easy terms. The Federalist legislature quickly forced the new bank to close down, but in so doing it created a powerful political issue; for Republicans were able to call the Federalist bank an undemocratic monopoly.

In the campaign that followed, the Republicans also exploited regional animosity. Farmers in the interior were tired of being ruled by the Exeter Junto and demanded that the capital be moved from Exeter to Concord. They enthusiastically supported

2. Fisher Ames to Rufus King, Sept. 24, 1800, *The Life and Correspondence of Rufus King*, ed. Charles R. King (New York, 1894–1900), III, 306; Dixon Ryan Fox, *The Decline of Aristocracy in the Politics of New York 1801–1840* (New York, 1919), p. 5; George Sullivan, *Oration, Pronounced at Exeter on the Fourth Day of July, 1800, in Commemoration of the Anniversary of American Independence* (Exeter, N.H., 1800), pp. 12–13.

Judge Timothy Walker of Concord, who was the Republican candidate for governor. Republicans appealed to both financial and sectional tensions as they toured back country towns, describing the prosperity and easy credit that the new bank would have brought.[3]

The Federalist press complained bitterly about the Republican activity: "Jog around the country then, ye disorganizers—publish your electioneering pieces—hold your private meetings—foment malicious falsehoods—exert every nerve—make use of every species of intrigue—but, before any person you propose is chosen Governor, you ALL will be suspended by a single rope." Another article lamented that the "Federalists appear to be sleeping.— But the Jacobins are busy." Federalist papers printed a copy of the constitution of a "Democratic society," which planned to establish Republican committees of correspondence in many towns. Such organization, warned the Federalists, violated George Washington's warning against "self-created societies." The Federalists in one town finally seized a Republican "runner," strapped him to a Fandango (a miniature ferris wheel) and sent the unfortunate "Jacobin" spinning through the air.[4]

3. Mark D. Kaplanoff, "Religion and Righteousness: A Study of Federalist Rhetoric in the New Hampshire Election of 1800," *Historical New Hampshire*, 23 (Winter 1968), 3, 13. For the best summary of the gubernatorial and presidential voting statistics, see *Manual for the General Court, 1891* (Concord, N.H., 1891), pp. 150–157 (gubernatorial), 157–160 (presidential). This volume is henceforth referred to as *New Hampshire Manual 1891*. The results are also conveniently tabulated in A. J. Coolidge and J. B. Mansfield, *History and Description of New England. New Hampshire* (Boston, 1860), pp. 705–709. Gilman was governor 1794–1804, 1813–1815. For religious overtones to the election of 1800, see Kaplanoff, "Religion and Righteousness," pp. 3–6, 13–17. For a review of the voting results in the 1790's, see Mark D. Kaplanoff, "The Social and Economic Bases of New Hampshire's Political Change," unpublished thesis, Yale University, 1969, pp. 10–14. For evidence that Gilman had investments in the Bank of New Hampshire, see John Taylor Gilman, Ledger Number 1, 1774–1826, entries of Feb. 28, Mar. 5, June 5, 1800. For more on banking and the election of 1800 see Smith, "Banking in New Hampshire," pp. 44–46.

4. [Amherst] *Village Messenger*, Mar. 1, 1800; An Old Farmer, [Portsmouth] *Oracle of the Day*, Mar. 15, 1800; Kaplanoff, "Religion and Righteousness," pp. 13–17.

In the election, Republicans reduced Gilman's percentage of the vote from 86 percent to 61 percent, giving Walker 6,039 votes to 10,362 for the governor. The distribution of votes revealed social, economic, and regional patterns. Old, traditional Congregational towns remained loyal to Federalism, while the more enterprising, faster growing communities were most likely to vote Republican. Federalists swept the Connecticut and Merrimack river valleys as well as the Mount Monadnock area in the southwest between them (see Map 3). Republicans had about half of the vote in the rest of the large interior region and along the seacoast, where they captured Portsmouth.[5]

The regional split was neither new nor unique. At the convention in 1788 to ratify the United States Constitution, strongest backing for the new government came from the Connecticut Valley; opposition from the interior. In the state election of 1816 and in the presidential elections of 1828 and 1832, the Connecticut, Monadnock, and Merrimack regions backed first the Federalists and then the National Republicans; the rest of the interior was staunchly Republican or Democratic. The seacoast was unpredictable, voting Republican in 1816, National Republican in 1828, and Democratic in 1832; but Portsmouth was consistently Republican-Democratic and Exeter Federalist-National Republican.[6] The town vote in the various regions is shown in Table 1.

5. *Oracle of the Day*, Mar. 22, 29, April 5, 1800; *New Hampshire Manual 1891*, p. 151; Kaplanoff, "Social and Economic Bases," pp. 35–37, 39–49, 54–72, 82–98, 229–234. Kaplanoff's paper makes an important contribution to the study of voting patterns in the early nineteenth century. Using sophisticated methods, he concludes that the simple regional and economic interpretations of Frederick Jackson Turner and Charles Beard do not hold for New Hampshire. He correctly points out that the most important community in the seacoast region—Portsmouth—was Republican.

6. The first New Hampshire convention called to ratify the Constitution met in Exeter, but adjourned February 22, 1788, when Federalists despaired of getting a majority. The second convention met at Concord on June 17, 1788, and on June 21 voted 54–47 to ratify the Constitution. The action made the Constitution official because New Hampshire was the ninth state to ratify. Joseph B. Walker, *Birth of the Federal Constitution: A History of the New Hampshire Convention for . . . the Federal Constitution . . .* (Boston, 1888); Orrin G. Libby, *The Geographical Distribution of the Vote of the Thirteen*

Table 1. Voting by Towns in 1788, 1800, 1816, and 1828

Region	1788[a]		1800[b]		1816[b]		1828[c]	
	For the Constitution	Against the Constitution	Federalist	Republican	Federalist	Republican	National Republican	Democratic
Connecticut Valley	15	5	8	2	13	2	23	0
Monadnock Section	5	15	7	0	11	2	15	1
Merrimack Valley	15	16	11	5	15	12	22	11
Seacoast Region	17	7	12	12	9	16	16	9
Interior uplands and mountains	60	54	27	25	25	63	33	81
Total[d]	95	86	65	44	78	95	109	102

Source: For 1788, Libby, *Geographical Distribution*, pp. 110–111; for 1800, *Oracle of the Day*, Mar. 22, 29, April 5, 1800; for 1816, *Patriot*, Mar. 19, 26, April 2, 1816; for 1828, *Patriot*, Nov. 10, 17, 1828.

[a]The number cited for and against the Constitution is greater than the number of delegates at the convention. In determining the point of view of towns either not represented or sharing a representative at the convention, I have followed Libby, pp. 110–111.

[b]Gubernatorial election.

[c]Presidential election.

[d]The number of towns voting is not always complete because the newspapers sometimes omitted towns.

The election of 1800 cast a long shadow. Even though they lost, Republicans found a formula that would soon bring success at the polls and that would ultimately aid the Democrats of the Jackson period. Republicans appealed to the interior by running a candidate from Concord. They appealed to farmers by offering a bank and easy loans. They gained backing everywhere by accusing the opposition of monopoly and aristocracy. They labeled their opponents Congregationalists. New Hampshire men, in short, debated the same issues as Federalists and Republicans in 1800 that they would argue as National Republicans and Democrats in 1828. The election of 1800 started the first party system in New Hampshire; when the second party system developed a quarter century later, it was not far different. Both systems had at their roots important regional and economic differences within the state.[7]

Cheered by partial success, Republicans whittled away at the Federalist lead. In 1802 Langdon cut Gilman's majority to barely 2,000. Two years later the Republicans failed to get the governor's seat by only 235 votes; they succeeded in gaining control of the state legislature, and in the fall they carried the state for Jefferson. After that it was a rout: Langdon defeated Gilman in 1805 with a majority of 3,810 out of 28,384. The turnout of voters was remarkable: about 65 percent of those eligible cast ballots, a percentage that was almost as high as the turnout in the gubernatorial election of 1828. The interest in elections was not confined to state politics, for 26,721 persons voted in the

States on the Federal Constitution 1787–1788 (Madison, Wis., 1894), pp. 7–11, 53–54, 70–73, 110–111. For the detailed election results, see Table 1. For a similar pattern in the election of 1832, see Chapter VI. In that election, of the 142 towns voting for Jackson, 64 had been against the Constitution, 57 for it, and 21 did not indicate a preference. Of the 63 Clay towns, 38 were for the Constitution, 22 against, and 3 not indicated. Libby, Geographical Distribution, pp. 110–111; Patriot, Nov. 12, 19, 1832.

7. William A. Robinson, Jeffersonian Democracy in New England (New Haven, Conn., 1916), pp. 29–31. The vote in Concord was Walker 124, Gilman 104; in Portsmouth, Walker 436, Gilman 183. [Concord] Courier of New Hampshire, Mar. 8, 1800.

presidential election of 1808. A vigorous two-party system was operating in New Hampshire in the first decade of the nineteenth century.[8]

The Republican Party ruled the state until 1809. The movement of the capital from Exeter to Concord in 1807 helped the party by bringing the center of politics closer to the farmers of the interior, but Jefferson's embargo hurt Republicans by disturbing people along the seacoast. The embargo seemed to threaten Exeter shipbuilders, who built ocean-going vessels in busy yards along Water Street, and Portsmouth merchants who sent them across the Atlantic. Daniel Webster, who was starting a law career in Portsmouth, became the spokesman for the shipping interests. The embargo was so unpopular that Federalists regained control of the state in 1809 by electing Jeremiah Smith of Exeter governor. He, Webster, and Jeremiah Mason of Portsmouth—all lawyers with national reputations—and former governor Gilman represented the Congregationalist establishment in New Hampshire.[9]

In April 1809, barely a month after Smith's victory, Hill arrived in Concord to take over the *New-Hampshire Patriot* and

8. Robinson, *Jeffersonian Democracy*, pp. 48–49. The population of New Hampshire in 1805 was about 199,000, of whom about 43,780 were adult males. Population figures are conveniently gathered in De Bow, *Statistical View*, p. 40. For voting results see *New Hampshire Manual 1891*, pp. 151, 158. The New Hampshire voting record substantiates the position taken by Richard McCormick in his perceptive article "New Perspectives on Jacksonian Politics," *American Historical Review*, 65 (Jan. 1960), 288–301. There was no great democratic upsurge in the 1820's. Almost all adult males had been able to vote as early as 1800. Great numbers voted whenever they thought it worthwhile. I also agree with McCormick that party structure was an important factor in party politics. Langdon's organization in 1805 and Hill's in 1832 decisively influenced election results. I disagree, however, with McCormick's position in his *Second American Party System*, p. 14, that issues did not divide parties in America. In New Hampshire important differences divided Democrats from National Republicans and Whigs. These differences appear in this chapter and those that follow.

9. The legislature met in Concord from 1800 on. Kaplanoff, "Social and Economic Bases," p. 198. Claude M. Fuess, *Daniel Webster* (Boston, 1930), I, 3–121. In spite of the embargo, economic conditions in Portsmouth were good during these years. Maurice G. Baxter, *Daniel Webster & the Supreme Court* (Amherst, Mass., 1966), pp. 6–7; Robinson, "Hill," pp. 11–12.

to fight the establishment. Casting himself into the role of defending the common man against rich Federalist merchants, he called the Federalists Tories and denounced Governor Smith for driving into Concord with a military escort. Republicans, he said, always "refused to be introduced by parade or show." No one reminded Hill of this charge on another June day in 1833 when he led a magnificent parade into Concord for Andrew Jackson, or still later, in June 1836, when another parade greeted his own return from Washington. Hill never let up on the governor: in December he even attacked Smith for omitting the word "God" in his Thanksgiving proclamation.[10]

The Federalists fought back by suggesting that Hill had inherited insanity from his father and by claiming that his ancestry went back to the witches in Salem. Federalist newspapers rejoiced when Samuel Kimball, whom Hill had called an "ignorant pettifogger," assaulted him in Concord. He welcomed the attacks because they made him the underdog; "I have hit them," he once announced, "for they flutter." A few years later Federalists introduced a resolution in the New Hampshire House of Representatives charging Hill with libel and of "insulting members of the House." He retaliated by sending a memorial citing the Bill of Rights and by appearing in person on the floor of the House. The battle was a draw: the House refused to censure him, but would not expunge the motion.[11]

Within a year of his arrival Hill was a success. He turned a faltering newspaper into a money-maker that soon dominated state politics. He helped make the faltering Republican Party a winner. Aided by the repeal of the embargo, Langdon returned to Concord as governor in 1810 and 1811; another Republican, William Plumer of Epping, succeeded him on the eve of the War of 1812.[12]

10. Robinson, "Hill," pp. 11–18; *Patriot*, April 18, Dec. 5, 1809.
11. Bradley, *Hill*, pp. 25–26; Robinson, "Hill," p. 24; *Patriot*, Dec. 31, 1816.
12. *Patriot*, Mar. 20, 1810, Mar. 19, 1811, Jan. 7, 21, 28, Feb. 4, 25, 1812.

Historians have advanced many reasons for the coming of the War of 1812, including fear for the republic, party regularity, and sectionalism. All three to a degree apply in New Hampshire. Editor Isaac Hill and Congressman John A. Harper agreed that the republic would be in danger if it allowed further humiliation from Great Britain. Federalists were willing to accept humiliation in order to maintain peace, but Republicans in New Hampshire called for war. For them the war would be a crusade against both their Federalist and their British enemies. The sectional motif is the most compelling, for New Hampshire tended to divide between the interior, which favored war, and the Connecticut Valley and seacoast, which opposed it.

Pressure for war came early from the interior. In 1810 the *Patriot* in Concord began to publish anti-British letters and militant speeches from Congress. Some of the most aggressive speeches were given by Harper, who came from Meredith on the nothern shore of Lake Winnipesaukee. Harper, a good example of a frontier war hawk, worried that war would not come. Although he wanted the United States to acquire Canada, he wanted war even without territorial annexation. In 1811 Matthew Harvey in the hill town of Henniker demanded war with both Britain and France because they had "plundered" American ships. In the vote for war in 1812 the New Hampshire Senators and Congressmen split more along regional than along party lines. All three from the interior voted for war; three from the seacoast voted against the declaration, only one for it. The six Republicans split four-two for the war; the one Federalist, George Sullivan, voted against it, but many people considered Sullivan a Republican in 1812. The evidence is not conclusive. One Republican who opposed the war, Nicholas Gilman, was a former Federalist who preferred DeWitt Clinton to James Madison for President in 1812. And although Harper and Obed. Hall of Bartlett, who voted for war, represented frontier towns, Samuel Dinsmoor, who voted with them, came from Keene in the long-settled Connecticut Valley. The regional split was present in 1812, but it hid a complex situation.[13]

The split continued after war was declared. Opposition to the war was strongest in Portsmouth, where Daniel Webster spoke before a "peace" rally on the Fourth of July, 1812, and in the vicinity of Exeter, where over a thousand people attended a similar rally in Brentwood in August. George Sullivan stirred the Brentwood crowd with an address loaded with rhetorical questions: Why invade Canada to protect shipping when merchants were against the war? Why fight Britain when the real enemy was France? A committee, including Webster, then drew up the Rockingham Memorial, which hinted broadly at secession. The government's policy, said the memorial, had tended toward "the destruction of the COMMERCE of these States," but nothing in the "National Compact" would make Americans give up their right to sail the seas. It was strange, continued the memorial, that states with no seamen were the most sensitive to damage

13. The bibliography on the causes of the War of 1812 is enormous. For a start see Warren H. Goodman, "The Origins of the War of 1812, A Survey of Changing Interpretations," *Mississippi Valley Historical Review*, 28 (1941–42), 171–186; Marshall Smelser, *The Democratic Republic 1801–1815* (New York, 1968), pp. 216–225. For the argument that fear for the republic caused war see Roger H. Brown, *The Republic in Peril: 1812* (New York, 1964); for stress on partisanship see Bradford Perkins, *Prologue to War 1805–1812* (Berkeley, Calif., 1961); for emphasis on sectionalism see Julius W. Pratt, *Expansionists of 1812* (New York, 1925). A good discussion of John A. Harper can be found in Brown, *Republic in Peril*, pp. 56, 75, 121–124. Harper also looms large in Pratt's argument. See Pratt, *Expansionists of 1812*, pp. 49–52, 122, 126, 141, 148–149, 187. *Patriot*, Oct. 30, Nov. 6, 13, 1810, Dec. 17, 1811, June 30, 1812; Matthew Harvey, *An Oration Pronounced at Henniker, New Hampshire, July 4th, 1811* (Concord, N.H., 1811). Republican interior Congressmen Obed. Hall of Bartlett, John A. Harvey of Meredith, and Samuel Dinsmoor of Keene voted yea; so did Republican Senator Charles Cutts of Portsmouth. Republican Senator Nicholas Gilman of Exeter, Republican Congressman Josiah Bartlett, Jr., of Stratham, and Federalist Congressman George Sullivan of Exeter all represented seacoast nay votes. *Annals of the Congress of the United States,* 12th Congress, 1st Session (1811–1812), p. 297 (Senate vote, June 17, 1812), p. 1637 (House vote, June 4, 1812). Contemporary reference to Sullivan as a Republican is in Levi Bartlett to Ezra Bartlett, Mar. 17, 1805, Ezra Bartlett Papers, New Hampshire State Library.

done to that class. "A voice," it suggested, "beyond the Western Mountains" called for war. Webster and the committee were opposed to a "separation of the States," but said that when one part of the country tried to *"sacrifice* the interest of another; when a small and heated *Majority* in the Government . . . shall by hasty, rash, and ruinous measures, threaten to destroy essential rights," then it was time to act.[14]

On the other hand, Republicans of the interior supported the war. The *Patriot* demanded military action, and Republican governor Plumer sent units of the New Hampshire militia off to Lundy's Lane, Sackett's Harbor, and Ogdensburg. In Francestown, Woodbury drew up the Hillsborough Resolves in defense of the war, the interior's answer to Webster's Rockingham Memorial.[15]

The indecisive war become so unpopular in New Hampshire that Federalists returned John Taylor Gilman to office in 1813, 1814, and 1815 and elected Webster to Congress. Gilman would have sent delegates to the antiwar Hartford Convention had not the governor's council, Republican three to two, blocked the maneuver. Even then Webster tried to reverse the three-two ratio by insisting that the council election in Portsmouth had been illegal. When all failed, Charlestown and Hanover in the Federalist Connecticut Valley informally sent representatives to Hartford. On December 9, 1814, Webster delivered a strong speech in Congress against a bill to draft men into the army from the state militia. He proposed state nullification of the sort that he later denounced in his famous reply to Senator Robert Y. Hayne of South Carolina. "It will be the solemn duty of the State Governments," he said, "to protect their own authority

14. George Sullivan, *Speech at the Late Rockingham Convention with the Memorial and Resolutions and Report of the Committee of Election* (Concord, N.H., 1812). The *Patriot* accused the memorial of calling for separation of the states. *Patriot*, Aug. 25, 1812.

15. Bradley, *Hill*, pp. 39, 101; Robinson, "Hill," p. 24; J. Duane Squires, *The Granite State of the United States* (New York, 1956), I, 186; Capowski, "Woodbury," p. 18.

over their own Militia and to interpose between their citizens and arbitrary power."[16]

The wartime division in New Hampshire matched that of the Jackson period. Republicans of the interior, who supported the war, later voted for Jackson; aside from Portsmouth, seacoast and Connecticut Valley Federalists opposed both. The war was but the first in a series of struggles between Hill and Webster. It also provided the first opportunity to distinguish future Democrats from their opponents. War hawks Hill, Harvey, Dinsmoor, and Woodbury were by 1828 the four leading Democrats in the state; the same year, Webster, who was against the war, was helping unite National Republicans. One Republican circular in 1814 listed ten future Jacksonians among Republicans active during the war. At the end of the war Hill compared Republican loyalty with Federalist treason and took pains to praise that "dauntless soldier" Andrew Jackson. The "God of Battle," he wrote, was "on the side of *right* and *justice*."[17]

Republicans used political organization as well as rhetoric to defeat the Federalists. As Langdon had done in 1800, Hill, chairman of the central committee, sought to unite Portsmouth and Concord Republicans on a platform that would appeal to the farmers of the interior. With the war over, Langdon could bring disaffected Portsmouth Republicans back into the fold. At the same time William Plumer, who had once been a Federalist, could bring over wavering Federalists. Plumer had held almost every job in New Hampshire politics, including governor and United States Senator. Former governors Langdon, seventy-three, and Plumer, fifty-six, were voices out of the past.[18]

---

16. Daniel Webster, "Speech on the Conscription Bill Made in the House of Representatives, December 9, 1814," in Claude H. Van Tyne, *The Letters of Daniel Webster* (New York, 1902), pp. 56–68. Quotation on p. 67.

17. *Patriot*, Feb. 14, 21, 28, 1815; "Circular," Dec. 1814, Woodbury Papers, LC. In addition to Hill and Woodbury, Nathaniel Upham, William Pickering, John Harvey, John Page, John Steele, Jonathan Harvey, Thomas Chandler, and Matthew Harvey were among those listed as Republicans on the circular.

18. William Plumer, Jr., *The Life of William Plumer* (Boston, 1856), p. 429.

Levi Woodbury, only twenty-six, offered a fresh 'voice. When Hill needed help during the war in collecting money owed the *Patriot* by debtors in Hillsborough County, he turned to Woodbury, and the business association quickly became political. In 1814 Woodbury sat on the Hillsborough County Republican Committee, which sent delegates to the central committee in Concord. The central committee made plans for town and county nominations, sent out circulars and drew up an attack on the Hartford Convention. Woodbury not only made lists of Republicans but reported faithfully also on the Federalists of Francestown. He was chairman of the Hillsborough County Convention held in 1816.[19]

The Hill-Woodbury alliance was an uneasy one. When Governor Gilman removed Benjamin Pierce as sheriff of Hillsborough County, Hill denounced Gilman, but Woodbury's father defended the governor. Fearful of losing Levi Woodbury's support, Hill wrote him a conciliatory letter: "I know I have given cause to you at least to mistrust the sincerity of my friendship . . . . Rest assured sir, that at the time . . . I had a higher opinion of the private worth of your father than I had ever formerly entertained." In 1814 Hill anxiously wrote Woodbury about rumors that he was about to start a newspaper that might rival the *Patriot*. He prevailed on Woodbury not to get involved in any such venture.[20]

The two men had enough in common to hold them together most of the time. They were, first of all, Republicans with roots in the American Revolution. Hill often went out of his way to praise Revolutionary War hero Benjamin Pierce. "That good man," he said on one occasion, was "willing to sacrifice anything to the good of his country . . . would that all *Republicans* were what they ought to be." In a Fourth of July Address at Lynde-

19. Hill to Woodbury, Sept. 1814, Francestown Protest, May 19, 1814, Woodbury Papers, LC; Capowski, "Woodbury," pp. 17–39, 65–66.
20. William Claggett to Levi Woodbury, Jan. 29, Nov. 15, 1813, Woodbury Papers, LC, cited in Capowski, "Woodbury," pp. 40–48; Hill to Woodbury, Nov. 29, 1813, Feb. 7, 1814, Woodbury Papers, LC.

borough in 1815, Woodbury connected Republican beliefs such as frugality and rotation in office with the Puritan tradition and the Declaration of Independence. The two Republicans also shared an optimistic view of the future. Hill wrote Woodbury during the height of the War of 1812 that the nation was "dawning on a glorious era." Both were Freemasons, and Freemasons stuck together in New Hampshire politics. Although Woodbury's family background was more prosperous and stable than Hill's, Woodbury was no less a man on the make. They both wanted desperately to succeed in politics, and each would have preferred to do it alone. At times their careers came into conflict; yet in the end each found it necessary to rely upon the other.[21]

Republicans barely missed toppling Gilman from office in March 1815. The rest of the year became one long campaign to return the Republican Party to power. As the 1816 election approached, the *Patriot* accused the Federalists of disloyalty during the war and dubbed them Tories. Hill's masthead slogan read "Plumer and the Union of the States." It continued, "Don't give up the SHIP to Tories or Algerines. FREE TRADE AND SAILORS' RIGHTS."[22]

As in the past, Republicans linked Federalists with Congregational ministers, who were often unpopular because they received tax support from the towns. The *Patriot* opposed the "spirit of favoritism manifested towards a particular religious order," calling it the union of church and state. Congregationalists, who had once called Jefferson and Madison atheists, would revive the inquisition if given a chance. Hill urged Federalist Baptists to leave the party because they were in danger of a "deep and dark plan" to "subvert religious freedom." In a "Chronicle of the Federalists" published just before the election,

---

21. Levi Woodbury, *An Oration Pronounced at Lyndeborough, N.H. in Commemoration of the Independence of the United States of America, July 4, 1815* (Amherst, N.H., 1815); Capowski, "Woodbury," pp. 44, 50–51; Hill to Woodbury, Nov. 29, 1813, Sept. 30, 1814, Woodbury Papers, LC.
22. *Patriot*, Feb. 21, 1815, Feb. 27, Mar. 5, 1816; Coolidge and Mansfield, *New Hampshire*, p. 708.

the *Patriot* described the menace: "Moreover certain of the priests in the land, who were of the Federalists, multiplied, and they became numerous, insomuch that they devoured the substance of the people, by their idleness and sumptuous living."[23]

To extend his network and to combat the Federalist Washington and Benevolent clubs, Hill formed "Friends of Union" groups all over the state and made himself secretary. Already people referred to Hill and his Republicans as Democrats. Already the Republicans sounded like Democrats as they talked about rotation in office and praised the "farmers and mechanics" of the state. And in the organization were men like Hill, Woodbury, William Badger, Benjamin Pierce, and the Harveys—Matthew, John, and Jonathan—who a decade later would be Jackson Democrats.[24]

When Plumer defeated wealthy merchant James Sheafe, the Federalist candidate in March 1816, some called it a "revolution." The Republicans turned a 500-vote deficit in 1815 into 2,000 and then 7,000 vote victories in 1816 and 1817. The distribution of votes in 1816 repeated the earlier patterns and anticipated those of the Jackson era. Once again the leading Federalist regions were the Connecticut Valley, the Monadnock section, and the Merrimack Valley. Republicans took Portsmouth and over 70 percent of the upland, mountain, and seacost towns, but they could not carry Exeter.[25]

Plumer's election and James Monroe's overwhelming presidential victory in the fall marked the end for the Federalist

23. *Patriot,* May 2, 23, July 4, 11, 1815, Jan. 23, Feb. 13, 1816.
24. Bradley, *Hill,* p. 41; *Patriot,* Feb. 7, Nov. 14, 1815, Jan. 30, Feb. 6, Mar. 16, 1816.
25. The voting margins were actually 558 in 1815, 2,344 in 1816, and 7,059 in 1817. *New Hampshire Manual 1891,* p. 152. For details on the election of 1816 see *Patriot,* Mar. 19, 26, April 2, 1816, and Table 1. In one issue the *Patriot* carried a map showing Republican strength in the interior hill country (Mar. 19, 26, 1816). For more on the election, see *ibid.,* Jan. 23, Feb. 6, 1815, and Jan. 2, 1816. Cheshire County near the Connecticut River had twenty-four Federalist members of the lower house after the election of 1816 and only twelve Republicans; Hillsborough County in the uplands was 30–9 Republican.

Party and the beginning of the so-called Era of Good Feelings in both the state and the nation. After one more try, Federalists gave up running candidates for governor in New Hampshire. Even before that, Daniel Webster left the state to pursue his politics in Boston, leaving his brother Ezekiel, Jeremiah Mason, and Jeremiah Smith holding the fort and leaving Republicans to rule. William Plumer governed from 1816 to 1818, Samuel Bell of Chester from 1819 to 1822.[26]

In his inaugural address Governor Plumer sought to make the political revolution a springboard for political and social reform. First, he asked for organic changes: the legislature should improve the militia, should allow the people to select Congressmen by districts instead of by counties, and should return the Supreme Court to the form it had before 1813, when the Federalists altered it. Next, in good Republican tradition, he proposed an increase in the power of juries over judges and a reduction in state salaries. As a challenge to Congregationalists, he demanded that the state allow any religious society to incorporate so that it could receive tax support. As a challenge to Federalists, he set forth a plan to turn Federalist Dartmouth College into the University of New Hampshire. Woodbury wrote in his diary that Plumer had given a "most gracious speech" and that the "last election [had] produced . . . our America."[27]

At Monticello, Thomas Jefferson read the message and was as delighted as Woodbury. "Your message," he wrote Plumer, was "truly Republican"; he called its principles "sound." Praising Plumer's "unusual" suggestion to reduce salaries by starting with his own, Jefferson said, "I place economy among the first and most important of Republican virtues, and public debt is the greatest of dangers to be feared." Plumer must, he contin-

---

26. The Federalists continued to take part in New Hampshire politics, often siding with one Republican faction against another. Until 1820 Federalists ran for governor, but not as party candidates with full party backing. Stackpole, *History*, III, 65–78; *New Hampshire Manual 1891*, p. 152.

27. Plumer, *Plumer*, pp. 440-441; Woodbury Memorandum Book, Woodbury Papers, LC.

ued, press the attack against Dartmouth, for no institution was immune from regulation.[28]

The legislators acted promptly on Plumer's proposals. In twenty-five furious days they passed ninety-six laws, including one that slashed government salaries and another that reorganized the militia. To reward the party faithful, the legislature turned the state printing contract over to Hill, voted to build a new state capitol in Concord, and set up a new high court with Republican justices. The governor's choice of judges caused trouble. After selecting Samuel Bell of Chester and William M. Richardson of Portsmouth, Plumer sought to conciliate the opposition with a Federalist appointment, but Jeremiah Mason and other Federalists turned down the position. Plumer then enraged old Republicans by refusing to appoint Clifton Claggett of Portsmouth, who had been on the old Superior Court. When he finally decided on Levi Woodbury in December, a storm broke out against the "baby judge." Woodbury was not quite twenty-seven at the time, not yet married, and not yet from Portsmouth. To his diary Woodbury confided that Claggett and David L. Morril of Goffstown, just elected United States Senator, "cried out the loudest" against his appointment. Now Plumer had a Republican court, one that would vote against Dartmouth College in 1817.[29]

The Reverend Eleazar Wheelock received a royal charter in 1769 to establish a college in New Hampshire to educate Indians. A year later he built the first college building, a log cabin, in Hanover in the Connecticut River Valley. He called the college Dartmouth for the Earl of Dartmouth, who had contributed

---

28. Plumer, *Plumer*, pp. 440–441.
29. Capowski, "Woodbury," pp. 66–67, 73, 83; Lynn Turner, "William Plumer, Statesman of New Hampshire," unpublished dissertation, Harvard University, 1943, p. 1014; *Patriot*, July 2, 9, 16, 1816; Lynn W. Turner, *William Plumer of New Hampshire 1759–1850* (Chapel Hill, N.C., 1962), pp. 256, 261; Claggett to Woodbury, Oct. 21, 1816, Woodbury, "Diary," Dec. 8, 1816, Woodbury Papers, LC.

£200. By 1816 Hanover was a town of about 2,000, a Federalist, Congregationalist stronghold.[30]

Starting in 1810, a factional struggle at Dartmouth between non-Congregationalist president John Wheelock and the Congregationalist trustees, many of them clergymen, gave Hill, Woodbury, Plumer, and the Republicans the chance they had long awaited: to attack Dartmouth, Federalism, and Congregationalism, all at once. John Wheelock, son of the founder, had been president of Dartmouth since 1779, and the trustees had long resented his arbitrary ways. Under Wheelock, students had been required to attend a Presbyterian Church, rather than the Congregational Church that the trustees preferred. When he dismissed a teacher who preached at the Congregational Church, the trustees intervened. Other issues quickly arose. The trustees accused the president of opposing the severe disciplinary system of the college and of setting up classes not allowed in the charter. Wheelock said the trustees were selecting books and giving favorite instructors more power than the president. In 1815 Wheelock published two pamphlets summarizing his charges against the trustees. The trustees thereupon replaced him with a Congregationalist clergyman, Francis Brown.[31]

Republicans had a rare political opportunity. The Wheelock Federalists were so outraged at the trustees that they voted for Plumer in 1816, and the Republicans carried Hanover. Hill's boarding house in Concord became the center of intense lobbying, led by Wheelock, his nephew William H. Woodward, who had been treasurer of Dartmouth, and Colonel Amos Brewster, Woodbury's spokesman in Hanover. Ever since the summer of 1815, the newspapers carried charge and countercharge about Dartmouth College. When Federalist newspapers labeled Wheelock a

---

30. Squires, *Granite State*, I, 97–98.
31. *Patriot*, Aug. 1, 15, 1815, Sept. 5, 1815; Capowski, "Woodbury," pp. 68–72; J. M. Shirley, *The Dartmouth College Causes and the Supreme Court of the United States* (St. Louis, 1879), is a useful source on the case.

Unitarian or a Universalist, Hill answered that the former president was simply a "liberal," who "opposed the intolerance in certain factions of the Clergy." He accused the trustees of sacrificing Wheelock because he refused to make Dartmouth as "inquisitorial" as the theological seminary at Andover, Massachusetts. When Dartmouth students debated the desirability of religious tests for civil office (and the affirmative won), Hill said that the result proved that Dartmouth stood for religious intolerance.[32]

A brisk battle of pamphlets broke out. The trustees argued that the legislature could not alter the college charter, but Hill pointed out that Massachusetts had changed the Harvard charter and that the New Hampshire legislature had the power to "cherish the interest of literature and the sciences." The issue of the *Patriot* that greeted Plumer when he rode into Concord in June 1816, cited twelve reasons why the legislature should get rid of the trustees and take over the college. The main charge was that the trustees had dismissed Wheelock while the legislature was investigating the college.

Amid the debate the Hill side came up with the public interest argument that Jacksonian Democrats later used against monopolies. When the Federalist Concord *Gazette* said that the legislature would not intervene if a bank removed its president, the *Patriot* replied that a bank was a private business, but Dartmouth College was by its nature a public institution. The state could intervene in the affairs of the college in order to protect the people. The "public good," said the *Patriot,* "imperiously requires, and the general vote demands, the application of a speedy and adequate remedy." Dartmouth existed not "for the benefit of individual proprietors, or any individuals whomsoever: but for the public good." The trustees were simply "public agents or stakeholders for the public."[33]

32. *Patriot,* Sept. 5, 1815, April 23, 1816.
33. *Ibid.,* May 14, 28, June 4, 11, 1816. The *Patriot* argued that if the legislature failed to control Dartmouth, the college could teach anything and could destroy students' morals.

The legislature passed the Dartmouth College Act, making Dartmouth the state university of New Hampshire with a new board of trustees. Nine of the twenty-one trustees, including Woodbury, Matthew Harvey of Hopkinton, and Moses Eastman of Salisbury, were from the hill district. Hill and Plumer were making certain that the men from the interior had a say in the affairs of the new university. Three of the new trustees, Woodbury, Harvey, and Henry Hubbard of Charlestown, were later important cogs in the Democratic organization. Hill's activities in the Dartmouth College affair helped provide a nucleus for the Democratic Party, both by strengthening the machine and by providing issues later used in other contexts.[34]

The affair demonstrates the importance of issues in early American politics. The New Hampshire newspapers were filled with articles discussing the role of Dartmouth College and the power of the state legislature to control corporations. Like many others, Woodbury took the struggle very seriously, for he considered the case a microcosm of the political and social problems besetting all New England. When he found it impossible to get the new trustees to meet, he wrote in anguish: "At all events in some mode or other a triumph of liberal principles both in religion and politics must be effected." And in the *Patriot* Hill hammered away for the right of the legislature to regulate in the public interest the only college in the state. The groups and issues were hardly as simple as he painted them: it was not the rich against the poor; nor was religious liberty at stake. Yet as the battle developed, Hill, Woodbury, Harvey, and other future Democrats represented the common people of the state against Jeremiah Mason, Jeremiah Smith, and Daniel Webster, who spoke for a privileged institution. Just as John Langdon had exploited a battle over banking in 1800, Hill turned a struggle over education and religion to his own political advantage. He portrayed the battle as one against monopoly and privilege. The

34. John K. Lord, *A History of Dartmouth College* (Concord, N.H., 1913), II, 89–90, 682–683.

sides in 1816 were like those in 1800 and those that would line up again in 1828.[35]

During the winter the new trustees of the state university restored John Wheelock as president, but President Brown of the college refused to turn over the keys. Most of the students—"prone to mischief," said Hill—rallied around Brown; in August, sixty of them even seized the meeting house and kept it away from the university the entire month. At the end of the summer in 1817 there were two graduations: eight received diplomas from the university; thirty-nine from the college. That fall students loyal to the college plotted to make off with the books from the two libraries. When university professors reached the libraries and found the doors locked, they smashed their way in with axes. The books were gone, and what was worse, a number of the students, armed with clubs, seized the professors and locked them in a closet. Local authorities, either sympathetic with the students or afraid of them, promptly indicted the teachers for cutting down the doors.[36]

Before the scuffling, the old trustees, in February 1817, sued William H. Woodward, treasurer of the university, to recover the charter, records, and seal of the college. After a preliminary hearing in May, the Superior Court heard the case in September in Exeter. While the old Federalist triumvirate of lawyers, Smith, Mason, and Webster, presented their briefs before a crowded courtroom, three Republican justices, Richardson, Bell, and Woodbury, listened. Mason contended that since Dartmouth was a private, eleemosynary institution, it was not subject to state regulation. Such control, he argued, would violate the clause in the federal Constitution that denied states the right to impair "the Obligation of Contracts." Smith filled out Mason's arguments, leaving it to Daniel Webster to sum up. Webster spoke

35. Woodbury to Eleazar Wheelock Ripley, Sept. 20, 1816, Woodbury Papers, LC.

36. *Patriot*, Sept. 5, 1815, Mar. 4, 18, Sept. 2, Nov. 18, Dec. 9, 1817, Dec. 23, 1819.

for an hour and finished with one of his grand perorations comparing the "murder of Dartmouth College" with that of Caesar by Brutus. The predominantly Federalist audience was deeply moved, many to tears, but one skeptic was heard to sneer: "I guess he's being pathetic, ain't he?"

In their defense of Woodward and the university, George Sullivan and Ichabod Bartlett maintained that Dartmouth was a public institution. Since Dartmouth College received its charter to provide education for the public, the state legislature had the right to regulate it in the public interest.[37]

The Republican judges agreed with the Republican lawyers. Woodbury remarked that Webster's speech was "more language than light." In his opinion for the court, Richardson defined as public any "corporation, all of whose franchises" were "exercised for publick purposes." On this basis Dartmouth was public and thus liable to public regulation. It was against "sound policy," he said, "to put institutions of great learning within the absolute controul of a few individuals, and out of the controul of the sovereign power . . . It is a matter of too great moment, too intimately connected with the publick welfare and prosperity to be thus entrusted in the hands of a few." Richardson was following the public interest doctrine advanced by the *Patriot* and was anticipating the position stated by United States Chief Justice Roger B. Taney in the Charles River Bridge case: "While the

37. The briefs of Mason and Smith are printed in 65 New Hampshire Reports, 473–502, 524–563; those of Sullivan and Bartlett, *ibid.*, 520–524, 563–593. The most recent analysis of the legal arguments in the Dartmouth College case appears in Baxter, *Webster & the Supreme Court*, pp. 65–109, but Baxter does not relate the case to politics. For the arguments of the lawyers, see Timothy Farrar, *Report of the Case of The Trustees of Dartmouth College against William H. Woodward* (Portsmouth, N.H., 1819). The politics of the case is treated in William G. North, "The Political Background of the Dartmouth College Case," *New England Quarterly*, 18 (June 1945), 194–196. Baxter argues persuasively that Woodbury heard the case even though the docket says he did not sit. Baxter, *Webster*, p. 72. Mason's part in the case is covered in G. J. Clark, ed., *Memoir, Autobiography and Correspondence of Jeremiah Mason*, rev. ed. (Kansas City, Mo., 1917), pp. 163–167. The *Patriot* describes the Exeter scenes in the issues of Nov. 4, 11, Dec. 30, 1817. See also *ibid.*, June 3, 1817.

rights of private property are sacredly guarded," said Taney, "we must not forget, that the community also have rights."[38]

On March 10, 1818, Webster led off for the college in a final appeal before the Supreme Court of the United States. In his speech he followed Mason's thesis that Dartmouth was not a public institution, but "an *eleemosynary* corporation," a "private charity" not subject to public control. After a brief reference to the contract clause that Marshall considered so important, he moved to his dramatic climax. "Every college," he declared, was "in danger if Dartmouth falls." If their fate depended upon "the rise and fall of popular parties," colleges would become "a theatre for the contention of politicks." Then came a long Latin quotation and finally his famous peroration. No exact record remains of the peroration, but according to Professor Chauncey Allen Goodrich, who was there, part of it went as follows:

> Sir, you may destroy this little Institution . . . But if you do so, you must carry through your work! You must extinguish, one after another, all those great lights of science which, for more than a century, have thrown their radiance over our land!
> It is, Sir, as I have said, a small College. And yet, there are those who love it.

At this point, according to Goodrich, Webster broke down, tears filled his eyes, and Chief Justice Marshall was close to tears himself. There was little the defense could do to save the state university.[39]

When the Court met eleven months later, in February 1819, to announce its decision, Marshall moved quickly to the first of his two main points. If the funds of Dartmouth College were public

38. Richardson's opinion is printed in 65 New Hampshire Reports, 624–643. Turner, *Plumer*, pp. 298–299; Albert Beveridge, *The Life of John Marshall* (Boston, 1919), IV, 234–236. The Charles River Bridge decision is in 11 Peters 536–553, the Taney quotation on p. 548. The New Hampshire Court did not announce its decision until Nov. 6, 1817. Baxter, *Webster*, pp. 75–76.

39. 4 Wheaton 551–624; Baxter, *Webster*, pp. 76–88; Beveridge, *Marshall*, IV, 236–251.

property, the university and the Republicans were right, but if they were private, then the college and Webster were the victors. The college won. Using Mason's and Webster's own words, Marshall declared Dartmouth a "private, eleemosynary institution," with "objects unconnected with government." Second, the contract clause of the Constitution prevented New Hampshire from altering the charter of the college. No man would ever found a college, said the Chief Justice, "believing that it is immediately to be deemed a public institution, whose funds are to be governed . . . by the will of the legislature."[40]

Outside of New Hampshire the case caused little stir, but within the Granite State, Federalists were elated and Republicans crushed. When the bad news came, Hill declared: "It renders permanent the spirit of intolerance and high-handed party persecution . . . ." "Has Justice," he cried, "fled to brutes, and have men lost their reason?" Like the War of 1812, the Dartmouth College case was a landmark in the emergence of the Democratic Party in New Hampshire. In the years to come Democrats linked their opponents with treason in the war and privilege in the case.[41]

The Dartmouth College case was also part of a drive for religious equality in New Hampshire. In his inaugural address Plumer implicitly attacked Congregationalism when he asked that the state incorporate all religious sects. During the campaign of 1816, Hill had been much more direct. The headline of the *Patriot* on March 9, 1816, read: "RELIGIOUS FREEDOM, THE RIGHTS OF THE BAPTIST, QUAKER, METHODIST AND OF ALL DENOMINATIONS in room of a Law Religion, imposed by an intolerant sect." For years Hill and the *Patriot* had fought for religious toleration.

In the legislature decisive leadership came from Reverend Daniel Young, a Methodist preacher from Lisbon, nestled in the White Mountains near Franconia Notch. Woodbury described

40. 4 Wheaton 624–654, especially 630, 647; Beveridge, *Marshall*, IV, 261–272.
41. *Patriot,* Feb. 16, 1819.

him as a man of "open countenance, considerable talents." In 1816 Young proposed repeal of the act of 1791 allowing towns to support "religious societies." Under the 1791 statute, a majority of the voters in a town could designate a church (usually Congregational) as the established one. The town would then support it by assessing all taxpayers in the community. Only those who could prove that they were supporting another officially recognized sect could be exempted from contributing to the established church. Even then towns were slow to grant exemptions. To be recognized, the local sect had to petition the state legislature, which often delayed, particularly if the new sect were Catholic or Universalist. Many people belonged to no church at all, but they too were assessed to support the established one. Daniel Young, Methodist, William Plumer, Deist, and Isaac Hill, Episcopalian, wanted a change.[42]

The change came gradually. Young mustered three votes for reform in the twelve-man Senate in 1816, six in 1817, and finally a majority in 1818. The Toleration Bill passed the House in 1819 and became law. The new act allowed a town to establish several religious societies instead of one. Once a church was incorporated, the town would support it by assessing its members. The new act also prescribed that persons who did not wish to belong to any of the established sects could be exempted simply by filing papers stating that they were of a different faith or of no faith at all. The act did not stop towns from supporting churches; it simply "democratized" establishment and protected dissenters. Many future Jacksonians supported the Toleration Act, including John Brodhead and Joseph Hammons, who were elected to Congress in 1829. Republicans opposed the 1791 law because it gave Congregationalists, who were often Federalists, an unfair advantage. Republicans were attacking monopoly, privilege, and Federalism just as they had in the Dartmouth College case and just as Demo-

42. Charles B. Kinney, Jr., *Church and State: The Struggle for Separation in New Hampshire, 1630–1900* (New York, 1955), pp. 78–100; *Patriot,* Mar. 9, 1816; Woodbury, Memorandum Book, 1816–1817, Woodbury Papers, LC.

crats would later attack monopoly, privilege, and whiggery in the war on the Bank of the United States.[43]

The Toleration Act was passed the same year in which debate began over slavery in Missouri. At first New Hampshire Republicans went on record against slavery. When James Tallmadge of New York proposed in 1819 that Congress prohibit the further importation of slaves into Missouri, most people in New Hampshire responded sympathetically. Early in December a meeting in Portsmouth voted to keep slavery out of Missouri. On Christmas Eve, Hill proclaimed: "The step which shall be taken by the present Congress will mark an era in the history of *Slavery in the United States*—it will determine whether as a nation, we will tolerate an evil which *can* be remedied, or whether we will wipe away the foulest stain on our national character."

By February 1820, the political aspects of the Missouri debates had forced Hill and Woodbury to change their minds. Hill declared that he hated to see the Missouri bill "reviving sectional prejudices." It was, he insisted, an attempt to create "a Northern and a Southern interest . . . for sinister party purposes." He was referring to fears that Tallmadge, Rufus King, DeWitt Clinton, and other New Yorkers were trying to use the antislavery sentiment as a means of uniting northern Federalists and Republicans in one party. Martin Van Buren was so frightened by the prospect that he took steps to recreate the New York-Virginia alliance, which had formed the basis of the old Republican Party under Jefferson. From 1820 on, Hill, Woodbury, Van Buren, and other Republicans took every opportunity to show their sympathy for the South and its institution of slavery. They sought to create a new party based on the old North-South alliance.[44]

43. Kinney, *Church and State*, pp. 100–118; *Patriot*, June 22, 29, July 6, Aug. 3, 17, 24, 1819. *The Spirit of the Republican Press*, Jan. 21, 1829.
44. *Patriot*, Nov. 30, Dec. 21, 1819, Feb. 1, 15, 22, 29, Mar. 7, April 18, 1820; [Portsmouth] *New Hampshire Gazette*, Dec. 21, 28, 1819 (henceforth called *Gazette*); William Plumer to William Plumer, Jr., Feb. 21, 1820, William Plumer Papers, LC; Glover Moore, *The Missouri Controversy, 1819–1821* (Lexington, Ky., 1953), pp. 186–199. By April, 1820, the *Patriot* had dropped its opposition to slavery in Missouri.

Van Buren's fears in New York and Hill's in New Hampshire were exaggerated. If Federalists were fishing in troubled Missouri waters in 1819 and 1820, they failed to catch anything worthwhile. In New Hampshire, Smith and Mason, two leading Federalists, were unwilling to fight for abolition in Missouri. They preferred to spend their time amalgamating with dissident Republicans to stop the growth of Hill's political machine. Mason therefore lost considerable favor among his Boston Federalist friends who were strongly opposed to slavery in Missouri.[45]

Although it would take six more years to transform the Republican Party into the Democratic Party, the roots of the New Hampshire Democracy, which had been planted in 1800, were growing well in 1820. The term "Republican" would be preferred for another decade, but the word "Democrat" began to appear. In 1818, for example, the *New-York Evening Post* commented that the "Democracy of N. H." was a "low crowd." New Hampshire Republicans paid increasing attention to Andrew Jackson. Between 1818 and 1820 the *Patriot* first defended Jackson for seizing Pensacola, then carried his biography, and finally produced a laudatory article.[46]

New Hampshire Republicans continued to sound as Democrats would sound a decade later. During the Panic of 1819, Republicans showed the same hostility toward paper money that some Democrats would exhibit during the Bank War. In a letter to the *Patriot* one writer declared that the state should incorporate a bank only if it agreed not to issue bills of credit. Similar attacks continued during the depression year of 1820, when Hill con-

45. Clark, *Memoir of Mason*, pp. 231–232; Moore, *Missouri Controversy*, pp. 186–187; Shaw Livermore, *The Twilight of Federalism: The Disintegration of the Federalist Party* (Princeton, N.J., 1962), pp. 91, 95, 104. I concur with the findings of Richard Brown that the Missouri Compromise helped sharpen party lines and contributed to the rise of the Democratic Party. Like Van Buren, Hill and Woodbury looked South. Richard H. Brown, "The Missouri Compromise, Slavery, and the Politics of Jacksonianism," *South Atlantic Quarterly*, 65 (1966), 55–72. See also Everett S. Brown, ed., *The Missouri Compromises and Presidential Politics 1820–1825 from the Letters of William Plumer, Junior* (St. Louis, 1926).

46. *Patriot*, April 4, July 21, 1818, Jan. 5, May 4, 1819, Dec. 5, 1820.

tended that the banks of New Hampshire suffered less than those elsewhere because they had kept "within bounds."[47]

Hill and his followers also suggested the Democratic line on internal improvements. In 1820, the Superior Court rendered the same "public interest" decision in a bridge case that it had given three years earlier in the Dartmouth College case. In its decision the court allowed a toll bridge across the Connecticut River at Claremont even though it interfered with an earlier ferry grant. The grant gave Benjamin Sumner the "sole right" to carry passengers across the river, but Woodbury and the court argued that even if the new bridge should "fringe the rights of the owner of the ferry," it should be built because it was in the "public interest." Taney gave a similar decision in the Charles River Bridge case in 1837.

Like Democrats later, Republicans recognized the need for improved transportation in the growing state. Although they were generally opposed to internal improvements at federal expense, they were eager to have state and private projects. The first boat from Boston over the Middlesex Canal and the Merrimack River arrived in Concord in 1815 and set everyone's imagination stirring. The *Patriot* outlined elaborate plans for a forty-mile canal from Concord east to Exeter, where it would connect by river with Portsmouth and the Atlantic Ocean. Others planned a road from Boston to Quebec. Hill summed it up with a five-point plan, which included a canal from Lake Winnipesaukee to Portsmouth and another from the Merrimack River to the Connecticut River. If the Republicans had had their way, New Hampshire would have been crisscrossed by roads and waterways. The road to Quebec was built; the canals were not.[48]

47. New Hampshire had ten banks in 1820 and twenty-one in 1831. In 1825 the legislature chartered only two of the many banks proposed. New Hampshire Republicans also anticipated Jacksonian opposition to the Supreme Court when the *Patriot* condemned Marshall's assertion of authority in *Cohens v. Virginia. Ibid.*, Oct. 19, Nov. 16, 1819, Dec. 19, 1820, July 4, 1825; John J. Knox, *A History of Banking in America* . . . (New York, 1900), pp. 337–338.

48. *Patriot*, June 27, 1815, Feb. 4, 1817, Sept. 15, 1818, Nov. 23, 1819, Dec. 5, 1820.

Republicans were as much interested in social reforms as Democrats were a decade later. One condition that particularly embarrassed them was imprisonment for debt. After a speech by Governor Plumer, the legislature passed a law forbidding imprisonment for any debt less than $13.34. The law was designed to get seventy-year-old Captain Moses Brewer, a hero of the Revolution, out of jail, but he was soon back in because he could not pay the $300 in expenses that he had incurred. After Hill publicized the case, saying that Brewer was "immured in a dungeon twelve feet square," Benjamin Pierce, later the first Democratic governor of New Hampshire, paid the $300 out of his own pocket to release Brewer from his "Bastille." The *Patriot* came out strongly against solitary confinement in jail; it favored retention of an eighteenth-century act against usury; and it got the Senate to pass a resolution in favor of appropriating $1,000 to send deaf and dumb children to an asylum in Hartford, Connecticut. Prodded by the *Patriot*, the legislature instructed New Hampshire Congressmen to demand federal money for education in any state where the national government had not set aside land for that purpose.[49]

Republican politics was also a school for Democratic tacticians. The *Patriot* continually showed reverence for those who had fought in the Revolution. When General John Stark, the New Hampshire hero of the Battle of Bennington, died at the age of ninety-three, the *Patriot* was wreathed in black, saddened that "the immortal Stark" was "no more." Hill suggested that only Revolutionary War veterans should be presidential electors, so that the "voice of the Revolution" could speak once more. During the War of 1812, said the *Patriot*, Federalists had shown none of the patriotic Revolutionary spirit. The *Patriot* also never failed to appeal to farming sentiment. It carried column after column of farm advice, adorned its articles with agrarian maxims, and

---

49. Hill praised Benjamin Pierce for his generosity, then lectured his readers on the reasons for indebtedness, which he blamed on "extravagance" and "foreign finery." *Patriot*, June 9, Aug. 11, Nov. 17, 1818, Sept. 4, 1819, June 4, 11, 25, July 2, 1821.

printed hundreds of letters from farmers. The Republican Party was a farmers' party dedicated to the Revolution.[50]

Freemasonry was often connected with the Republican Party and later with the Democratic Party. The number of Masons doubled between 1823 and 1826; the increase may have helped the rise of the Democratic Party, which began about that time. During the election of 1824, Hill, who was senior grand warden in the Masons, received a letter asking for thirty-five copies of a circular to go out to all grand masters. From 1824 to 1855 the governor—usually a Democrat—was a Mason twenty-four out of thirty-one years. When William Morgan disappeared in 1826 in western New York, the *Patriot* refused to believe that Masons had carried him off and argued that it was a plot to sell anti-Masonic books.[51]

By the early 1820's the Republicans were well organized. Every June the Republican legislators met in caucus in Concord and nominated candidates for governor and lesser offices. The Central Committee, whose secretary was Hill, sent out printed circulars to county committees, which chose candidates for the state legislature. The structure dated back to the days of John Langdon at the start of the century. In the next few years the organization would be tested by a severe intraparty battle; and out of that would come the Democratic Party.[52]

On the eve of the formation of the second two-party system in New Hampshire, Isaac Hill and his followers formed a sturdy link between the Republicans of 1800 and the Democrats of 1828. In the fight against Dartmouth College, Hill used rhetoric that

50. *Ibid.*, Dec. 22, 1818, Jan. 12, Feb. 16, 1819, Oct. 8, Dec. 31, 1821, May 13, 1822, April 19, Aug. 2, 1824, Sept. 25, 1826; *Gazette*, Oct. 29, 1823.

51. Of twenty-nine Masons holding office 1800–1805, sixteen were Republicans, thirteen Federalists. Kaplanoff, "Social and Economic Bases," p. 153; J. F. Dana to Hill, Oct. 31, 1824, Hill Papers; Charles B. Heald, "Thirty-nine of the Sixty-six Governors of New Hampshire Were Freemasons," *The Masonic Craftsman*, Feb., 1948, pp. 23–25; *Patriot*, Oct. 16, Dec. 25, 1826.

52. For the early Republican organization in New Hampshire see Noble E. Cunningham, *The Jeffersonian Republicans in Power: Party Operations, 1801–1809* (Chapel Hill, N.C., 1963), pp. 142–145. See also McCormick, *Second American Party System*, pp. 55–56.

echoed the Republican campaign of 1800 and anticipated Democratic slogans in the 1830's. Republicans in 1820 already showed the same sympathy for slavery, concern for the public interest, and belief in humanitarian reform as did Democrats a decade later. The roots of Jacksonian Democracy went back to the start of the century.[53]

53. Lee Benson denies that there was continuity in New York state politics and considers "the Federalist-Whig, Republican-Democrat formula" invalid. Benson, *The Concept of Jacksonian Democracy: New York As a Test Case* (New York, 1961), pp. 4–6, 62–63, quotation on p. 62. Contrary to Benson, I find far more evidence of continuity than of discontinuity in the politics of New Hampshire.

III

The Rise of the

Democratic Party, 1822-1829

In June 1822, the Republican legislative caucus in Concord nominated war hawk Samuel Dinsmoor for governor; a month later the Tennessee legislature nominated Andrew Jackson for President. The choice of the two Democrats symbolized the end of the political Era of Good Feelings and the emergence of the Democratic Party; the nomination of two men so closely connected with the War of 1812 suggests the link between the Democratic Party and the past. In New Hampshire the rise of the Democratic Party began in 1822 with a regional battle between Isaac Hill and Levi Woodbury.

In 1822 Hill was doing well. New Hampshire had "waded through the trial of political warfare," and was "more decidedly Republican than any other state in the Union." Hill's own *New-Hampshire Patriot* was the state's leading Republican newspaper. Amply backed by federal and state printing and mail contracts, it had become a prosperous enterprise. His bookstore and other investments were also profitable. He was a state senator from 1820 to 1822. As secretary of the Republican Central Committee he pulled political strings in New Hampshire.[1]

1. The quotations are from *Patriot*, Mar. 11, 1822. In my account of New Hampshire politics, 1823–1824, I have drawn from Vincent J. Capowski, "The Era of Good Feelings in New Hampshire: The Gubernatorial Campaigns of Levi Woodbury, 1823–1824," *Historical New Hampshire*, 21 (Winter 1966), 3–5.

Levi Woodbury by 1822 had also risen rapidly. Associate Justice of the state Superior Court and son-in-law of Asa Clapp, Woodbury was a man to be reckoned with. By settling in Portsmouth he strengthened his political position. When he moved there in 1819, former governor Plumer of Epping and newly elected governor Samuel Bell of Chester led the seacoast Republicans. By 1822 Plumer had retired, and Bell, who had just been elected United States Senator, would soon be spending most of his time in Washington. The way was open for Woodbury. Outside of the state his political acquaintance had also grown. He was a close ally of William King, a political power in Maine, and in Washington John Quincy Adams had reason to support him. When Portsmouth Federalists attacked Adams' policies as Secretary of State, Woodbury on the Fourth of July, 1821, gave a "Vindication" of Adams. Though more a defense of nationalism than of Adams—"I am an AMERICAN . . . I am a Republican," he had concluded—it had pleased the Secretary of State. In 1823 Adams considered sending Woodbury to England to talk with Foreign Secretary George Canning about his proposals for the western hemisphere. Woodbury had become the ranking Republican along the seacoast.[2]

Portsmouth Republicans needed a powerful leader because Hill and other Republicans from the middle of the state had wrested power from the seacoast and threatened its economy. Interior Republicans had once supported plans for a canal from Portsmouth to Lake Winnipesaukee and on to the upper Connecticut River. Concord Republicans turned against the canal because they feared being bypassed. Traffic from Boston would go by barge to Portsmouth and thence by river and the canal well around Concord to the Connecticut River above Hanover. They preferred to spend the money on the Merrimack River so that traffic would flow from Boston up the Middlesex Canal to the

2. Levi Woodbury, *A Vindication of Mr. Adams' Oration* (Concord, N.H., 1821); Capowski, "Woodbury," pp. 108–116; William Plumer, Jr., to Woodbury, Feb., 1822, Woodbury Papers, LC.

Merrimack, then to Concord, and eventually by canal to the Connecticut. Since the Union Boat Company, of which Hill was a director, had two-thirds of the Merrimack trade to Boston, Hill grew hostile to a Portsmouth canal.[3]

Republicans from the hill country also showed their power by demanding the creation of a new county in the Concord region and by insisting on a governor from the interior. They disliked going to Portsmouth on legal business, and they resented the fact that all governors had come from the seacoast. "To run for governor," Hill concluded, "a man must remove either to Portsmouth or Exeter, erect or purchase a large, three-story house, keep his coach, four horses, and servants." Hill brought the sectional tiff to a head in 1822 when he forced the caucus to nominate Dinsmoor of Keene, in western New Hampshire, for governor.[4]

The regional antagonism drove a wedge between Hill and Woodbury when Portsmouth Republicans, in January 1823, prevailed on Woodbury to run against Dinsmoor. Outside of Portsmouth, Republican patriarchs such as Plumer, Bell, and Benjamin Pierce preferred Woodbury. According to Plumer, Dinsmoor was "much too feeble—much shame to the Republicans for nominating him." In Concord a group called "North-enders," angry at Hill because he helped pick a south-end site for the new state house in 1816, joined in. Hill's opponents in Concord also established the *New Hampshire Statesman* to challenge the *Patriot*. To make things worse, Hill's partner and political ally, Jacob Bailey Moore, left the *Patriot* to join the opposition.[5]

All over the state—in Keene, in Hanover, in Exeter—Federalists like Ezekiel Webster did their best to promote disharmony in

3. *Patriot*, Nov. 11, 1822.
4. Capowski, "Era of Good Feelings," pp. 5–6; *Patriot*, Feb. 3, 1823.
5. Plumer's statement is from his letter to William Plumer, Jr., Jan. 13, 1823, Plumer Papers, LC. Capowski, "Era of Good Feelings," pp. 6–10; Plumer to Woodbury, Jan. 28, 1823, Benjamin Pierce to Woodbury, Jan. 20, 1823, Woodbury Papers, LC; William Plumer to William Plumer, Jr., Dec. 30, 1822, Plumer Papers, LC; William Plumer, Jr., to Jacob Moore, Jan. 25, 1823, Jacob Bailey Moore Papers, Houghton Library, Harvard University; Livermore, *Twilight*, p. 119.

the Republican Party. Moore commented on the new Federalist threat: "No enemy openly appears—he darts about unseen . . . . We have now a hydra to combat, more terrible than even the monster at Hartford." Plumer believed that the Federalists had it "absolutely in their power to settle the question."[6]

Hill responded by taking the offensive. When the Portsmouth *Gazette* accused him of dominating the state, the *Patriot* replied: "Shall Portsmouth dictate?" When the *Gazette* said that Dinsmoor was hardly intelligent enough to be governor, Hill charged that the newspaper opposed Dinsmoor just because he was loyal during the War of 1812, whereas many people in Portsmouth were not. Hill warned that if Woodbury won, Concord would be saddled with a $10,000 tax for a canal from Alton Bay, on Lake Winnipesaukee, to Portsmouth.[7]

Hill also tried to mend fences with William Plumer, who reported that Hill appeared "considerably alarmed at the opposition that is made to him and his paper." Plumer became increasingly apprehensive about the violent tone of the *Patriot*. "Hill's last two papers," he wrote, "contain much rant and abuse against Woodbury and others, who for a long period have been his best friends." After failing to win the old governor over, Hill unwisely refused to print an article by Plumer against Dinsmoor. Plumer simply took the manuscript back and sent it to the *Portsmouth Journal,* which stood behind Woodbury. The affair was embarrassing for Hill.[8]

Woodbury won the election by over 4,000 votes. When Ezekiel and Daniel Webster claimed that the Federalists had elected

6. Moore to Dr. N. Carter, Oct. 5, 1823, Moore Papers; William Plumer to William Plumer, Jr., Feb. 17, 1823, Plumer Papers, LC; Livermore, *Twilight,* p. 119.

7. Bradley, *Hill,* pp. 57–58; Robinson, "Hill," p. 32; *Gazette,* Feb. 18, Mar. 4, April 1, 1823; *Patriot,* Oct. 7, 1822, Jan. 7, Feb. 3, 24, Mar. 3, 1823; Edward J. Gallagher, "Luther Roby, Early New Hampshire Publisher," *Historical New Hampshire,* 2 (Sept. 1946), p. 4.

8. *Patriot,* Mar. 3, 17, 24, 1823; Turner, *Plumer,* pp. 325–327; William Plumer to William Plumer, Jr., Feb. 3, 17, 1823, N. A. Haven to William Plumer, Feb. 19, 1823, Plumer Papers, LC.

Woodbury, Hill, a bad loser, agreed. But although Federalism was helpful, regional issues made the difference. Portsmouth, for example, voted 900-34 for Woodbury. The election revealed a deep schism in Republican ranks and gave the new governor the opportunity to form a new party out of dissident Republicans and old Federalists. With bases in Francestown and Portsmouth and friends in all parts of New Hampshire, he had a unique opportunity.[9]

A new party might have blocked the eventual rise of the Democratic Party, but Woodbury chose instead to follow Samuel Bell's advice to conciliate the regular Republicans. When he wrote Hill suggesting peace, the latter indicated that he was grateful for the overture. "Your friendly concessions," he replied, "considering the higher ground on which you stand before the public, are greater than I had reason to anticipate." Hill added that "the contest was one of uncommon severity"; the whole "artillery" had been directed at him, but he admitted that he could be "accused of too much severity." His main interest was "the welfare and unity of the great republican party." Both men seemed willing to forget the past.[10]

Woodbury tried to reassure Republicans with a Jeffersonian inaugural address. He sought, he said: "the general diffusion of knowledge, equality of rights, liberty of conscience, and a strict accountability of all public servants." He supported free schools. Calling the "sturdy yeomen" the backbone of the nation, he favored the "promotion" of agriculture. As Republicans, and later as Democrats, Hill and Woodbury could agree on all those points. Then the governor went about pleasing Hill in more

9. *Patriot,* Mar. 17, 24, 1823; Livermore, *Twilight,* p. 119; Woodbury, "Woodbury," pp. 5, 299; *New Hampshire Manual 1891,* p. 152.

10. Capowski, who is writing a biography of Woodbury, says that Hill's letter shows him to be unforgiving. He points as evidence to the military tone of the letter ("high ground," "artillery"). I think the letter reveals more of an attempt at conciliation than one could have expected from Hill. For Hill, politics was a form of warfare, and opponents were to be crushed. Bell to Woodbury, Mar. 29, 1823, Hill to Woodbury, April 9, 1823, Woodbury Papers, LC; Capowski, "Era of Good Feelings," pp. 14–16.

practical ways. With Woodbury's backing, the legislature voted to form Merrimack County in central New Hampshire out of parts of Hillsborough and Rockingham counties. Woodbury appointed Hill's brother-in-law, Richard H. Ayer, sheriff of the new county. The appointment outraged the large majority of Federalists and anti-Hill Republicans, who had supported the governor. In general, Woodbury appointed Republicans rather than Federalists to most positions.[11]

By conciliating the Republicans, Woodbury lost Federalist backing, but even so he was unable to get Hill's endorsement. Caught in the middle between the Republican-Federalist camp and the Republican-Democratic camp, Woodbury had little chance of success. When he decided to run again in 1824, Hill opposed him, for he suspected that Federalists still lurked behind the Portsmouth movement. "I find," he wrote, "the Republican cause in these pretended days of good feelings, has more to fear than it had when *grim visaged war put on her sable front.* Our ancient political enemy, having cast off her odious name, is acting more effectively against us than she did when every Republican knew her by the mark in her forehead. She is constantly sowing dissentions [*sic*] in the Republican ranks."[12]

Trusting neither Woodbury nor the Federalists, Hill sought another candidate. Since he no longer controlled the legislative caucus, he called for a nominating convention. When his calls went unheeded, he and the party regulars turned to county caucuses to select an opponent for Woodbury. One such group gathered at Fogg's Tavern in Epping and nominated David L. Morril for governor. When Republicans in Cheshire County,

11. Jefferson might not have approved of Woodbury's words in favor of manufacturing. *Patriot,* June 9, 1823; Capowski, "Era of Good Feelings," pp. 16–23. Woodbury confided to himself in his diary, "Sunday Exercises," Nov. 23, 1823, that many had turned against him because of "suspicions and jealousies of my personal attachment to Mr. Hill." Woodbury Papers, LC.

12. Hill to John F. Parrott, Nov. 10, 1823, John F. Parrott Papers, NHHS; Capowski, "Era of Good Feelings," pp. 23–24.

Concord, and Hanover also nominated Morril, Hill decided that he had found the man to defeat Woodbury.[13]

Morril, born in Epping during the Revolution, was son and grandson of Congregational ministers. Educated at Phillips Exeter Academy, he first practiced medicine, next became pastor of the Congregational Church in Goffstown, and then served as United States Senator, 1817-1823. As a Congregational minister and former Federalist, Morril was a strange man for Hill to support. According to the *New Hampshire Gazette* in Portsmouth, Methodists, Quakers, and Baptists (the heart of Hill's following), did not like Morril because he was a "Calvinist" and a "priest of the standing order." The *Gazette* embarrassed Hill by intimating that Morril would bring about the repeal of the Toleration Act if elected. Hill's position became even more difficult when a number of Federalists came out for Morril. But to defeat Woodbury, Hill was willing to use a Congregationalist candidate and Federalist votes.[14]

Fortunately for Hill, loyalty to the governor was waning. Two future Jacksonians deserted him. At Bowdoin College, Franklin Pierce was highly amused when he heard that Woodbury would probably not be reelected. He wrote: "to have the chair of state *twitched* from under him before he has hardly taken his seat, I fear, will throw the feble [*sic*] judge into a high fever." In Charlestown, Henry Hubbard, one of the governor's aides, called a county convention, which nominated Samuel Dinsmoor, but Dinsmoor turned the nomination down. Federalist Jeremiah Mason remarked that Woodbury had "discovered *great talents,* & much industry, in destroying his *own popularity* in the short term of a few months." Federalists, aware that Woodbury had remained firmly Republican, nominated Jeremiah Smith as their own candidate for governor. In view of all his handicaps, it is remark-

13. *Gazette,* June 10, 1823; *Patriot,* Jan. 12, Feb. 9, 16, 1824.
14. Stackpole, *History,* III, 78; *Gazette,* Feb. 24, 1824. Hill's willingness to accommodate Federalists can be seen in his letter to Samuel Bell, Dec. 12, 1823, Samuel Bell Papers, NHHS (henceforth called Bell Papers).

able that Woodbury did as well as he did. Morril had a 3,000 vote margin over him in March, but no one had a majority. In June the legislature elected Morril governor.[15]

Woodbury felt that he had lost because he had "erred in trusting" Hill's "promises of friendship." Hill, he moaned, had "grossly betrayed" him and "had not the magnanimity" to do him justice. The election proved to Woodbury that "Federalists and apostate democrats" could control the state "by combination and terror." He was at least partly correct, because Federalists were stronger in 1824 than they had been at any time since 1816. Jacob Bailey Moore declared that they were showing themselves openly and were laughing at the division within the Republican Party.[16]

For Woodbury the two-year battle had ended in defeat. He was angry, but determined to stay within the party. Hill had won, but he realized that he needed Woodbury in order to secure political control of the state. Woodbury's decision not to join the Federalists and Hill's willingness to take him back made it possible to organize the Democratic Party in the next two years.

Formal reconciliation between Woodbury and Hill came during the fight to elect a United States Senator from New Hampshire, a battle so intense that it continued for three consecutive sessions of the state legislature—June and November 1824 and June 1825. The Federalists, who were numerous in the lower house, flaunted their power and were able to get the House to nominate Jeremiah Mason. Standing six feet seven inches tall

15. Franklin Pierce to Colonel John McNeil, Jan. 10, 1824, Pierce Papers, NHHS. For the Mason quotation see William Plumer to William Plumer, Jr., Feb. 2, 1824, Plumer Papers, LC; E. M. Cutting to Woodbury, Feb. 27, 1824, Woodbury Papers, LC; Moore to Woodbury, Feb. 27, 1824, Moore Papers; Capowski, "Era of Good Feelings," pp. 25–29. Woodbury still showed tremendous strength in Portsmouth, where he polled 726 votes to 18 for Morril and 14 scattered, but his total vote of 11,741 was down from 16,985 the year before. The vote at the state legislature in June was Morril 146, Woodbury 64. *Patriot*, April 5, May 10, June 7, 1824; *Gazette*, Mar. 8, 16, 23, April 13, 1824; Stackpole, *History*, III, 78; *New Hampshire Manual 1891*, pp. 152–153.

16. Woodbury, "Sunday Exercises," Mar. 16, 1824, Moore to Woodbury, April 7, 1824, Woodbury Papers, LC; Capowski, "Era of Good Feelings," pp. 29–30; Woodbury to Moore, Mar. 4, 1824, Moore Papers.

and possessing a brilliant mind, Mason was respected as the leading Federalist in the state. His glance was sharp and penetrating,
his tongue sarcastic, and since he did not tolerate weakness, he
was feared and hated. After graduating from Yale in 1788, he had
pursued a legal career in New Hampshire and was for four years
(1813–1817) United States Senator. In the Dartmouth College
case Mason had helped Webster defend the college. Now Webster
and John Quincy Adams were supporting Mason's attempt to
return to the Senate, and Hill could not afford to have Mason
win. Before the upper house could vote, the June session ended.[17]

When the legislature reconvened in November, Hill, who was
secretary of the Senate, went to work to get someone other than
Mason elected Senator. Under his prodding the Senate first chose
incumbent Senator John F. Parrott, then Samuel Dinsmoor,
finally William Plumer, Jr., but the House accepted none of
them. In spite of Hill, the Senate temporarily voted 7-5 to confirm the House choice of Mason, but Senator Nehemiah Eastman
succumbed to Hill's pressure and changed his vote. The session
closed with the Senator unchosen.[18]

Not since 1816 had there been such political fury in New
Hampshire. William Plumer, who described the debate as *"rude
& indecorous,"* blamed the bitterness on the Federalists, whose
intrigue had "done more to perpetuate *party spirit*" than any
event in the past eight years. Mason himself told Daniel Webster
that the "spirit of Jacobinism" was "pretty thoroughly roused."
Among Republicans there was little unity. Josiah Butler complained that Hill insisted on his own personal choice for Senator
and said that Jacob Bailey Moore was the only man who could
stop him. With considerable understatement Butler remarked
that Hill had "nothing of the conciliatory spirit or moderation."
William Claggett pointed out that Hill could not unite the party;

17. Livermore, *Twilight*, p. 192; Stackpole, *History*, III, 15–16; Reid, "Doe's
World"; Capowski, "Woodbury," pp. 168–169; Woodbury to Samuel Bell,
Jan. 1, 1825, Bell Papers.
18. Reid, "Doe's World"; *Patriot*, Jan. 3, 1825; *Gazette*, Dec. 14, 1824, Mar.
1, 1825; Clark, *Memoir of Mason*, pp. 288, 289.

while Woodbury urged Moore to start a newspaper in Concord to challenge Hill and to appeal to both Republicans and Federalists. Moore himself favored Woodbury as Senator.[19]

Hill worked energetically in the March election to get his followers elected to the legislature. Mason reported to Webster that Hill was "traversing the state, like a flying dragon, attending all the caucuses, & organizing his regulars," even using the mails illegally. The *Patriot* announced that the "very existence" of the Republican Party was at stake. In March his victory was complete: Morril was reelected governor and Hill Republicans gained a majority in the legislature. Future Jacksonians such as Matthew Harvey, John Brodhead of Newmarket, Thomas Chandler of Bedford, and Benning Bean of Moultonboro were swept into the Senate. They were "Hillites," said the *Concord Register*, "Patriot men," "Democrats of the Hill stamp." Hill wrote serenely that the *Patriot* had not been the "aggressor" in the "severe election," that it was "purely a way of self defense." "If anyone supposes," he continued, "that I war personally with federalists, they greatly mistake; I am not that person who is destitute of the common kindly feeling of human nature."[20]

Reassured by the election results, Hill was ready to deal once again with Woodbury. In March Portsmouth had sent Woodbury to the House, and in June the House chose him as Speaker. The temperature of the hottest June in years matched that inside the state house as the legislature renewed the battle over the Senate seat. The struggle went on for five ballots, but finally Hill and Woodbury came to an understanding. They joined forces, and Woodbury was elected United States Senator. From that point on the two Democrats worked together building the state party.[21]

19. William Plumer to William Plumer, Jr., Dec. 27, 1824, Feb. 7, 1825, Plumer Papers, LC; Mason to Webster, Feb. 20, 1825, Daniel Webster Papers, LC; Josiah Butler to Moore, Dec. 6, 1824, William Claggett to Moore, Dec. 30, 1824, Woodbury to Moore, Dec. 27, 1824, Moore Papers; Moore to Woodbury, Jan. 5, 1825, Woodbury Papers, LC.

20. Mason to Webster, Feb. 20, 1825, Webster Papers, LC; *Patriot*, May 30, June 6, 13, 1825; Hill to John Kelly, May 6, 1825, Hill Papers.

21. *Gazette*, June 14, 1825; *Patriot*, June 13, July 25, 1825; Clark, *Memoir of Mason*, p. 289.

In national politics New Hampshire Republicans looked in different directions. William Plumer, Samuel Bell, and others, who would be National Republicans in 1828, looked north and supported John Quincy Adams in the election of 1824. Plumer was the only elector in 1820 to cast a vote against James Monroe for President, hoping that his vote for Adams would start a groundswell for the New Englander. In the gubernatorial election of 1823, many of the Federalists and Republicans backing Woodbury wanted Adams for President.

Isaac Hill, who had started to look south during the Missouri debates in 1820, continued to seek his political future in that section. When the Republican Congressional caucus nominated Secretary of the Treasury William H. Crawford of Georgia for President in February 1824, Hill endorsed the selection. Plumer warned Hill that he was backing a losing candidate, but he replied obstinately that Adams' "principles were federal." In supporting the southerner Crawford, Hill joined future southern Democrats against the "amalgamating" northern Federalists and Republicans.

Martin Van Buren took the same position in New York, defending Crawford, while the followers of DeWitt Clinton supported Adams. The politics of Van Buren and Hill were similar in the 1820's. In the debate over Missouri both were inclined to heed the interests of the South. In their separate states they were forming the political machines that would help send to the White House southerners Jackson and Polk and northerners Van Buren and Pierce.[22]

22. Lynn Turner, "The Electoral Vote against Monroe in 1820," *Mississippi Valley Historical Review*, 42 (1955), 250–273; William Plumer to Moore, Jan. 25, 1823, Moore Papers. Hill's statement about Adams is in William Plumer to William Plumer, Jr., Feb. 3, 1823, Plumer Papers, LC, cited in Capowski, "Era of Good Feelings," p. 11. William Plumer, Jr., wrote from Washington that Crawford's friends were backing Morril (Hill's man) for governor in New Hampshire. Brown, *Missouri Compromises*, pp. 107–108. Robert Remini, *Martin Van Buren and the Making of the Democratic Party* (New York, 1959), pp. 36, 58–72. In his authorized biography of Hill, Cyrus Bradley makes it clear that Hill joined southerners in backing Crawford. Bradley, *Hill*, pp. 96–97.

Woodbury was drawn in both directions. In 1820 he had shown southern sympathies, but in 1823 Adams men had backed him for governor. Before the campaign of 1824, Charles G. Haines of New York, a Clintonian who had once lived in New Hampshire, wrote him suggesting that New York and New Hampshire Republicans join forces against Van Buren and Hill. "It is time," he said, "that your state should be rescued from the shackles, cast around her, by little minds." Woodbury replied that although he preferred Adams, he saw no need to come out openly. In both 1823 and 1824 Woodbury had the chance to split his party by joining a fusion of Federalists and Republicans, but in each case he chose not to. By resisting the overtures of New Hampshire Federalists and New York Clintonians, Woodbury was soon able to join forces with Van Buren and Hill.

In spite of Hill, the New Hampshire Republicans nominated Adams for President in 1824 over Crawford by an overwhelming margin. The voters ratified the decision by giving Adams over 9,000 votes in November to barely 600 for Crawford. Hill's setback in the Granite State only matched Van Buren's in New York, which also went for Adams. "Van Buren looks like a wilted cabbage," laughed one opponent. Both men bounced back fast, however, and before long had shifted their support to Jackson.[23]

As Woodbury and Hill drew together, so too did Portsmouth and Concord Republicans. The new Portsmouth-Concord turnpike had sharply increased overland trade between the coast and the interior. Where previously a stage a week could not be supported, now two lines ran three stages weekly. Hill now called Concord a funnel through which goods from upstate New Hamp-

23. Charles G. Haines to Woodbury, Feb. 14, 1823, Woodbury to Haines, June 17, 1823, Woodbury Papers, LC. For a thorough discussion of Woodbury and the Adams campaign, see Capowski, "Era of Good Feelings," pp. 10–12, 24–25. In the New Hampshire Republican legislative caucus in June 1824, the vote for presidential nomination was Adams 161, Crawford 4, Jackson 1. Moore to Woodbury, June 9, 1824, Woodbury Papers, LC. The popular vote in New Hampshire in November was Adams 9,389, Crawford 643. Svend Petersen, *Statistical History of the American Presidential Elections* (New York, 1962), p. 143; *Gazette*, Sept. 14, 1824; Remini, *Van Buren*, pp. 73–81.

shire flowed to Portsmouth as well as to Boston. Meanwhile, steep hills and high expenses dissipated enthusiasm for a canal from Portsmouth to Lake Winnipesaukee. It was not needed, and it was never built. For the time being disputes over transportation ceased to divide the coast and the interior.[24]

Amid the good feeling Hill set about disengaging himself from Governor Morril, whom he had supported in order to defeat Woodbury, but whose Congregationalist background was a political liability. As an alternative there was General Benjamin Pierce. A noisy, foul-mouthed, hard-drinking tavern keeper, Pierce had chased the redcoats out of Concord, withstood several British charges on Bunker Hill, and suffered with Washington at Valley Forge. After the Revolution he settled in Hillsborough, where he brought up his son Franklin. Both Benjamin Pierce and his tavern were popular in southwestern New Hampshire.[25]

Although four county conventions split two and two between Morril and Pierce for the Republican nomination, Hill did not hesitate. Morril, said the *Patriot,* was a "physician and a divine"; had he "ever faced the cannon's mouth, or seen the British bayonet, or Indian tomahawk, or broad scalping knife reeking with the blood of his countrymen?" Pierce had. He was "the last hero of the Revolution whom we shall ever have an opportunity to honor with our votes." In 1825, fifty years after the start of the Revolution, it was good politics to have a Revolutionary War hero on your side. When Lafayette visited Concord that year, reviving memories of the past, Pierce marched at the head of two hundred soldiers of the Revolution to greet him, amid "tears of

24. Hill advised Concord people not to oppose a Portsmouth-Winnipesaukee canal, saying that competition was healthy. *Patriot,* April 23, May 9, 21, 28, June 6, 27, Oct. 3, 1825; Edward J. Gallagher, "Luther Roby," pp. 1–16; *Gazette,* June 10, 1823, May 4, 1824.

25. Roy Nichols, *Franklin Pierce: Young Hickory of the Granite Hills,* rev. ed. (Philadelphia, 1958), pp. 9–12, 31–33; Benjamin Pierce, "Autobiography" (n.p., n.d.); *Dedication of a Statue of General Franklin Pierce . . .* (Concord N.H., 1914), pp. 23, 75–77; *Patriot,* Feb. 27, 1826; Amos Tuck, *Autobiographical Memoir of Amos Tuck* (Exeter, N.H., 1875), p. 61; Elmer E. Charlton, *New Hampshire As It Really Is* (Claremont, N.H., 1856), p. 523; John R. Irelan, *The Republic* (Chicago, 1888), XIV, 15–17.

joy and sorrow" and the strains of Yankee Doodle. The Democratic Party would look to the Revolution just as the Republican Party had done. In the March 1826 election Federalists made Hill's shift easier by backing Morril. Even though Pierce lost, Hill had realigned the party structure and broken his one link with Congregationalists and Federalism.[26]

At the same time Hill and his followers moved into the Jackson camp. When Franklin Pierce graduated from Bowdoin and arrived in Portsmouth in 1825 to work in Woodbury's office, he was already for the Old Hero. On the Fourth of July that year young Pierce offered a toast to Jackson at a Portsmouth celebration. The *Patriot* accused the Adams administration of "proscribing" friends of Jackson and called Adams' supporters in New England former Federalists. In 1826 "Senex" began a series of intemperate articles against Adams in the *Patriot*. The Portsmouth *Gazette,* anti-Hill during the Hill-Woodbury fight, now joined the *Patriot* against Adams and Clay.[27]

In the spring and summer of 1826 Hill's Democratic organization grew. Committees of correspondence prepared for the coming election, and the party set up a new newspaper in Dover. To arouse statewide support for Benjamin Pierce, Hill revived the practice of calling a legislative caucus. After the Jacksonians nominated Pierce, they held a mammoth Fourth of July celebration in which the toasts looked back on fifty years of freedom and forward to victory in 1827. The Democrats also began to communicate with the party in New York. Van Buren praised the "Republicans" of New Hampshire for nominating Pierce and offered to stump the state for him. In the *Patriot*, Hill wrote

26. *Patriot,* Jan. 10, June 27, 1825, Feb. 13, Mar. 13, 1826; Nichols, *Pierce,* p. 31. William Plumer thought Hill did well considering the number of Federalists who opposed him. Plumer to Woodbury, April 5, 1826, Woodbury Papers, LC. Hill to Samuel A. Peason, Mar. 6, 1826, Mellen Chamberlain Collection, Boston Public Library; Livermore, *Twilight,* p. 224. Capowski, "Woodbury," p. 184.

27. *Patriot,* Sept. 29, 1823, April 10, 24, May 8, 1826; William Plumer to Woodbury, April 5, 1826, Woodbury Papers, LC; David L. Morril to Clay, Mar. 8, 1826, Henry Clay Papers, LC; Nichols, *Pierce,* pp. 29–30.

optimistic accounts of Democratic successes in the Empire State. Shortly after the party caucus, he took off for New York to visit Van Buren and to tour battlefields of the Revolution.[28]

The vigorous Democratic drive in 1825 and 1826 brought a strong reaction. Charles W. Cutter of the pro-Adams *Portsmouth Journal* tried ridicule: "Mr. Hill," he wrote, "has made some noise." Cutter claimed that there were but ten Jackson men of influence in New Hampshire, but he admitted that Hill was allied with Democratic editors in New York, Nashville, and Cincinnati. Morril, Moore, and Salma Hale of Keene took the Hill movement far more seriously, for each one used the word "revolutionize" to describe what Hill was doing to politics in New Hampshire. In Washington, Henry Clay, who also knew how to play politics, took the government printing contract away from the *Patriot* and left Hill "raving": "Of all the profligate politicians that have appeared in this country—we will not even except Aaron Burr—there is no man who has ever exceeded Henry Clay." Of the anti-administration papers in New Hampshire, only the Portsmouth *Gazette* kept its federal printing contract.[29]

Considering Hill's barrage, the administration was remarkably forbearing. In spite of protests, the *Patriot* retained a federal contract worth $6,000 to $8,000 a year to transport the mail in New Hampshire. Furthermore, the contract enabled the *Patriot* to circulate at no expense. Moore complained that Hill had even made threats against those carrying other newspapers. Edward Everett of Massachusetts vainly protested about him to Post-

28. Hill to Henry Lee, Sept. 16, 1828, Massachusetts Historical Society, *Proceedings*, 43 (1909), 70; Robert Remini, *The Election of Andrew Jackson* New York, 1963), pp. 83–84; Van Buren to Woodbury, July 11, 1826, Woodbury Papers, LC; Capowski, "Woodbury," pp. 209–210; *Patriot*, Feb. 27, June 26, Aug. 7, 14, 21, 28, Sept. 4, Oct. 9, 16, 1826, Jan. 29, 1827.

29. Cutter sent his remarks to the Chillicothe (Ohio) *Supporter and Gazette*. The *Patriot* printed the comments with appropriate rejoinder. *Patriot*, Nov. 13, 1826. David L. Morril to Clay, Mar. 8, Sept. 18, 1826, Clay Papers, LC; Salma Hale to John Bailey, April 29, 1826, John Bailey Papers, New-York Historical Society; Moore to Bell, Feb. 9, 1827, William Plumer to Bell, Jan. 12, 1827, Bell Papers; *Patriot*, Aug. 13, 1827. Clay also terminated the printing contract of the Democratic Maine *Eastern Argus*. Remini, *Election*, pp. 79–80.

master General John McLean in 1828. By employing Hill to carry the mail, he said, the Postmaster General gave him "the means of distributing a paper, which is infamous among the infamous, *gratis* .... you put it in the power of a wretch, capable of putting his name to the filthy libel which I exposed last winter, to hold himself up as your agent, enabled by you to distribute his venom throughout the community." McLean, who was disloyal to Adams, answered calmly that Hill had the contract because he made the lowest bid. The Postmaster General added that Hill was "now engaged in decided opposition to the Administration, but he strictly performs his contracts."[30]

In Washington, Daniel Webster sought ways to check Hill. Webster wrote Clay in June 1826 fearful that Hill and Woodbury would be able to carry New Hampshire in 1828. To his old friend Mason, Webster complained that Hill could not "be trusted in any promise or engagement which should bind him to a course of honest and liberal politics and manly feeling." He was so contrary that "even if the road led away manifestly from his own interest, he would follow it." In May 1827, Webster wrote Clay again, distressed that for two years the Republicans had failed to put Hill down even though four-fifths of the Republicans of New Hampshire favored the administration. They should appeal, said Webster, directly to the people. He saw the need for determined action.[31]

More and more the responsibility for checking the Democratic Party lay with United States Senator Samuel Bell. Once Hill's ally in the years after the War of 1812, Bell had moved to the other side. In the summer of 1826 while Hill was organizing Democrats, Bell was creating an opposition. He hurried home from Congress in May to help set up Republican newspapers, including the hard-hitting but badly named *Butterfly* in Dover

30. Jacob Moore to Bell, Feb. 16, 1827, Bell Papers; Edward Everett to John McLean, Aug. 1, 1828, and McLean to Everett, Aug. 8, 1828, Massachusetts Historical Society, *Proceedings,* Third Series, 1 (1907-1908), 360–370.

31. Webster to Clay, June 8, 1826, April 14, May 18, 1827, Clay to Bell, April 18, 1827, Clay Papers, LC; Clark, *Memoir of Mason,* p. 298.

and the *New Hampshire Journal,* edited by Moore, in Concord. John Quincy Adams wrote Bell that no state would give him more pain to lose than New Hampshire. "Your approbation," he concluded, "has been among my most cheering encouragement." After withdrawing the printing contract from the *Patriot,* Clay followed Bell's advice and turned the contract over to Moore's *Journal.* Knowing he had a difficult task ahead of him, Bell moved warily. To Webster he confided in 1826 that he was prepared to attack Hill, but feared that Hill would pretend to conform with all Republicans and prevent an open split.[32]

Hill's behavior and character made the Senator's task easier. Bell himself was convinced that Hill would never forgive him for defending the administration and would subject him to "a most vindictive and unprincipled persecution." Hill's former partner, Jacob Moore, who also expected an attack, insisted that he would not be a "slave" to Hill. When another of Hill's old cronies, Postmaster Joseph Low of Concord, refused to come out against Adams, Hill warned that there would soon be a new postmaster. Bell was so outraged that he described Hill as a "despot," whose "sham Republicanism" must be exposed. The affair helped draw Republicans such as the Plumers, Bell, Moore, and Morril closer together; but it also cost Low his job in 1829.[33]

The 1827 gubernatorial campaign was a curious one. The Republicans fought hard against the Democrats and ran a full ticket except, oddly, in the battle for governor, where they did not dare oppose the popular General Pierce. Bell and both Plumers agreed the preceding fall that to renominate Morril against Pierce would simply allow Hill to call the Republicans Federalists. From time to time the Republican press taunted Pierce for his lack of education, but the Democrats had an effective rejoinder. Though not well educated, Pierce was a man of

32. John Quincy Adams to Bell, Sept. 8, 1826, Bell Papers; Clay to the editor of the *New Hampshire Journal,* Dec. 7, 1826, Bell to Moore, Dec. 9, 1826, Moore Papers; Clark, *Memoir of Mason,* p. 298.
33. Bell to Moore, Jan. 4, Feb. 24, 1827, Moore Papers; Moore to Bell, Jan. 11, Feb. 9, 12, 16, 1827, Bell Papers.

"moral worth," who was "learned at war," which was "of more practical value . . . than all the speculative learning of the schools." In June, Benjamin Pierce, dressed in Revolutionary War garb with a three-cornered hat, rode into Concord as the first Jacksonian Democratic governor of the state. Hill took a seat in the state Senate.[34]

The Bell party faced a dilemma over Federalist backing. Some, like Morril, welcomed the Federalists, whereas others, like the Plumers, feared their support. But Webster and Clay spelled out the situation to Bell in the spring of 1827. Without Federalist votes, they argued, he could not defeat Hill, and if Bell did not take the lead in organizing a new party, then the Federalists would do it and he would have to join in as a follower. First, Webster said, the Bell Republicans should hold a "Friends of the Administration" meeting of Republicans and Federalists who supported John Quincy Adams. Second, said Clay, they should secure a resolution in the legislature supporting the Adams administration. According to Webster, the Federalists, who made up a third of the New Hampshire legislature, were willing to cooperate but were waiting for the Republican Adams men to take the lead.[35]

But Bell was not willing to make such an open break. Instead of calling an "amalgamation" meeting, he called a "Republican" meeting, at which Morril, Bell, and Henry Hubbard spoke. The meeting irritated the Federalists, who felt excluded, particularly when it "vindicated" Adams from charges of being a Federalist and described him as more Republican than Jackson. The resolution in the legislature was worded to appeal to Democratic Republicans as well as to Adams Republicans; but not to Fed-

34. *Patriot,* Jan. 29, Feb. 26, Mar. 12, 1827; Bell to Moore, Oct. 30, 1826, William Plumer, Jr., to Moore, Nov. 7, 1826, Moore Papers; Bell to Edward Everett, May, 19, 1827, Bell Papers.

35. Morril to Clay, Sept. 18, 1826, Clay Papers, LC; William Plumer, Jr., to Moore, Nov. 7, 1826, Moore Papers; Webster to Clay, April 14, May 18, 1827, Clay Papers, LC; Clay to Bell, April 18, 1827, Bell Papers; Capowski, "Woodbury," p. 219; Livermore, *Twilight,* p. 225.

eralists. It defended the Adams administration, calling it "strictly democratic." Jackson men, who hated Adams, and Federalists, who hated anything "democratic," then combined to vote the resoluton down. Webster wrote Clay that "Mr. Bell's good sense appears to me to have strangely deserted him." Though Bell needed Federalist support, he had adhered to *"exclusive caucuses and party discipline"* and thereby forced many men "of weight and influence" to stay away from the meeting. Federalist Ezekiel Webster was particularly angry. Martin Van Buren, on the other hand, was pleased with the failure of the Adams meeting. Woodbury summed up the summer of 1827 as a victory for the "Jacksonians" in New Hampshire.[36]

In Washington, where he had taken his seat in the Senate in December 1825, Woodbury was helping advance the cause of General Jackson. The first suggestion that Woodbury was unhappy with Adams came in January 1826, when he wrote that the President stood "aloof more than was expected from the antient and firm democracy of the country." He said that a Calhoun-Jackson alliance was entirely possible, though "public confidence in" Jackson's "talents as a statesman" was "by no means strong."[37]

During the same winter, Woodbury took part in a debate that helped shape the new Democratic Party. The controversy began in December 1825, when the administration proposed sending two delegates to the inter-American congress that was to be held in Panama. Since Adams and Clay supported the plan and future Jacksonians such as Van Buren, Calhoun, Woodbury, and Thomas Hart Benton opposed it, the debate crystallized opposition to the administration. Southern Congressmen were particularly opposed to the mission because they feared that slavery would be discussed

36. Capowski, "Woodbury," p. 219; Livermore, *Twilight*, pp. 224–226; Ezekiel Webster to Daniel Webster, June 14, 1827 (copy), Daniel Webster to Clay, June 22, 1827, Clay Papers, LC; Van Buren to Woodbury, July 5, 1827, Woodbury Papers, LC; Woodbury to R. Jarvis, Aug. 27, 1827, Robert Jarvis Papers, LC, cited in Livermore, *Twilight*, p. 226.
37. Capowski, "Woodbury," pp. 192–198; Elizabeth Woodbury to Mrs. Asa Clapp, Dec. 10, 1825, Woodbury Papers, LC; Woodbury to John J. Parrott, Jan. 10, 1826, Parrott Papers, NHHS.

at the congress, where republics controlled by Negroes would be represented. By voting against the mission, northern Jacksonians further cemented the alliance with the South that they had started during the Missouri Compromise. When the proposal passed the Senate, 24–19, most of the opposition came from the South. Four of the seven nay votes from the North were from Jacksonians Woodbury, Van Buren, John M. Berrien, and Mahlon Dickerson. When the appropriation passed the House, 134–60, all the nay votes except nine came from the South. The solitary nay vote from New England was that of Jacksonian Jonathan Harvey of New Hampshire.[38]

The debate also helped shape the new party system in New Hampshire because Democrats and National Republicans there took opposite sides. In his speech denouncing the plan, Woodbury claimed that the Panama Congress would become a permanent league, involving its members in fruitless wars. If the United States took part in such an unconstitutional arrangement, the Constitution would be nothing but a "nose of wax." The *Patriot* agreed that Latin America was planning a "league" and condemned Webster for supporting it. Democrat Benjamin Pierce congratulated Woodbury for his effort. On the other side, Senator Samuel Bell and all the New Hampshire Congressmen except Harvey backed the Panama Congress. The National Republican *Portsmouth Journal* pointed out the political implications of the split within the state's delegation.[39]

Woodbury, always cautious, tried for a while to maintain the fiction that he had not deserted Adams. He insisted that he was

38. *Gazette*, Aug. 14, 1827; Martin Van Buren, *Autobiography of Martin Van Buren*, John C. Fitzpatrick, ed., American Historical Association, *Annual Report, 1918*, II (Washington, D.C., 1919), 201; Remini, *Van Buren*, pp. 105–113; *Register of Debates in Congress*, 19th Congress, 1st Session (1825–1826), pp. 667, 2514.
39. *Patriot*, April 10, 17, 24, May 1, Sept. 25, Dec. 18, 1826, Jan. 1, 1827. Pierce to Woodbury, April 12, 1826, Plumer to Woodbury, April 5, 1826, Woodbury Papers, LC; Clark, *Memoir of Mason*, p. 298; Levi Woodbury, *Writings, Political, Judicial, and Literary; Now First Selected and Arranged by Charles Levi Woodbury* (Boston, 1852), I, 67–84.

still for the President as long as Adams was Republican, and he denied that he was "in the secrets of any party." In the spring of 1826 Webster still considered Woodbury for Adams, but by June, Webster was convinced that he had gone over to Hill and Jackson.[40]

As Woodbury committed himself to Jackson, he drew closer to Van Buren and Calhoun. Van Buren was friendly enough to ask the Woodburys to visit his "watering place" in New York. The Calhouns entertained them at dinner on several occasions. Calhoun also wrote Woodbury a revealing letter in which he attacked Adams for reviving the Federalist doctrines of 1798. He predicted a union of the South and middle states against the administration and asked Woodbury if New England would join. At the end he remarked that he had written without using his frank because he wished to "avoid the curiosity in some of the post offices." When the Twentieth Congress began in December 1827, the Woodburys started what came to be known as the "Woodbury Mess" at Mrs. Peyton's Boarding House in Washington. Here Jacksonians from all sections dined together: Van Buren and Gulian Verplanck of New York, Littleton Tazewell and John Randolph of Virginia, Calhoun and Powhatan Ellis of the deep South, John Bell and Hugh White of Tennessee, Tristam Burges and Mahlon Dickerson of the mercantile North. The New Hampshire Senator helped to draw the Jacksonians together.[41]

Woodbury soon found himself directly between Calhoun and Van Buren. When interest in him for Vice-President sprang up in New England, he wrote that the two Democrats were "shy" of him as a "competitor." On the tariff he was less committed than

40. Woodbury to William Plumer, Mar. 20, 1826, in *The Granite Monthly*, 5 (1881–1882), 404. For the quotation see Woodbury to William Plumer, May 17, 1826, Woodbury Papers, LC. Webster to Mason, Mar. 27, 1826, Clark, *Memoir of Mason*, p. 301; Webster to Clay, June 8, 1826, Clay Papers, LC. Josiah Butler wrote Woodbury from South Deerfield that he was unhappy with Woodbury's change of sentiment about Adams. Butler to Woodbury, April 21, 1826, Woodbury Papers, LC; Capowski, "Woodbury," pp. 196–203.
41. Van Buren to Woodbury, July 11, 1826, Calhoun to Woodbury, Sept. 21, 1826, Thomas Hart Benton to Woodbury, Aug. 3, 1828, Woodbury Papers, LC.

Calhoun, who wanted a low tariff, and Van Buren, who favored some protection. Instead of following either, Woodbury listened to Isaac Waldron of Portsmouth, who wrote that high duties on iron, hemp, and duck would hurt the merchants of that city. The Senator then voted against the Tariff of Abominations of 1828. Politicians and historians have debated whether Woodbury was on Calhoun's side or Van Buren's, but he was on neither.[42]

As the election year of 1828 approached, both parties moved to gain control of New Hampshire. Before returning to Congress in December of 1827, Bell finally called a convention of Friends of the Administration, Federalist as well as Republican, to meet in Portsmouth. The seaport was a promising National Republican base because few politicians there had ever liked Hill. One politician, Jeremiah Mason, had long favored doing away with the distinction between Republican and Federalist. Another, Port Collector Timothy Upham, wrote that even Republicans sympathetic to Governor Pierce were taking part in the anti-Hill caucus. Democrats later charged that Mason and Upham spent large sums of money opposing Hill in 1828. With this kind of support the administration party nominated John Bell, formerly a Federalist and the brother of Samuel Bell, for governor.[43]

The National Republicans were well organized. Immediately

42. Woodbury, "Sunday Exercises," April 7, 1827, Woodbury Papers, LC. Hayne of South Carolina also voted nay on the tariff; while Benton of Missouri joined Van Buren in voting yea. *Register of Debates in Congress*, 20th Congress, 1st Session (1828), p. 766. Capowski, "Woodbury," pp. 224–226; Isaac Waldron to Woodbury, Feb. 7, 1828, Woodbury Papers, LC; Remini, *Election*, pp. 77, 80, 84; Remini, *Van Buren*, p. 242. Charles Sellers considers Woodbury a Calhoun man. Charles Sellers, *James K. Polk, Jacksonian* (Princeton, N.J., 1957), pp. 116–117; Carl B. Swisher, on the other hand, sees him as a Van Buren man. Carl B. Swisher, *Roger B. Taney* (New York, 1935), p. 138.

43. After much debate Bell and the others arranged to have Republicans call the meeting, but invited both Republicans and Federalist friends of the administration. Bell to William Prescott, Oct. 3, 1827, David Morril to Bell, Dec. 17, 1827, Bell Papers; Bell to Moore, Oct. 31, 1827, Timothy Upham to Moore, Nov. 6, 1827, Moore Papers; Clark, *Memoir of Mason*, p. 301; Livermore, *Twilight*, p. 226; *Portsmouth Journal*, Dec. 15, 1827; Col. John Decatur to Woodbury, Dec. 10, 1827, Woodbury Papers, LC; Capowski, "Woodbury," pp. 222–223.

after Christmas, meetings at Epping and Hillsborough also nominated John Bell. Moore's *New Hampshire Journal,* which earlier had reached barely 1,200 people a year, had 3,800 subscribers in January of 1828. The party distributed pamphlets all over the state reciting tales of misdeeds by Isaac Hill and Andrew Jackson. Salma Hale from Keene even suggested slyly that the National Republicans circulate ballots with General Pierce's name at the top and the Adams slate below. The Bells and the Plumers, who had once admired Benjamin Pierce, turned sharply against the old general, calling him Hill's senile tool. Franklin Pierce was worried about his father's chances.[44]

Hill opened the 1828 Democratic campaign with a speech on January 8 addressed to the common man. The Democrats held a dozen celebrations of the Battle of New Orleans that day, and from then on January Eighth rivaled the Fourth of July in political importance. The largest crowd gathered in Concord, where 600 Jacksonians paraded from the state house to the Old North Church to hear Hill give his speech. Though now a man of substance, Hill symbolized the common man, for he always wore a black printer's coat and everyone remembered his early poverty. For an hour he appealed to the farmers and artisans with a masterpiece of rhetoric, ridiculing the "polished education" of Adams and comparing it with the stern self-education of General Jackson. He concluded by asking what Adams' economic program had done for New England. Like many Jacksonian speeches in 1828, this one laid down no specific program, but it showed that Democrats were staking their future on the plain people of the North.

After the speech, the Jacksonians paraded back to a large hall near the state house for a 3:00 P.M. dinner. On one wall soldiers in coonskin caps crouched behind bales of cotton and fired at

44. Colonel John Decatur to Woodbury, Dec. 10, 1827; Capowski, "Woodbury," pp. 222–223; Bell to Moore, Dec. 27, 1827, Hale to Moore, Jan. 26, 1828, Moore Papers; Moore to Bell, Jan. 8, 1828, Bell Papers; Turner, *Plumer,* pp. 327–328; Pierce to Mrs. E. A. McNeil, Feb. 17, Mar. 19, 1828, Pierce Papers, NHHS.

British regulars, while on another, scrolls reading "The Declaration of Independence" and "The Declaration of War 1812" flanked pictures of Thomas Jefferson and James Madison. The most prominent spot behind the head table was reserved for a gigantic picture of General Andrew Jackson himself. After several courses had passed down the table, the toasts got underway. First came tributes to Revolutionary War heroes, followed by toasts for stalwarts of the War of 1812. Toasts for "The Democracy of our country" followed several for freedom in Greece. Finally one Democrat shouted, "never let funds of states be taken away for internal improvements," and another gave a cheer for the "virtuous and enlightened yeomanry." As usual, New Hampshire Democrats were aware of their debt to the past, but at the same time claimed to represent the common man of the future.[45]

That evening 200 Democratic ladies and gentlemen gathered at the Eagle Hotel and Coffee House across from the state house for what was to become an annual ball. The opposition Portsmouth newspaper protested that many of the "ladies" were nothing but prostitutes, the opening charge in a dirty campaign. Even for the election of 1828, "prostitute" was a strong word.[46]

A day's ride west in Hillsborough, Governor Pierce and his son Franklin dominated the Jackson Day celebration. Benjamin Pierce, seventy-three, was preparing to run again for governor. Franklin Pierce, twenty-three, who was practicing law in Hillsborough, was campaigning for town moderator. Before noontime, 500 people gathered and marched in ragged fashion to Putnam's Tavern, where they sat down for dinner, after which the younger

---

45. The Jacksonian speeches in New Hampshire in 1828 confirm many of the insights of Marvin Meyers, *The Jacksonian Persuasion: Politics and Belief* (Stanford, Calif., 1957), and John W. Ward, *Andrew Jackson, Symbol for an Age* (New York, 1955). Yet I see Democrats in New Hampshire looking forward as well as back. Jacob Bailey Moore called Hill's speech a "violent philippic against Adams, Clay & Co." Moore to Bell, Jan. 8, 1828, Bell Papers; *Patriot*, Jan. 14, 1828; Isaac Hill, *An Address Delivered at Concord, N.H. Jan. 8, 1828, Being the 13th Anniversary of Jackson's Victory at New Orleans* (Concord, N.H., 1828); Bouton, *History of Concord*, pp. 403–404.

46. *Patriot*, Jan. 21, 28, 1828.

Pierce delivered his first formal address. A few days later, he wrote enthusiastically: "The cause of truth and republicanism yea more the cause of religion all are flourishing here."[47]

In seacoast Portsmouth and mountainous Wentworth, other loyal Democrats held Jackson Day dinners. Toasts to Levi Woodbury (the "North Star of Democracy") compared him with old John Langdon. Democrats uttered harsh remarks against Henry Clay and accused John Quincy Adams of reviving the "reign of terror" started by his father in 1798. In Wentworth Nathaniel Rix toasted "Ebony and Topaz," representing the spirits of darkness (Adams) and light (Jackson). Rix had named his son, born in 1811, James Madison Rix. Young Rix eventually became editor of the *Democratic Republican,* the strongest voice in northern New Hampshire. The spirit of 1828 combined the spirit of the Revolution, of 1798, and of 1812 with appeals to the common man.[48]

As election day approached, National Republicans stepped up their campaign. They circulated a booklet entitled *The Wise Sayings of the Honorable Isaac Hill,* to remind voters of statements Hill had made in the past when he was praising Adams and Clay and attacking Woodbury and Jackson. Handbills showing coffins of the six militiamen that Jackson had executed for desertion had more impact. As Bell poured coffin handbills into the state, Hill was forced to publish a special supplement to the *Patriot* defending the Old General.[49]

Democrats resorted to religious and class issues to put National Republicans on the defensive. By renewing their demand for a state university, Democrats recalled the Dartmouth College case and identified themselves with the old Republican crusade against Congregationalism, Federalism, aristocracy, and privilege.

47. Nichols, *Pierce,* 9–12, 31–33; *Statue of Pierce;* Pierce to Mrs. John McNeil, Jan. 16, 1828, Pierce Papers, NHHS.
48. *Patriot,* Jan. 28, 1828.
49. *New Hampshire Journal, The Wise Sayings of the Honorable Isaac Hill* (Concord, N.H., 1828); Bell to Moore, Feb. 29, 1828, Moore Papers; *Patriot,* Jan. 21, 1828.

National Republicans were obliged to answer Hill's boast that all Methodists were for Jackson. Senator Bell felt it necessary to explain how he had voted on a federal bankruptcy bill because he was concerned that his vote would underline Democratic charges that the National Republicans represented the well-to-do. Port Collector Timothy Upham described the social conflict in Portsmouth, where Jacksonians called themselves "Mechanics." He claimed that the National Republicans had "all the Merchants and nearly all the principal mechanics" on their side, but he feared that "many of the laboring people" had been "seduced" by Democratic "misrepresentations" and by Democratic "talk about *aristocracy & the oppression of the poor.*" Upham said that steps had been taken to "undeceive them," but concluded that the workers were "very ignorant." By "principal mechanics" Upham meant the prosperous highly paid craftsmen in the port; by his own testimony the others were Democratic. His patronizing statement about trying to "undeceive" the "very ignorant" reveals that social and economic lines were drawn.[50]

Bell defeated Pierce in March, 21,149 to 18,672; the National Republicans and Federalists captured two-thirds of the seats in the legislature; and even state senator Hill lost. In *The Second American Party System,* Richard McCormick rightly attributes the increase of 10,000 votes since 1826 to the return of Federalists to the polls. But he is less correct in wondering whether they voted for Pierce or Bell. When Federalists returned to the polls in 1828, they voted National Republican, not Democratic.[51]

There was continuity from Federalism to National Republicanism. Directly after the election Democrats were convinced that Federalist votes had determined the outcome. According to Franklin Pierce, the Federalists had resorted to the "most unparalleled exertions and unfair means" to carry the election. The

50. *Patriot,* June 4, 1827, Jan. 21, 28, Feb. 25, Mar. 3, 1828; *Gazette,* Feb. 5, 1828; Thomas Whipple, Jr., to Moore, Dec. 21, 1827, Bell to Moore, Jan. 19, 1828, Timothy Upham to Moore, [Dec., 1827], Moore Papers.
51. *Patriot,* Mar. 17, 24, 31, 1828; McCormick, *Second American Party System,* p. 59; Livermore, *Twilight,* p. 226; *New Hampshire Manual 1891,* p. 153.

Patriot said that Bell received 18,000 "old Federalist" votes and 3,000 "old Republican" votes, while Pierce could muster only 19,000 "old Republican" votes. Although the newspaper was exaggerating—even in 1816 the Federalists had been unable to secure 18,000 votes—Federalist votes did make the difference. The *Patriot* pointed out that of the 200 towns voting in both 1814 and 1828 all but 42 held to the same pattern: Republican towns in 1814 were Democratic in 1828, and Federalist towns in 1814 were National Republican in 1828. The interior of the state running from Goffstown west to Hillsborough and north to Lake Winnipesaukee and the White Mountains was heavily Republican in 1814 and solidly Democratic in 1828.[52]

In addition, almost all the leading National Republicans in New Hampshire had a Federalist past. Samuel Bell, John Bell, David L. Morril, Timothy Upham, John Prentiss, George Sullivan, Jeremiah Smith, and William Plumer had once been Federalists. Jeremiah Mason and Ezekiel Webster, who were still Federalists, fought hard for Bell. Mason and his old colleague Daniel Webster had pleaded with Samuel Bell for months to get him to unite Republicans and Federalists against the Democrats. David Morril wrote Henry Clay that all the Federalist newspapers in the state were on the amalgamation side. The Democratic newspapers could be expected to call the opposition "Federalist," as they did, but they were undoubtedly correct. National Republicans had to have Federalist support in order to defeat Hill, and they got it.[53]

52. Of the twenty-three towns that shifted from Federalist in 1814 to Democratic in 1828 all but two were in the interior. On the other hand, of the nineteen shifting from Republican to National Republican in 1828, all but one was outside of the interior. In short, Federalist towns in 1814 were likely to be National Republican towns in 1828, particularly outside of the interior of the state, which Hill dominated. Pierce to Mrs. Elizabeth E. McNeil, Mar. 19, 1828, Pierce Papers, NHHS; *Patriot*, Mar. 17, 24, 31, 1828.

53. Morril to Clay, Sept. 18, 1826, Clay Papers, LC. David Fischer gives biographies of nineteen "young" New Hampshire Federalists in his *The Revolution of American Conservatism*. By 1828 most were obscure, but six were for Bell, none for Pierce. David Hackett Fischer, *The Revolution of American Conservatism: the Federalist Party in the Era of Jeffersonian Democracy* (New York, 1965), pp. 233–239.

One successful Democrat in the election was Franklin Pierce, who won an upset victory in Hillsborough. For several years a local anti-Democratic politician named "King" Healy had controlled Hillsborough, but Pierce defeated Healy's candidate for moderator of town meeting. Pierce proudly reported that "The Adams men made their *mightiest* effort to elect Dr. Hatch Moderator but failed. . . . You never knew the Republicans in this town so zealous and so active. . . . The King . . . felt more mortified and chagrined at my being elected Moderator than . . . at anything else."[54]

News of John Bell's victory brought reactions from Washington. Governor C. P. Van Ness of Vermont, brother of John P. Van Ness, Chairman of the Democratic Central Committee in Washington, said that the anxiety in Washington over the New Hampshire election was "intense." "The Administration," he said, "actually trembled for the result." He told Hill that several of his "personal friends" in Washington, particularly Martin Van Buren and James Hamilton, Jr., "inquired anxiously" after him. Van Ness went on to reassure Hill: "they deeply appreciate your great services in the cause and will not forget you." The happiest man in Washington was Senator Samuel Bell, who wrote that his brother's victory would "forever prostrate the mischievous influence of Isaac Hill." "The election," he continued, "excited a great deal of interest here. The opposition had been taught to believe that the influence of Isaac Hill was irresistible in N.H."[55]

Turning his attention to the presidential campaign, Hill arranged a state Democratic convention, the first of its kind, in which 200 delegates met for two days in Concord in June. Before the session was over, the convention nominated eight presidential electors and six Congressmen, set up a ten-member committee of

---

54. Pierce to Elizabeth E. McNeil, Mar. 19, 1828, Pierce Papers, NHHS.

55. C. P. Van Ness to Hill, April 6, 1828, Hill Papers; Samuel Bell to Henry Hubbard, Mar. 24, 1828, Samuel Bell Papers, New-York Historical Society. D. Barker, an Adams man, wrote John Parker Hale, a Jacksonian, that he was "dismayed" at the success of the Jackson men in Rochester, New Hampshire, since he had thought there were only fifty of them there. D. Barker to Hale, Mar. 24, 1828, John P. Hale Papers, NHHS.

correspondence headed by Hill, and published an "Address," which denounced excessive spending and all forms of aristocracy. While this was going on, the National Republicans held a legislative caucus in Concord, and the legislature reelected Bell United States Senator over Hill. The second two-party system was operating in New Hampshire.[56]

Hill did everything possible to carry New Hampshire for the party. He was "malignant & unprincipled," to quote William Plumer, in his attacks on John Quincy Adams. Plumer wrote the President that the "deformity" of Hill's writing was "too gross to succeed . . . . it must produce a reaction." Hill's most vulgar and most amusing libel appeared in his *Brief Sketch of the Life, Character, and Services of Major General Andrew Jackson,* which appeared that summer. When Adams was minister to Russia, his chambermaid had written a letter home describing Tsar Alexander's love affairs. When Alexander read the letter, which had been intercepted, he was much amused and asked Adams if he could meet the girl. The meeting, which lasted ten minutes, was in the presence of the Tsarina and several others, and was entirely innocent. Yet in his *Sketch of Jackson,* Hill maintained that Adams had "procured" the girl for the Tsar's illicit pleasure, but that the "lascivious monarch" would not have her. How anyone could believe that stodgy John Quincy Adams had "procured" a girl is hard to understand, but the story circulated, particularly in the West, where Adams was called "the pimp of the coalition."[57]

In articles and speeches Hill defended Jackson from opposition attacks. According to the Adams campaign literature, Jackson had murdered seven militiamen, two British agents, two Indian chiefs, and one fellow American (in a duel). After defending Jackson on each individual charge, Hill made his main point:

56. Before the convention there were Democratic meetings at Ela's Tavern, Dover, as well as in Portsmouth. *Patriot,* April 14, 21, May 5, 1828; McCormick, *Second American Party System,* pp. 59–60; Reid, "Doe's World."

57. Plumer to Adams, April 16, 1827, Plumer Papers, LC, cited in Turner, *Plumer,* pp. 327–328; Isaac Hill, *Brief Sketch of the Life, Character and Services of Major General Andrew Jackson* (Concord, N.H., 1828), pp. 49–50. Remini, *Election,* pp. 117–118.

"Pshaw!" he burst out, "Why don't you tell the whole truth? On the 8th of January, 1815, he murdered in the coldest blood 1,500 British soldiers for merely trying to get into New Orleans for Booty and Beauty." Jackson papers all over the nation used Hill's "Pshaw" statement. Another of Hill's most important efforts was his Fourth of July Address in Portsmouth, where, according to the opposition, he arrived in "a handsome barouche" with a red flag and "fiddlers" and spoke under a picture of the Battle of Waterloo, which was supposed to be New Orleans.[58]

Woodbury joined Hill in Portsmouth that day, and the two worked together during the rest of the campaign. In August Woodbury boasted: "we have organized our forces in every quarter and have begun . . . to pour into every doubtful region all kinds of useful information." Even so, some Jacksonians were uncertain about Woodbury's party loyalty and his popularity with the rank and file. To quiet such criticism Hill wrote that the Senator got on well with all party members except for the "more humble" Democrats in Portsmouth. If only he would mix more with his hometown Democrats, groaned Hill, all would be well. Woodbury already had a good reputation as a Senator because he had worked hard to secure pensions for Revolutionary War veterans, but he was unable to appeal to the lower classes as effectively as Hill.[59]

Woodbury's strength in the party lay in his contacts with Democrats outside of the state. He had made himself popular with western Democrats when he was one of four northeastern Senators to vote against a bill protecting the Indians. Talk had already

58. Bowers, *Party Battles,* pp. 33–34; Hill, *Sketch of Jackson; Patriot,* April 9, 1828; *Gazette,* July 8, 1828; [Concord] *New Hampshire Statesman,* Sept. 27, 1828; Isaac Hill, *An Address Delivered before the Republicans of Portsmouth and Vicinity, July 4, 1828* (Concord, N.H., 1828).

59. John Decatur to Woodbury, Dec. 10, 1827, Mar. 11, 1828, Woodbury Papers, LC; *Patriot,* April 21, 1828; Hill to Henry Lee, Sept. 16, 1828, Massachusetts Historical Society, *Proceedings,* 43 (1909), 72; Woodbury to Gulian Verplanck, Aug. 29, 1828, Gulian Verplanck Papers, New-York Historical Society; Isaac Munroe to John B. Davis, Nov. 21, 1828, Massachusetts Historical Society, *Proceedings,* 49 (1916), 216.

started that if Jackson won, Woodbury would be Secretary of the Navy. Letters came in to Woodbury from prominent Democrats such as Thomas Hart Benton describing victory in Missouri and Gulian Verplanck announcing that New York was safe. Woodbury's weakness lay in his extreme caution. Just before the election he wrote to the editor of the *Patriot* that Adams had spent federal money to buy a billiard table for the White House, but concluded timidly that he did not want his "name known as connected" with the story.[60]

The union of Hill and Woodbury reassured Democrats that all differences between the back country and Portsmouth were over. This frightened National Republicans, who predicted that the two would become "prime ministers" of the state under some "wooden king" once they gained control of New Hampshire. To prevent that from happening, the National Republican Central Committee of Correspondence printed 10,000 reports of the "Administration" convention in June, while National Republican newspapers such as the *Statesman* in Concord and the *Journal* in Portsmouth bitterly fought the Democratic press.[61]

As in March, religious and social issues played an important part in the November election, and Federalists continued to support the National Republicans. According to Hill, the Jackson party represented the lower classes, while the opposition stood for the old Federalist aristocracy. He accused "wealthy" Federalists of threatening to sue "poor" debtors if they voted Democratic. In most villages, said Hill, two or three "federal lawyers or federal orthodox clergymen or aristocrats" ruled over the "middle class" artisans and sturdy farmers. He pointed out that former gover-

60. Woodbury in turn wrote Van Buren describing the New Hampshire campaign. Benton to Woodbury, Aug. 3, 1828, Verplanck to Woodbury, Aug. 18, 1828, Thomas Ritchie to Woodbury, Sept. 3, 1828, Woodbury to John Farmer, Oct. 22, 1828, Woodbury Papers, LC; Woodbury to Van Buren, July 1, 1828, Van Buren Papers, LC.

61. *Statesman*, 1828, *passim;* [Keene] *New Hampshire Sentinel*, Nov. 21, 1828; Central Committee to County Commissioners, n.d., Moore Papers; Charles E. Perry, "The New Hampshire Press in the Election of 1828," *The Granite Monthly*, 41 (1929), 454–458.

nors Gilman, Smith, Bell, Morril, and Plumer, all once Federalists for John Adams, were now National Republican-Federalists for John Quincy Adams. In a pamphlet entitled *Letter from a Farmer,* Hill argued that a vote for Jackson was a vote for the spirit of 1776 and a vote against disloyalty in 1812. It was a vote for the people and a vote against the aristocracy. Hill was using rhetoric, but there was truth in his words.[62]

Even the opposition sometimes agreed with Hill. The *Statesman* said that the Jackson Party was made up of debtors, "acreless men," ready for revolution. And when National Republicans denied charges that they were aristocrats, they came off second best. Jacob Moore, for example, maintained that many Methodist ministers were for Adams, but the *Patriot* laughed, saying that in the past Moore had "sneered" at Methodists. His effort merely showed, said the *Patriot,* that the "same spirit of intolerance and bigotry in politics and religion still animates the leaders of the *federal party."* Woodbury underscored Hill's charges of class warfare by reporting that all the old Federalist leaders were for Adams. The Democrats were "poor devils in purse," he complained, while the opponents were "talented—wealthy and cunning." Hill, Woodbury, and the National Republican *Statesman* agreed that a social conflict divided New Hampshire.[63]

Despite the efforts of Hill and Woodbury, New Hampshire voted for Adams in November. The result was expected: Franklin Pierce, for example, predicted that Adams would win. The National Republican-Federalist alliance was well organized and had carried the state in March. With Adams, a New Englander, on the ticket the alliance had an important advantage. Adams, after all, had won all the New England states in 1824. Andrew Jackson's only comment on hearing about New Hampshire was that,

62. *Patriot,* July 30, Sept. 3, 24, Nov. 19, 1827, Oct. 20, 1828, Mar. 9, 1829; Turner, *Plumer,* pp. 329–333; Hill, *Sketch of Jackson;* Isaac Hill, *Letter from a Farmer in the County of Rockingham to His Brother in the County of Merrimack, in New Hampshire* (Concord, N.H., 1828). Hill made a particularly vicious attack on old William Plumer accusing him of taking part in a secessionist plot in 1804.

63. *Patriot,* Sept. 15, Oct. 6, 1828; *Statesman,* Oct. 4, 1828; Woodbury to Van Buren, July 1, 1828, Van Buren Papers, LC.

considering the odds, Isaac Hill had "done wonders." With 24,124 votes for Adams and 20,922 for Jackson, the total of 45,046 was the greatest in the history of the state (Table 2).

Table 2. Total Vote Cast in New Hampshire Elections

Year	Vote	Estimated population	Estimated number of adult males	Percentage of adult males voting[a]
1805[b]	28,443	199,000	43,780	65
1816[b]	38,332	232,000	51,119	75
1816[c]	28,802	232,000	51,119	56
1824[b]	30,348	254,000	55,880	54
1824[c]	10,032	254,000	55,880	18
1828[b]	39,897	264,000	58,861	67
1828[c]	45,046	264,000	58,861	76

Source: *Journal of the House of Representatives of the State of New Hampshire, passim; New Hampshire Manual 1891,* pp. 151–153, 158–159; Petersen, *History of Elections,* p. 143; Coolidge and Mansfield, *New Hampshire,* pp. 705–709.

In most cases I have used the official results, which are reported in the *Journal* of the House and Senate. The actual number of persons voting in the gubernatorial elections is somewhat higher than the figure given because the legislative committee often refused to accept returns from three or four towns for technical legal reasons. The *New Hampshire Manual 1891* lists the official gubernatorial figures from the *Journal.* It is difficult to determine presidential results because each elector received a slightly different popular vote. I have followed the practice of the *Manual* in using the figure for the elector who received the highest vote. Scattering votes are included in the total. In 1824 I have followed the figures given in Petersen, *History of Elections,* because the statistics in the *Journal* and in the *Manual* are ambiguous. To determine the percentage of adult males voting (Negroes could vote), I found the number of males 21 and over in the United States Census Reports and extrapolated for the particular years. In 1830, New Hampshire had 131,184 white males (about 60,150 males 21 and over) and 137,537 white females. There were 279 free colored males, 323 free colored females, and 5 Negro slaves. The total population was 269,328. United States Census Office, *Abstract of the Returns of the Fifth Census,* pp. 4, 48. For population see also DeBow, *Statistical View,* p. 40.

[a]The highest percentage of adult males to vote was 78% in 1814.
[b]State election.
[c]Presidential election.

Compared to the 10,032 voting in the presidential election of 1824, it marked a tremendous increase.[64]

64. Pierce to Mrs. Elizabeth E. McNeil, Sept. 11, 1828, Pierce Papers, NHHS. For Jackson's comment see Frederic Austin Ogg, *The Reign of Andrew Jackson, A Chronicle of the Frontier in Politics* (New Haven, Conn., 1919), p. 111.

Richard McCormick has properly pointed out that the increase in voters in 1828 does not seem so large when that election is compared with elections at about the time of the War of 1812. But the turnout in each of the two 1828 elections was, first of all, far greater than in any other election in the 1820's. In addition, the percentage voting in the presidential election of 1828 was higher than that in any previous election except one— the gubernatorial election of 1814. In 1828, the rhetoric, if not the issue, of class warfare and the strong feelings aroused by Isaac Hill and Andrew Jackson brought voters back to the polls. McCormick is correct in saying that Jacksonian Democracy did not bring democracy to the United States; but in New Hampshire, at least, he underestimates the role of issues and Jackson in bringing out the voters.[65]

Both sides agreed that Federalists voted for Adams. In the voting, old Federalist areas such as the Connecticut and Merrimack Valleys gave Adams solid support. Franklin Pierce and Hill used a new epithet, "Twaddlers," to describe the Federalists and National Republicans. They "embrace," said Pierce, "everything . . . mean and abject." And after it was determined that the National Republicans had lost the national election, Samuel Bell wrote Jacob Moore that they must at least keep New Hampshire in their hands. To do so, said Bell, they must nominate some Federalist candidates for seats in Congress.[66]

Immediately after the election one observer commented that the size of the Jackson vote in New Hampshire surprised many

65. My results are very similar to those of Richard McCormick, who estimates the percentage voting in New Hampshire in the presidential election of 1828 to be 76.5 percent. My estimate of a 78 percent turnout in 1814 is slightly lower than McCormick's figure of 80.8 percent, but I concede that the percentage in 1814 was higher than that in 1828. See McCormick, "New Perspectives," pp. 292–295, and McCormick, *Second American Party System*, p. 14.

66. For a regional breakdown of the voting, see Table 1. Pierce to Colonel John McNeil, Nov. 11, Dec. 15, 1828, Pierce Papers, NHHS; Hill to Woodbury, Nov. 27, 1828, Woodbury Papers, LC; Bell to Moore, Nov. 19, 1828, Moore Papers. Adams carried every town in the Connecticut Valley and two-thirds of the Merrimack Valley.

in Washington. "Watch out," he warned, or "Hill will have control of the state" in 1829. He was correct. Federalists and National Republicans, who voted in November because they were frightened at the prospect of a Jackson victory or because they favored a New England son, showed less interest in the state election in March. As the opposition alliance fell apart, the Democratic machine grew stronger. The winter months were filled with Democratic meetings and dinners. Toasts were raised to Jackson, to the Battle of New Orleans, to the American Revolution, and to the yeomanry of New Hampshire. In March, Benjamin Pierce was elected governor with 22,615 votes to 19,583 for John Bell. National Republican editor Charles Cutter mourned that "the wildfire of Jacksonism [had] spread through the State . . . it must burn itself out." Cutter had to wait a long time for the fire to go out. Pierce was governor, four out of five governor's councilors and nine out of twelve senators were Democrats, and six Jacksonians were on their way to Congress. The Democrats had taken over New Hampshire.[67]

In 1829 the new party system in New Hampshire was reminiscent of the old. The interior and Portsmouth still opposed the Connecticut and Merrimack valleys. Federalists had largely become National Republicans. The rhetoric of class warfare was as prominent in 1828 as it had been earlier. Democrats favored the South as Republicans had before. Although Democrats did not propose a specific platform in 1828, they did offer a point of view that clearly distinguished them from their opponents. Jacksonians stressed democracy, opposed privilege, appealed to the common man, and harkened back to the Revolution far more than did National Republicans. Ideology contributed to the rise of Jacksonian Democracy.

67. Isaac Munroe to John B. Davis, Nov. 21, 1828, Massachusetts Historical Society, *Proceedings*, 49 (1916), 216; *Patriot*, Jan. 19, Mar. 16, 1829; *Gazette*, Mar. 17, 1829; *New Hampshire Manual 1891*, p. 153.

V

Jacksonians in
Washington, 1829-1832

With victory theirs, the New Hampshire Jacksonians began to descend on Washington, where life away from home was both lonely and gay. Before Woodbury's wife Elizabeth joined him in the capital, he wrote her wistfully: "I have an anxious desire for thy company to the South." When Isaac and Susan Hill came to Washington in 1831, they left their children at home. That winter Susan Hill wrote many letters back to Concord, worrying about them.[1]

But dinner parties brightened the evenings, as even obscure New Hampshire Congressmen received many invitations. Congressman John Weeks for example, was invited to tea or dinner at the White House on at least four occasions within the first year. Susan Hill reported having a good time at one of President Jackson's levees and said that the President had been in "excellent spirits." When Woodbury accepted a post in the cabinet and Elizabeth Woodbury came to Washington to stay, the couple bought a house in fashionable Lafayette Square across from the

---

1. Woodbury to Elizabeth Woodbury, May 20, 1827, Dec. 5, 1828, Hill to Woodbury, April 4, 1829, Woodbury Papers, LC; Hill to Jackson, May 12, 1829, Andrew Jackson Papers, LC; Susan Hill to her children, Jan. 29, Feb. 23, 1832, Hill Papers.

White House. The Woodbury dinner parties, which Jackson, Calhoun, and others attended, became famous.[2]

Even before Hill departed for Washington after the presidential election of 1828, he began to angle for a federal job. In a letter to Postmaster General John McLean about patronage he said that he would soon be in Washington to "accept" a position. After receiving a letter from Hill, editor Duff Green of the *United States Telegraph* replied that he would like to help him, but thought that Woodbury had first claim on an opening for a New Englander. Shortly after the New Year, Hill arrived in Washington to advance his own cause. There he met almost daily with editors Green and Amos Kendall, and politicians Andrew J. Donelson and Major William Lewis of Tennessee. And whenever he could, he joined General Jackson at Gadsby's Hotel. Jackson greeted him warmly, and repeated amid great laughter some of the best jabs the *Patriot* had made against Adams during the campaign. The two were soon friends, and Hill wrote home that Jackson had "a fund of humor in his makeup. But most of his sallies . . . [were] likely to be a bit cruel." Kendall assured Hill that the General had "confidence" in him.[3]

The President showed his confidence by appointing Hill second comptroller in the Treasury Department, where he examined accounts, certified the balance, and countersigned requisitions. For his efforts he received the excellent salary of $3,000 a year and was able to appoint eight clerks with salaries ranging from $1,000 to $1,700. Hill was also a member of the Kitchen Cabinet,

2. John M. Weeks Papers, NHHS; Susan Hill to her children, Jan. 1, Feb. 23, 26, 1832, Nov. 21, 1833, Hill Papers; John P. Hale to Lambert, April 3, 1837, Hale Papers, NHHS; Harriet Martineau, *Society in America* (London, 1837), I, 152; Wilhelmus B. Bryan, *A History of the National Capital* (New York, 1916), II, 7; Elizabeth F. Ellet, *Court Circles of the Republic* (Philadelphia, 1869), pp. 226–233.

3. Hill to McLean, Nov. 27, 1828, John McLean Papers, LC; Green to Hill, Dec. 17, 1828, Green Letterbook, LC; Remini, *Election,* p. 199; Robinson, "Hill," pp. 76–78; Ogg, *Reign of Jackson,* pp. 111, 116. Hill's description of Jackson is from Hill's letter to an editor of the *Patriot,* Feb. 28, 1828, quoted in Buell, *Jackson,* II, pp. 208–209. I have not found the original, but feel that the letter accurately describes the relationship between Hill and Jackson.

which advised Jackson, where he ranked behind Kendall, Donelson, Van Buren, Attorney General Roger B. Taney, and Francis P. Blair, editor of the Washington *Globe*. Contemporary opinion considered Hill the administration "hatchet man," who presided over the spoils system. For that reason the opposition took him seriously. The *National Journal*, for example, ran a series of attacks on Hill; while the *Lynchburg Virginian* blamed him for Jackson's decision to run again in 1832. A popular ballad chanted:

> King Andrew had five trusty 'squires,
> Whom he held his bid to do;
> He also had three pilot-fish,
> To give the sharks their cue.
> There was Mat [Van Buren] Lou [McLane] and Jack [Branch]
>   and Lev [Woodbury],
> And Roger, of Taney hue,
> And Blair, the book,
> And Kendall, chief cook,
> And Isaac, surnamed the true.[4]

Like Hill, Woodbury also hoped for a job in the new administration. Samuel Bell reported that Woodbury "looked toward the Navy Department with a very wishful eye." When nothing developed, said Bell, Woodbury hung "his lip . . . like a motherless colt." Van Buren had suggested Woodbury for the position, but it went to Senator John Branch of North Carolina instead. When Woodbury arrived in New York to complain, he found Van Buren in bed. He went up to the bedroom, repeated criticisms he had heard about the cabinet appointments, and let out his disappointment. Van Buren considered his outburst all the

---

4. Bradley, *Hill,* p. 82; *Statesman,* April 17, 1830; Richard Longaker, "Was Jackson's Kitchen Cabinet a Cabinet?" *Mississippi Valley Historical Review,* 44 (1951), 94–108. Longaker plays down Hill's role, but the evidence of the Bank War and party patronage suggests that Hill was important. *Patriot,* Oct. 4, 1830; for the ballad see Ben: Perley Poore, *Perley's Reminiscences of Sixty Years in the National Metropolis . . .* (Philadelphia, 1886), I, 103. Ogg, *Reign of Jackson,* p. 221.

"more imposing" because he was aware of his "usual discretion in speaking of such things."

Van Buren was particularly incensed because two men whom he preferred—Woodbury and Louis McLane—had lost positions to two of Calhoun's friends, Branch and Samuel Ingham. He considered it a Calhoun cabinet with himself the only person in it from a state north of Pennsylvania. To placate Woodbury, Jackson offered him the very next job. "The President regards," declared Van Buren, "the Mission to Spain as the second in point of importance in the present condition of our foreign relations." The offer, Van Buren recalled later, "filled Mr. Woodbury with exaggerated notions of our estimate of the importance to the administration that he should be conciliated." Cautious as usual, Woodbury thought it over a long while before turning it down. Four years, he felt, was too long an exile, and his family did not care to go. When Hill heard of the offer, he reported acidly that Woodbury would not be satisfied with the Spanish post. "It is not in the nature of the man," said Hill, "to be satisfied."[5]

Since they represented an organization that depended on patronage, Hill and Woodbury actively participated in the distribution of the spoils. Historians once exaggerated the extent of political removals under Jackson, but recent estimates put the figure at only about 10 to 12 percent of federal officeholders. In New Hampshire, however, it was much higher. Removals were wholesale; the spoils system actually worked there the way historians once said it did everywhere. Though a small state, New Hampshire ranked second in number of postmasters removed within the first year. According to *Niles' Register* in April 1830, New York had 131 removals, New Hampshire 55, and Ohio 51. Somewhat later that year *The Concord Directory* reported that 101 of the 231 postmasters in New Hampshire were new. In

5. Bell to Moore, Feb. 20, 1829, Moore Papers; Van Buren, *Autobiography*, pp. 229–230, 252–256; Bowers, *Party Battles*, pp. 42–45; *Gazette*, April 7, 1829; Hill to McLean, April 20, 1829, McLean Papers, LC.

Concord, William Low replaced Hill's old enemy General Joseph Low; in Portsmouth, Woodbury's ally Abner Greenleaf took over the post office. The administration also appointed new customs collectors such as John T. Gibbs in Dover, new judges, and many other new federal officials. The early removal of Timothy Upham as port collector in Portsmouth was particularly dramatic because Upham, a Federalist, had fought hard for Adams. Kendall was delighted with Upham's demise and said that his example should be publicized. Like Van Buren's Albany Regency, Hill's Concord Regency carried out the spoils system effectively. The *Patriot* called it the "will of the people."[6]

Hill was the number-one spoilsman in New Hampshire. In his letter to McLean in November 1828, seeking a job for himself, Hill wrote that nine-tenths of the postmasters in New Hampshire were not Democrats. He agreed that no one who did "his duty faithfully and impartially" should be removed for "reasons merely political," but he concluded that offices were "created for the benefit of the people, and not for the aggrandizement of the individuals holding them." The same day he wrote Woodbury that it was about time they had some postmasters of the "right sort" in New Hampshire. To another friend he wrote that the "barnacles" would have to be "scraped clean off the ship of state." The Adams barnacles, he added, had "grown so large and stick so tight that the scraping process will doubtless be fatal to them."

Hill found at the start that it was not easy to make a large number of removals because many of the candidates had no better credentials than those in office, but before long heads were rolling. Hill's correspondence reveals his part in the hiring and firing. In a letter to Congressman John Weeks, Hill reported

6. Leonard White, *The Jacksonians: A Study in Administrative History* (New York, 1954), p. 308; *Niles' Register*, 38 (April 3, 1830), p. 105; *Patriot*, Aug. 10, Sept. 7, Nov. 9, 1829; *Statesman*, May 9, 23, Aug. 22, 1829, Jan. 16, April 3, 1830; Kendall to Blair, Mar. 18, 1830, Blair-Lee Papers, Princeton University Library; *The Concord Directory . . . 1830* (Concord, N.H., 1830), pp. 23–24.

that he had asked the President to appoint Governor Matthew Harvey federal judge in New Hampshire. Would Weeks write Jackson via William B. Lewis suggesting Harvey? Since Jonathan Harvey was leaving Congress, he added, "Why not replace one Harvey as governor with another?" Hill promised to write Congressmen Brodhead, Chandler, Hubbard, and *"perhaps"* Hammons. Matthew Harvey did become federal district judge, but Jonathan Harvey never became governor.[7]

Hill tried to arrange a job with the Washington *Globe* for John Kelly of Northwood. Editor Blair would pay Kelly a dollar a day and his expenses plus travel down and back. Although the pay was low, Hill urged Kelly to take it because there might be a better job later and Kelly could earn extra money by sending news to other Jackson newspapers. A letter from Henry Y. Simpson to John Parker Hale in 1834 gave further evidence of Hill's influence on patronage. Even though Simpson had cleared Hale's appointment as federal attorney with Thomas Hart Benton, he still urged Hale to get Judge Nathaniel Upham to write Hill. "The facts are these," concluded Simpson. "Isaac Hill can control this appointment" and he "puts more reliance on Upham in this sort of thing than anyone."[8]

Woodbury also played the part of office broker. On Christmas Day, 1828, he wrote David Henshaw in Boston: "Who should we take care of, unless it be those who have endured the heat & dust of the battle?" Letters poured in on Woodbury asking for jobs. Overwhelmed, he later protested that he had not controlled patronage. Although he had been asked about appointments and had made his views known, he was often disregarded. Some of the New Hampshire appointments, he added, were bad ones. Woodbury was probably covering up, but the perceptive William

7. Hill to McLean, Nov. 27, 1828, McLean Papers, LC; Bowers, *Party Battles*, p. 66; Hill to Woodbury, Nov. 27, 1828, April 2, 1829, Woodbury Papers, LC; Hill to John M. Weeks, May 7, 1829, Aug. 3, 1830, Hill Papers.

8. Hill to John Kelly, Aug. 29, 1831, Hill Papers; Henry Y. Simpson to John Parker Hale, Feb. 2, 1834, Hale Papers, NHHS; *Gazette*, Dec. 1, 1829; *Patriot*, Dec. 21, 1829.

Plumer, Jr., considered his importance overrated and said that Hill was far more "efficient" in changing the politics of New Hampshire.[9]

In Portsmouth the squabble over replacing Timothy Upham as port collector got Hill into trouble. By nominating John P. Decatur, he displeased Abner Greenleaf, editor of the *New Hampshire Gazette,* who wanted the job. Matters became worse when Greenleaf was appointed postmaster instead of Samuel Cushman and when Cushman was made United States attorney for New Hampshire instead of two other candidates. Portsmouth Democrats, never loyal to Hill, wrote President Jackson asking him to withdraw Decatur's nomination. By January 1830, the Decatur issue had moved to the fighting stage. When a thousand Portsmouth Democrats voted to sever all connection with Decatur, who had already taken over the collector's job, fifty of the customs house workers, loyal to their new boss, challenged the vote and scuffled with their opponents. Hill stuck with Decatur to the end in spite of advice from the *Patriot* and the *Gazette,* but the Senate refused to ratify the appointment of either Decatur or Cushman, and the jobs eventually went to other Jacksonians.[10]

In spite of the setback, Hill continued to control appointments, and his influence spread to other states. Although the Whig complaint that Hill had Connecticut in his pocket was rhetoric, he certainly wielded power in Vermont. One Vermonter complained

9. Woodbury to Henshaw, Dec. 25, 1828, Chamberlain Collection, Boston Public Library; Weeks to Woodbury, Dec. 1, 1828, Hill to Woodbury, Dec. 11, 1828, D. M. Durell to Woodbury, Jan. 26, 1829, Samuel Cushman to Woodbury, Jan. 14, 1829, Edward Cutts to Woodbury, Feb. 6, 1829, John Elwyn to Woodbury, Feb. 6, 1829, Badger to Woodbury, Mar. 2, 1829, Atherton to Woodbury, Mar. 16, 1829, John Dix to Woodbury, May 23, 1829, Woodbury Papers, LC; Woodbury to Francis Baylies, Jan. 7, 1830, Massachusetts Historical Society; Plumer to Bell, Feb. 24, 1830, Bell Papers.

10. Greenleaf denied any involvement in the effort to make him port collector, but he was not convincing. *Gazette,* Jan. 5, 1830. Hill to John Langdon Elwyn, April 13, 1829, Hill Papers; *Statesman,* May 2, 1829, Feb. 20, 1830; Thomas Laighton to John Weeks, Nov. 19, 1829, Lewis Loomis to Weeks, Feb. 27, 1830, James Thorne to Weeks, April 12, 1830, Weeks Papers, NHHS. William Pickering became collector and Daniel M. Durell, and later John Parker Hale, U.S. Attorney.

that Democrats there were angry about certain appointments. Since he knew that Hill had "intimate knowledge of affairs at Washington relative to appointments" in the state, he wanted his advice.[11]

Amid the patronage, Hill and Woodbury were involved in the party split between Van Buren and Calhoun, which came into the open in April and May of 1830. On April 13 both New Hampshire Democrats were at Brown's Indian Queen Hotel to attend the Jefferson Day Dinner, which was designed to unite the southern and western wings of the party behind Jeffersonian principles. Woodbury, who was second vice-president at the dinner, quoted from Jefferson in his carefully prepared toast. Hill's toast was more Biblical. "Democracy:" he started, " 'Wherefore do I take my flesh in my teeth, and put my life in mine hand? Though he slay me, yet will I trust in him'." But unity vanished as President Jackson shocked Calhoun and the state-rights Democrats with his stern toast: "Our Federal Union: It must be preserved." Hill, one of the few to know ahead of time what Jackson would say, reported that "all hilarity ceased." Calhoun's "glass so trembled in his hand that a little of the amber fluid trickled down the side." After all had been seated, Calhoun "slowly and with hesitating accent offered the second volunteer toast: 'The Union! Next to our Liberty Most Dear!' "[12]

Another toast at the dinner pointed to immediate difficulty for Hill. Duff Green offered a toast to "Isaac Hill, although rejected by the Senate, he will be rewarded by the people." The day before the dinner the Senate had refused to ratify Hill's appointment to the Treasury Department. The Senate had already rejected another Democratic editor, Henry Lee, as consul general to Algiers; before long it came close to turning down two more: Amos Kendall, as auditor in the Treasury Department, and Mordecai Noah, as surveyor and inspector of the port of New York. Within the next four years it would also reject among

11. *Patriot,* April 20, 1835; D. Azro A. Buck to Hill, Nov. 13, 1833, Hill Papers.
12. *Niles' Register,* 38 (1830), 153–154; Buell, *Jackson,* II, 240–242.

others Martin Van Buren as minister to Great Britain and Roger B. Taney as Secretary of the Treasury. The political repudiation of so many high-ranking officials during the Jackson years marked an important change, for the Senate had customarily ratified such appointments. It showed the extreme partisanship of the second party system.[13]

Hill had held his job in the Treasury Department for a year before the Senate got around to voting on confirmation, but he was well aware of the forces against him. In January 1830, he refused to intervene in appointments because his own situation was one of "so much delicacy." Franklin Pierce also knew that Hill was in difficulty. The Federalists of New England, he wrote, would like Andrew Jackson better if he got rid of Hill and others who "sat at naught 'good society'." Behind the move to unseat the editors were, first of all, National Republicans and ex-Federalists, who resented the vicious attacks on John Quincy Adams during the last campaign. Adams, himself, called the *Patriot* "one of the most slanderous newspapers . . . particularly against me, in the whole country." Within the Democratic Party, opposition came from Calhoun Democrats—men like Littleton Tazewell and John Tyler of Virginia—who sought to defeat Van Buren by opposing his editor friends. When on April 12 the Senate rejected Hill 33-15, John Tyler said jubilantly: "On Monday we took the printers in hand." Even though the whole power of the government was "thrown on the scale," he continued, only "two squeezed through." The new patronage ideas of the Democrats had suffered a severe setback.[14]

13. Green's toast is in a letter from Hill to Gideon Welles, April 20, 1830, Gideon Welles Papers, LC; Sidney H. Aronson, *Status and Kinship in the Higher Civil Service: Standards of Selection in the Administrations of John Adams, Thomas Jefferson, and Andrew Jackson* (Cambridge, Mass., 1964), pp. 161–163. In addition to those mentioned, Charles Biddle, Jr., Henry Gilpin, Benjamin Tappan, and James B. Bryce were among those turned down by the Senate. Noah was rejected first and later confirmed; Calhoun broke a tie vote to save Kendall. The story of the rejections is told in a colorful way in Bowers, *Party Battles*, pp. 82–87.

14. Hill to Stark, Jan. 13, 1830, Hill Papers; Pierce to General McNeil, Jan. 4, 1830, Pierce Papers, NHHS; *Senate Executive Journal*, IV (1829–1837), 90;

The furor following Hill's rejection widened the Van Buren-Calhoun rift. Duff Green, loyal to Calhoun, tried to convince Hill that Van Buren had been responsible for the rejection, but Hill blamed it on Calhoun. So did Amos Kendall, who feared a Calhoun-McLean ticket in 1832. Jonathan Harvey maintained that if Hill had agreed to support Calhoun, he would have been confirmed. According to Harvey a strong Calhoun faction refused to support the President for fear of helping Van Buren. From Connecticut Gideon Welles reported Federalists as saying: "your party is breaking up or Hill would have been confirmed."[15]

So many protests over the treatment of Hill, some inspired by Kendall, began to arrive in Washington that the opposition was taken by surprise. James W. Webb, editor of the *Courier and New York Enquirer,* called Hill the "friend of his country and of its republican institutions." During the War of 1812, he went on, while others were plotting treason, "his voice was heard in the Granite State and in the mountains of Vermont, animating the people, and arousing them to a just sense of their danger and the blessings of freedom." In addition, the *Boston Statesman* and the *Baltimore Republican* protested against the Senate's action.[16]

Writing from Hillsborough, Franklin Pierce reflected the sentiment in New Hampshire. Major Caleb Stark, that "uncouth, abusive old Devil," had called on horseback; both were "mortified at Hill's rejection." Pierce believed that it had "produced

Stickney, *Autobiography of Kendall,* p. 371; Charles F. Adams, ed., *Memoirs of John Quincy Adams* (Philadelphia, 1874–77), VIII, 217. Tyler wrote that he and Tazewell voted against the editors on the principle that the press should not get rewards. "The Sedition law," he said, "was no more obnoxious than a system of rewards . . . by means of the public offices." Tyler to Robert W. Christian, May 13, 1830, and Tyler to Conway Whittle, May 22, 1853, Lyon G. Tyler, *The Life and Times of the Tylers* (Richmond, Va., 1896), I, 408–410.

15. Stickney, *Autobiography of Kendall,* p. 371; Hill to Welles, April 20, 1830, Welles to Hill, April 24, 1830, Welles Papers, LC; Harvey to Welles, May 5, 1830, Gideon Welles Papers, Connecticut Historical Society; Harvey to William Prescott, April 27, 1830, Jonathan Harvey Papers, NHHS; Kendall to Francis P. Blair, April 25, 1830, Blair-Lee Papers, Princeton.

16. Harvey to Welles, May 5, 1830, Welles Papers, Connecticut Historical Society; Bradley, *Hill,* pp. 95–106; Bell to Moore, April 19, 1830, Moore Papers; Wheaton, "Woodbury," p. 23.

an astonishing sympathy in Hill's favor" because the "honor of the state" had been attacked. Hill, therefore, had an "advantage before the publick," a "sway over popular feeling" at a "very important crisis in politicks." Young Democrat Charles G. Atherton of Dunstable warned Woodbury that the state considered Hill's defeat a slap in the face delivered by southern Democrats.[17]

Long before his rejection, Hill had worked out a solution. He had written a friend in Portsmouth that if either Woodbury or Bell resigned from the Senate, he "would consider it the highest honor that could be conferred on him by his state to be able to fill their place! but this sub rosa." Woodbury's term would expire in March of 1831; in June 1830, the Democratic legislature would be choosing a successor. According to Major Stark, Hill "sigh[ed] for a place in the Senate." After consulting with Jackson, Kendall wrote the New Hampshire Democrats that the President had "entire confidence" in Hill and looked upon "his rejection as a blow aimed at himself." The party, he suggested, should "wipe away the stigma cast upon this just and true man, by the unjust and cruel vote of the Senate." Hill, Kendall, and Jackson all wanted New Hampshire to elect Hill to the Senate. The next move was up to Woodbury.[18]

Woodbury's position concerning Hill was equivocal. In the Portsmouth patronage controversy, he had refused to help Hill with the Decatur-Cushman appointments because Abner Greenleaf and Dana Drown—Woodbury's closest associates in Portsmouth—had opposed them. Many believed that Woodbury, though voting for Hill, had quietly supported the southern Senators against him. The Tylers, Tazewells, and Calhouns dined frequently with the Woodburys. Charles G. Atherton told of rumors that the New Hampshire Senator had not worked hard

17. Pierce to John McNeil, April 27, May 11, 1830, Pierce Papers, NHHS; Atherton to Woodbury, April 22, 1830, Woodbury Papers, LC.
18. Hill to John Langdon Elwyn, April 13, 1829, Hill Papers; Bradley, *Hill*, p. 100; Stark to Woodbury, April 22, 1830, Woodbury Papers, LC.

enough for Hill, and Woodbury's cousin Luke advised him to make public who blocked the confirmation or else end up taking the blame. It was up to the Senator to clear the air.[19]

Characteristically, he hesitated, took no direct action; the affair became yet another episode in the Hill-Woodbury rivalry. Through an intermediary he told Hill that he would resign his seat but only if the nomination was not reconsidered in the Senate. When Kendall heard the news, he was skeptical and told Hill that there was reason to doubt Woodbury's "sincerity." Hill and Kendall sent the intermediary back to ask Woodbury if he would announce his intentions to the New Hampshire legislature. Instead, according to Kendall, "Mr. W. wrote a letter of resignation which was exhibited to Mr. H. and his friends, with a request that they would recommend Mr. W. as minister to Russia!" When Hill and Kendall balked at that, Woodbury did not send the resignation. Kendall then planted articles in the newspapers saying that Woodbury intended to resign. Two weeks later he again offered to resign if Jackson would promise him a job, but although the President held out a future appointment as Secretary of the Navy, he refused anything immediate. As Woodbury delayed resigning, Hill became convinced that his old ally was plotting against him.[20]

Nothing shows the pressure under which Woodbury labored more than the rough drafts of his letter of resignation. Dated May 15, the first draft is a confusion of crossed-out words and sentences. He expressed his "wish not to be considered a candi-

19. Woodbury voted for Cushman and against Decatur. Woodbury to Decatur, Dec. 18, 1829, Decatur to Woodbury, Dec. 10, 1827, Mar. 11, 1828, Cushman to Woodbury, Jan. 14, 1829, John Elwyn to Woodbury, Feb. 6, 1829, William Badger to Woodbury, Mar. 2, 1829, Hill to Woodbury, April 4, 1829, Atherton to Woodbury, April 22, 1830, Benjamin Evans to Woodbury, May 14, 1830, Luke Woodbury to Levi Woodbury, May 17, 1830, Woodbury Papers, LC.

20. Kendall to Blair, June 24, 1830, Blair-Lee Papers, Princeton. John Hubbard did urge the President to offer Woodbury the Russian post, but Jackson said it was not available. Hubbard to Woodbury, May 30, 1830, Woodbury Papers, LC. Hill revealed his suspicions in letters to Gideon Welles. Hill to Welles, May 7, 23, 1830, Welles Papers, LC.

date for re-election," but then crossed out an offer to resign immediately. While he was dickering with the President, Woodbury got southern Democrats Felix Grundy and Robert Hayne to write open letters stating that he worked hard to secure Senate ratification of Hill's appointment. As Hayne put it, the rumor that Woodbury had opposed Hill was false; he had instead shown "great anxiety" regarding his appointment. But try as he might Woodbury could not still the talk that he had sabotaged Hill.[21]

Still undecided, Woodbury mailed his letter saying that he would not run. It reached Concord on June 6, just before the legislature met. At the same time he made a flying trip back to Portsmouth to sound out his followers. When Abner Greenleaf and others on June 5 urged him to be a candidate, he sent another letter suggesting that perhaps he would run after all if the party wanted him. According to Kendall the maneuvering showed how "mercenary" Woodbury was; actually it simply exposed his indecision.[22]

The Hill-Woodbury struggle renewed the old Concord-Portsmouth fight. In January 1830, the party machine in Concord had fumbled patronage for the seacoast city. Then in the March election it fought off a National Republican-Federalist-Portsmouth challenge when Matthew Harvey defeated Timothy Upham for governor. All spring the battle raged between the Concord *Patriot* and the Portsmouth *Gazette* over the Senate seat. The *Gazette* said that Woodbury should not resign unless he received a better job; the *Patriot* charged that the Senator had opposed Hill; the *Gazette* retorted that Hill was trying to keep Woodbury out of the cabinet. The Concord Regency sent out a circular blaming him for the rejection and accusing him of wanting to be Vice-President under Calhoun. Federalists

21. Woodbury to Governor Benjamin Pierce, May 15, 1830, Grundy to Woodbury, May 18, 1830, Hayne to Woodbury, May 21, 1830, Woodbury Papers, LC.

22. Abner Greenleaf and others to Levi Woodbury, June 5, 1830, Woodbury to Democrats of Portsmouth, N.H., June 5, 1830, Woodbury Papers, LC; *Niles' Register,* 38 (1830), 332; Kendall to Blair, June 24, 1830, Blair-Lee Papers, Princeton.

exulted. Jeremiah Mason wrote Daniel Webster hopefully that perhaps neither Democrat would be elected in June, but Webster urged old Federalists to vote for Woodbury.[23]

Hill won. The New Hampshire House chose him over Woodbury 117 votes to 22, with 81 scattered. The Senate voted 9-3 for Hill over Woodbury, who had National Republican votes. A year later Hill wrote with great satisfaction that three Democrats in Merrimack County who voted against him were not reelected. He boasted that his enemies were "in the condition of a body of troops beaten in the field having stacked their weapons, and retiring with ability only to utter impotent curses and execrations." A delighted Andrew Jackson later wrote his friends in Tennessee about the election. In New Hampshire, he said, "they put their favorite Woodbury aside" and elected Hill "as the most pointed rebuke" they could give "to the outrage committed by the Senate" in rejecting Hill.[24]

Everyone seemed to turn on Woodbury. Samuel Bell termed Hill's election a "disgrace," but preferred him to Woodbury. With all his "talents and great industry," Woodbury had proved himself an "unscrupulous and thoroughgoing partisan and demagogue." He had more ability than Hill and would be more mischievous in the Senate, where Hill would simply be held in "contempt." William Plumer agreed: "Woodbury's insatiable political ambition," he said, had made him "play the demagogue," and caused him to lose respect. Amos Kendall considered the Senator's career over, for "Who but a fool would throw himself against the torrent of public feeling in favor of Mr. Hill? He is ruined with the President and overwhelmed at home." Hill said that Woodbury would have a hard time getting the confidence of the party again. He would even have trouble being elected to

23. *New Hampshire Manual 1891*, p. 153; *Gazette,* April 27, May 25, June 1, 1830; Mason to Webster, May 13, 1830, Clark, *Memoir of Mason,* pp. 321–322; Joseph Low to Samuel Bell, April 27, 1830, Bell Papers.

24. *Gazette,* June 22, 1830; *Patriot,* June 21, 1830; Kendall to Blair, June 24, 1830, Blair-Lee Papers, Princeton; Hill to General McNeil, Mar. 10, 1831, Hill Papers; *Statesman,* June 12, 1830. For the Hill quotation, see Hill to Gideon Welles, Aug. 11, 1830, Welles Papers, LC. Jackson to members of the Tennessee Legislature, Sept. 1832, Bassett, *Correspondence of Jackson,* IV, 479.

the state senate. "What a pity," he concluded, "that avarice and ambition, prompting to duplicity and treachery" should ruin such a "man of talents." National Republicans and Democrats agreed that Woodbury was talented, ambitious, and ruined.[25]

Woodbury was not ruined; he was simply perplexed. He insisted that he had planned all along not to run for the Senate, fearing that it would split the party. He could not understand why people said he was not sincere, just because he did not openly support Hill. He was hurt by the lies being circulated about him, some saying that he was in league with Calhoun. When Woodbury began his final session of Congress in December 1830, he found that he was being ignored on party matters. Woodbury was not the demagogue that his opponents painted him to be. He had served the party well and had reason to resist being shunted aside. Somewhat inept and always hesitant, he found himself, as in 1824, temporarily on the outside.[26]

Woodbury continued to maneuver for a new position. In August 1830, Felix Grundy assured him that Jackson would offer him a job. Attorney General John Berrien promised to intercede on his behalf when the Old General returned to Washington. Virgil Maxcy predicted that Jackson would discharge Secretary of War John Eaton and replace him with Woodbury. At first no offer came from the administration, for no one was sure of the New Hampshire Senator. James A. Hamilton warned Van Buren that Woodbury "was engaged in the cabal with Calhoun and Tazewell" and would "probably be false." When, however, the President reorganized the cabinet in favor of Van Buren in the spring of 1831, Woodbury was offered the position of Secretary of the Navy, which he promptly accepted. In so doing

25. Bell to Plumer, June 10, 1830, Plumer to Bell, June 18, 1830, Bell Papers; Kendall to Blair, June 24, 1830, Blair-Lee Papers, Princeton; Hill to Welles, Aug. 11, 1830, Welles Papers, LC. For the Hill quotation, see Hill to Azariah Flagg, Feb. 17, 1831, Flagg Papers, New York Public Library.
26. Woodbury to Virgil Maxcy, June 15, 1830, Miscellaneous Woodbury Papers, New York Public Library; Woodbury to Henshaw, Woodbury Papers, LC.

he apparently went over to the Van Buren side. At the same time, his correspondence and entertainment notes show that he remained on friendly terms with Hayne, Calhoun, and Tazewell of the South. Nothing could make Woodbury commit himself wholly to one side.[27]

The ascendancy of Van Buren and Kendall brought Hill even closer to the center of power, for he had been committed to them from the start. When in the spring of 1831 William B. Lewis and others set about making Van Buren Vice-President, they turned to Hill for help. They thought that if the party held a national nominating convention in 1832, they would be able to muster party support behind a Jackson-Van Buren ticket. Since such a convention was unprecedented, they asked Hill and Kendall, who was visiting in Concord, to arrange for the New Hampshire legislature to pass a resolution asking for a convention. The promptness with which the legislature passed the resolution showed the tight discipline of the Concord Regency.[28]

As the new party alignment emerged and Hill joined the Senate in December 1831, both he and Jackson felt vindicated. In

27. Kendall was afraid that Hill would be miffed at Woodbury's appointment, but Hill denied it. Hill to Kendall, April 26, 1831, Miscellaneous Hill Papers, Houghton Library, Harvard University; Grundy to Woodbury, July 7, Aug. 24, 1830, Berrien to Woodbury, Sept. 11, 1830, Maxcy to Woodbury, Sept. 16, 1830, Jackson to Woodbury, April 21, 1831, Woodbury to Jackson, April 26, 1831, Calhoun to Woodbury, Dec. 20, 1831, John Randolph to Woodbury, Dec. 22, 1831, Littleton Tazewell to Woodbury, Dec. 29, 1831, Jan. 10, 1832, Vote of New Hampshire Nominating Convention, Jan. 13, 1831, Woodbury Papers, LC; Hamilton to Van Buren, May 1, 1831, Van Buren Papers, LC. Woodbury had also taken the precaution of being elected to the New Hampshire Senate and had to resign from that. Woodbury to Governor of New Hampshire, May 2, 1831, Woodbury Papers, LC. Woodbury served as Secretary of the Navy, May 23, 1831–June 30, 1834.

28. James Parton, *Life of Andrew Jackson* (New York, 1860), III, 381–384; Samuel R. Gammon, *The Presidential Election of 1832* (Baltimore, 1922), pp. 95–96; Robinson, "Hill," pp. 90–91; Van Buren, *Autobiography*, pp. 583-584; *Daily Globe,* July 2, 1831. When the Senate rejected Van Buren's appointment as minister to Great Britain, Hill wrote Van Buren a long letter pledging his own continued support. The *Patriot* warned of a threatening Webster-Calhoun alliance and predicted that Van Buren would be the next Vice-President. Hill to Van Buren, Jan. 29, 1832, Van Buren Papers, LC; *Patriot,* Jan. 16, 30, Feb. 1, 1832.

the White House the President spent hilarious moments as witnesses described the discomfiture of Senators hostile to Hill. When the new Senator delivered his first speech, he read from a prepared text instead of speaking from notes or memory as Webster and Clay did. Hill was determined not to be humiliated as he had been in the New Hampshire legislature when he tried to give off-the-cuff speeches. His three-hour effort was a halting, illogical performance in which he often veered off to make a personal attack on some old enemy. After he let fly one volley at Henry Clay, Senator Samuel A. Foot of Connecticut rebuked him for his "abusive" attack and Senator George Poindexter of Mississippi accused him of using "objectionable" words. When Clay demanded that Hill read the words over again, he refused, denied that he had slandered anyone, and called Clay a liar. It was an inauspicious start.[29]

In addition to playing politics, the New Hampshire Jacksonians managed to exercise influence over legislation. Aside from National Republican Senator Samuel Bell, all of the state's Senators and Representatives were Democrats during Jackson's first term. Henry Hubbard was a particularly important Congressman; both Woodbury and Hill played major roles in the Senate. The index to the *Congressional Globe* for the years 1829–1831 carried more references to Woodbury than to any other Senator except Benton and Hayne. During his first two years in the Senate, Hill gave major addresses on the tariff and the Bank of the United States.[30]

New Hampshire Jacksonians, who had sided with the South in the Missouri and Panama controversies, voted with the South

29. On another occasion, *Niles' Register* ridiculed Hill's speaking by reporting that he had read a "somniferous paper" in the Senate. The newspaper added that Hill had read the paper "in" the Senate, not "*to* the Senate, for friends and enemies 'cleared out' to avoid the punishment of hearing it." *Niles' Register*, 46 (1834), 34; Bradley, *Hill*, pp. 116–121; Ogg, *Reign of Jackson*, p. 129; *Register of Debates*, 22nd Congress, 1st Session (1831–1832), pp. 907–919, 930.

30. *Register of Debates*, 21st Congress, 1st and 2nd Sessions (1829–1831), index. Congressman Churchill C. Cambreleng of New York praised Hill's tariff speech as "*an excellent* one." Cambreleng to Van Buren, Feb. 13, 1832, Van Buren Papers, LC; Robert Remini, *Andrew Jackson and the Bank War* (New York, 1967), p. 95; *Niles' Register*, 42 (1832), 395.

and West on the economic issues of the Jackson years. Sympathy toward the West appeared in the discussions on public land policy. When Senator Foot moved in 1830 that Congress consider "limiting" the survey of western land, Woodbury helped block the measure by proposing that the word "limiting" be changed to "extending." He was also the only eastern Senator to support Benton's graduation bill reducing the price of western land. Even though the bill was defeated, his vote won Benton's gratitude and increased Woodbury's stature in the party. Benton was also pleased when New Hampshire Democrats refused to support Clay's bills to distribute to the states the proceeds of the sale of public land. Hill, one of only two Senators from North Atlantic states to oppose Clay's plan, considered distribution a plot to clean out the Treasury in order to justify a high tariff and a high price for land. In the New Hampshire legislature Democrats turned back a resolution in favor of distribution.[31]

New Hampshire Democrats continued to side with the South and West in the dispute over the Georgia Indians, partly for a parochial reason. The *Patriot* backed Georgia in imprisoning two missionaries to the Indians, primarily because the clergymen were Congregationalists. The same newspaper also agreed with the state when it executed the Indian Corn Tassel for murder. During the spring of 1832 the *Patriot* carried on a running battle with the National Republican *Statesman,* which defended the Indians and Congregational missionaries. For a short time the Georgia issue was more important than the debates over the tariff and the bank.[32]

31. *Patriot,* Feb. 1, Mar. 8, May 18, 1830, Sept. 3, 1832, Feb. 11, 1833; Isaac Hill, *Speech on the Bill to Appropriate . . . the Proceeds of the Sales of the Public Lands . . .,* United States Senate, Jan. 22, 1833; *Gazette,* Dec. 17, 1833; Thomas Hart Benton, *Thirty Years' View* (New York, 1854), I, 651, 657.

32. During the dispute the *Patriot* was particularly harsh in its attacks on the Marshall Court, which handed down the decision against the state of Georgia. *Patriot,* Jan. 25, 1831, Jan. 16, Mar. 26, 1832. The opposition *Statesman,* however, was on the side of the Indians and the missionaries. When Georgia attacked the Indians, it protested that "cupidity" was being "gratified." *Statesman,* June 5, 1830. For the prominence of the Indian issue see *Patriot,* June 18, 1832.

In the controversy over Jackson's veto of the Maysville road in Kentucky, the New Hampshire Democrats showed hostility to internal improvements at federal expense. Hill bragged that the opposition had retreated after Jackson's veto but later complained that "millions had already been expended" upon the National Road. He said that he saw "no end to the prodigality and waste of the public treasures" on such an "expensive undertaking." The *Patriot* and *Gazette* defended the veto, calling the bill unconstitutional and saying that it would have taken money away from New Hampshire. Jonathan Harvey warned Congressman John Weeks that he should oppose internal improvement bills because the people were against them.[33]

As good Jeffersonians, New Hampshire Jacksonians opposed the protective tariff, particularly because it raised prices paid by New Hampshire farmers. In one of his first speeches in the Senate, Hill argued that the tariff on twenty-eight items used by farmers cost them $102.65 in 1825 compared to $28.99 in 1791. Henry Clay's American system, he added, was a device to "build up a manufacturing aristocracy ... at the expense of the farmers and mechanics of the country." Clay derided Hill for being the only Senator in the Northeast to oppose tariff protection. But New Hampshire Democrats were not dogmatic on the tariff. Hill and five of the six Congressmen voted for the compromise (but high) tariff of 1832.[34]

Although New Hampshire went along with the South on land, Indians, internal improvements, and tariffs, it would not tolerate nullification. The remedy for excessive tariffs, counseled the *Patriot,* was the ballot box, not independent state action. After Jackson issued his proclamation to South Carolina in December

33. Hill to Welles, Aug. 11, 1830, Welles Papers, LC; *Gazette,* June 29, 1830; *Patriot,* May 24, June 21, 1830; Harvey to Weeks, Jan. 10, 1832, Weeks Papers, NHHS.
34. The *Patriot* opposed protection. *Patriot,* Nov. 16, 1829, Jan. 25, Feb. 8, 10, 1830. Hill's speeches are in *Register of Debates,* 22nd Congress, 1st Session, pp. 227–256, and *Congressional Globe,* 24th Congress, 1st Session (1835–1836), Appendix, p. 181. See also *Gazette,* Sept. 6, 1831, Feb. 14, 1832, Feb. 19, 1833; Benton, *Thirty Years' View,* I, p. 319.

1832, New Hampshire Democrats rallied behind their leader. Franklin Pierce praised his "bold and independent course," the *Patriot* said that Jackson's statement "completely disarm[ed] nullification," and the state legislature drew up a strong resolution condemning nullification. New Hampshire Jacksonians liked to look back on the spirit of '98, but they were not extreme state-righters. Like their President they interpreted the Constitution strictly, but believed that ultimate authority rested in the nation. They were strict construction nationalists.[35]

New Hampshire Jacksonians supported the program favored by most Democrats, particularly those from the South and West. They backed cheap land and Indian removal. They opposed internal improvements, distribution, tariff protection, and the Bank of the United States. Based upon strict construction of the Constitution, it was a negative program, one that would win out down to the Civil War.

But their negative legislative record in Washington should not hide the willingness of Jacksonians to use power in a positive way. New Hampshire Democrats used their influence in Washington to put the spoils system into operation back home. They also used their power to attack the Bank of the United States, both in New Hampshire and in Washington.

35. Jackson to Woodbury, Sept. 1, 11, 1832, Woodbury Papers, LC; *Patriot,* Aug. 2, 1830, Dec. 24, 1832, Jan. 21, Feb. 18, 1833; Pierce to John McNeil, Dec. 24, 1832, Pierce Papers, NHHS.

V

The Bank War, 1829-1837

Two days after Christmas in 1799 the New Hampshire legislature passed an act declaring "all notes of the New Hampshire Union Bank . . . null and void." The act aroused many of the plain people of the state. Until 1799 the Portsmouth New Hampshire Bank, a Federalist Bank and the only bank north of Boston, had "claimed," in Isaac Hill's words, "the exclusive right of banking" in the state. When Portsmouth Republicans organized the Union Bank and began to make small loans to farmers on easy terms, they were challenging Federalists. The act of December struck down the Union Bank, but it created an issue that helped sweep the Republicans into office.[1]

Throughout the United States as in New Hampshire, party politics and banking were closely related. In an expanding econ-

---

1. The New Hampshire Bank, chartered in 1792 with a capitalization of $160,000, was the seventh bank set up in the United States. Bray Hammond, *Banks and Politics in America from the Revolution to the Civil War* (Princeton, N.J., 1957), pp. 144–145; Knox, *History of Banking*, p. 337. Hill's statement is in his speech on the Bank of the United States in the Senate, June 8, 1832, *Register of Debates*, 22nd Congress, 1st Session (1832), p. 1059. Kaplanoff, "Religion and Righteousness," pp. 4–6; Gilman Ledger, Davis Library, Phillips Exeter Academy, Exeter, N.H. The bank act can be found in Isaac Long, Jr., pub., *The Laws of the State of New Hampshire . . . 1830* (Hopkinton, N.H., 1830), Title XXV, Banks, pp. 126–127. See notes in Chapter 2 for additional details. Smith, "Banking in New Hampshire," pp. 44–46.

omy, the desire to gain control over money and credit was one reason for political activity. By the late 1820's politics and banking came together in the fierce battle over the Second Bank of the United States. Historians have interpreted this struggle differently. Arthur M. Schlesinger, Jr., argued that the Jacksonian attack on the Bank was a social battle "between 'the humble members of society' and 'the rich and powerful'." Bray Hammond, on the other hand, considered the Bank War an attempt by small businessmen and bankers to take power away from an old established monopoly, the Bank of the United States. According to Hammond, the war was "a blow at an older set of capitalists by a newer, more numerous set." Since the New Hampshire Jacksonians were deeply involved in the Bank War, their experiences provide an opportunity to evaluate the differing interpretations.[2]

Despite the act of 1799, banking expanded rapidly in New Hampshire after 1800. Unable to block the demand for banks, Federalists reluctantly granted a charter to the New Hampshire Union Bank in 1802 and chartered five more banks in 1803, none of them in the interior of the state. Four were in the southeast; the other two in the Connecticut River Valley. As soon as Republicans gained power in 1805, they brought banking to the hill country by chartering a bank in Concord. Like Democrats later, they sought to widen access to credit for their constituents.[3]

With her new banks, New Hampshire caught up with the rest of the nation: whereas in 1800 she had only one of the twenty-eight commercial banks in the United States, in 1804 she had seven of fifty-nine. Banking capital in New Hampshire expanded from $160,000 to almost $1,000,000. The growth was not without risk; in 1809 the state suffered a severe banking crisis in which four banks closed. Hill, who arrived in Concord shortly before

2. Arthur M. Schlesinger, Jr., *The Age of Jackson* (Boston, 1945), pp. 90–91; Hammond, *Banks and Politics*, p. 329.
3. *Laws of New Hampshire . . . 1830*, Title XXV, Banks, p. 128; Knox, *History of Banking*, pp. 337–338; Farmer and Moore, *Gazeteer, 1823*, p. 40; Stackpole, *History*, III, 7, 72.

the disaster, never forgot it. During the War of 1812, nine banks were operating in New Hampshire. These are listed below with their location and date of charter. None were added until after 1820.[4]

New Hampshire	Portsmouth	1792
New Hampshire Union	Portsmouth	1802
Portsmouth	Portsmouth	1803
Strafford	Dover	1803
Exeter	Exeter	1803
Cheshire	Keene	1803
Coos (later Grafton)	Haverhill	1803
Concord	Concord	1806
Rockingham	Portsmouth	1813

After the War of 1812, the Second Bank of the United States established a branch in Portsmouth in 1817. In spite of the Panic of 1819, hostility to the Bank was at first not strong in New Hampshire. In 1820 the legislature refused to ratify a federal amendment that the Bank should restrict its activities to the District of Columbia. The same year in the state House of Representatives Jeremiah Mason proposed a resolution that Ohio could not tax its branch of the Bank of the United States. But some sentiment against the Bank had developed because Hill was able to have Mason's resolution postponed in the Senate.[5]

Manufacturing expanded with banking. Industrialists built the first cotton mill at New Ipswich in 1804 and the first woolen mill at Keene shortly after the War of 1812. Expansion acceler-

4. Hammond, *Banks and Politics*, pp. 144–145; Knox, *History of Banking*, pp. 306–311, 320–321, 337–338. The capitalization of New Hampshire banks was less impressive than the number of banks. In 1811 the actual capitalization was somewhat less than $1,000,000, compared to a total state bank capitalization of $42,610,600 in the United States. Farmer and Moore, *Gazeteer 1823*, p. 40. Norman W. Smith, "The 'Amherst Bubble,' Wildcat Banking in Early Nineteenth Century New Hampshire," *Historical New Hampshire*, 20 (Spring 1965), 27–40.

5. The Supreme Court decided against Ohio in *Osborn v. Bank of the United States* (9 Wheaton 738). *Patriot*, July 2, Aug. 27, 1820; Stackpole, *History*, III, 72.

ated in the 1820's, mostly in the southeast. By 1827 cotton mills had appeared on the Salmon Falls River in Somersworth, on the Cocheco River in Dover, on the Oyster River in Newmarket, and on the Squamscott River in Exeter. The first large factories on the Merrimack River were started at Dunstable in 1823 and at Manchester in 1831. The forty mills and 114,000 spindles in New Hampshire in 1831 represented perhaps one-tenth of the cotton spinning and weaving industry in the United States.[6]

Hill later condemned this "manufacturing mania," blaming it on the tariff of 1824 and on loans from the Bank, but he had participated in the boom. In 1826 he confessed that he had raised $4,500 to pay assessments on his factory stock, had $2,000 out on loan to his Montpelier, Vermont, newspaper, and had $2,000 tied up in his Concord block. Although admitting that he should not have taken on so much in one year, he said that he bought the factory stock in exchange for real estate and had to make advances to prevent a "sacrifice." He also had $800 invested in a factory at Hooksett. Since he could not secure a loan, he was unable to pay what he owed a Boston bookseller.[7]

Banking kept up with manufacturing. Between 1820 and 1831 the number of commercial banks increased to twenty-one and their capital rose from $939,936 to $2,065,310. In addition, the state chartered six savings banks. As in manufacturing, the boom was concentrated in the southeast, where eight of the seventeen new banks were located. Even more significant, only three of the twenty-one commercial banks were in the hill district, where the

6. Stackpole, *History*, III, 182–184; Edwin D. Sanborn, *Sanborn's History of New Hampshire from Its First Discovery to the Year 1830* (Manchester, N.H., 1875), p. 376; Victor S. Clark, *History of Manufactures in the United States* (New York, 1929), I, 544; Squires, *History*, I, 287–297; Callender, *Selections*, p. 469.

7. Hill, "Speech on the Bank of the United States," *Register of Debates*, 22nd Congress, 1st Session (1831–1832), June 8, 1832, p. 1067. Hill pointed out to the bookseller that he had been "as constant and as long a customer" as the seller had had. Hill to Robinson and Lord, Sept. 18, and Dec. 4, 1826, Hill Papers; Hill to Woodbury, Aug. 4, 1828, John Rogers to Woodbury, May 27, 1828, Woodbury Papers, LC.

lack of credit worried Hill. He complained that his bank in Concord was unable to fill half of the requests for loans because banks in Boston and the branch in Portsmouth were demanding repayment of loans. As he put it, the Merrimack County Bank could not "discount" more than half of the "good papers" presented because of "close quarters" from Boston and Portsmouth.

As chairman of the House Committee on Banking in 1826, Hill opposed credit expansion along the seacoast. In the three preceding years the legislature had chartered banks in Amherst, Claremont, Derry, two in Dover, and two in Portsmouth; thirteen more were asking for incorporation. Since Hill thought that there were already enough banks, he moved that the House postpone consideration of all applications. When the House rejected his motion and moved to consider a bank for Somersworth, close to Dover, a battle developed between Hill and Joseph Doe, who supported the bank. Even though Doe outtalked him, Hill had his way and Somersworth did not get its bank. But the legislature chartered several more banks by 1831.[8]

The branch bank of the Bank of the United States took part in the banking boom. The branch had been put in Portsmouth because it was the commercial center of the state, but interior businessmen would much rather have had it in Concord to ease the credit shortage. The first president defrauded the branch of $20,000 in United States pension funds. When his successor, James Shapley, could not recover the money, the central office in Philadelphia had to absorb the loss. Nicholas Biddle, president of the Bank, began to expand the loans of the entire system in the 1820's; Shapley followed his lead in Portsmouth. After the New Hampshire banking boom blew up in a local panic in 1828, Hill blamed it on the Bank. He accused Biddle of sending in "addi-

8. Knox, *History of Banking*, pp. 338–344; Farmer and Moore, *Gazeteer 1823*, p. 40; Hayward, *Gazeteer of New Hampshire 1849*, p. 190; *Laws of New Hampshire*, 1823–1831; *Niles' Register*, 40 (1831), 320; Hill to Robinson and Lord, Sept. 18, Dec. 4, 1826, Hill Papers. Two of the interior banks were in Concord, the other on Lake Winnipesaukee. Smith, "Banking in New Hampshire," p. 253; Reid, *Chief Justice*, pp. 22–24.

tional capital of some three hundred thousand dollars." "The flush of money," he later recalled, "threw out an inducement to every man . . . to embark in manufacturing establishments: property was to be made hand over hand . . . . Several invested not only all their own money, but all their credit could procure from the banks." Hill, who could not be trusted to speak accurately about the Bank, exaggerated its role. Branch loans at Portsmouth expanded somewhat more rapidly than those throughout the system, but no more so than at Providence or Hartford. And the new mills along the seacoast increased the need for additional capital.[9]

More important than the amount of lending was the policy on repayment and the location of the borrowers. Since 1822 the branch had been making so-called accommodation loans, that is, loans with little security, with payment extended over three years and four months—10 percent due every four months. The loans were renewed so often that Biddle called it a "permanent debt." According to Mason, later president of the branch, at least $80,000 to $90,000 of the generous loans were granted to "persons

9. The quotation from Hill is taken from *Register of Debates* (1832), p. 1067. For an account of the New Hampshire Bank War, see Smith, "Banking in New Hampshire," pp. 175–197. Ralph C. H. Catterall, *The Second Bank of the United States* (Chicago, 1903), pp. 93–113, 176, 379; Biddle to Secretary of the Treasury S. D. Ingham, July 18, 1829, House of Representatives, *Report on the Bank of the United States,* Report no. 460, 22nd Congress, 1st Session (April 30, 1832), p. 442; Biddle to Robert Lenox, July 6, 1829, Reginald C. McGrane, ed., *The Correspondence of Nicholas Biddle Dealing with National Affairs, 1807–1844* (Boston, 1919), pp. 72–73; Thomas P. Govan, *Nicholas Biddle: Nationalist and Public Banker* (Chicago, 1959), pp. 85–87; House of Representatives, *Executive Documents,* 22nd Congress, 1st Session, IV, doc. no. 147, pp. 8–9. The total for bills discounted on personal security is shown in the following tabulation. (Figures are from *ibid.,* pp. 8, 12, 14, 53, and House Report no. 460, p. 442.)

	June 1822	June 1826	June 1828
Bank of the U.S.	$22,387,614.62	$27,090,326.25	$29,101,574.16
Portsmouth Branch	311,178.52	504,926.62	428,643.55
Providence Branch	276,679.83	468,238.55	850,400.73
Hartford Branch	273,534.45	483,853.76	472,867.85

in the interior of the state . . . most of whom were not engaged in business." Hill stated that "farmers and country traders" had been "induced to make loans at this branch," because the terms were better "than could be had at the local banks." He himself borrowed $1,000. When the friendly policy changed in 1828, interior farmers and Hill became angry.[10]

Starting in 1826, Biddle began to warn President Shapley to reduce his accommodation loans, but Shapley was unwilling to change the "tradition." The panic of 1828 forced Biddle's hand. By the summer of that year, according to Biddle, the Portsmouth branch had "got into a very bad way" and was "nearly prostrated" with losses of over $100,000 in defaulted loans. He decided to replace Shapley and to change the loan policy.[11]

When Biddle asked the advice of Daniel Webster regarding a new president, Webster replied that the only man who could save the branch was his old colleague Jeremiah Mason. Within five days Biddle assured Webster that the job was Mason's, saying that "the Portsmouth office" had been "arranged agreeably to your recommendation." Yet a year later, with Mason under attack, Biddle told Secretary of the Treasury Samuel D. Ingham that "Webster had not the slightest agency in obtaining for him the appointment." Aware that Ingham was close to Hill, he felt obliged to deny that Webster had nominated Mason.[12]

Mason's appointment, in the midst of the bitter presidential campaign, infuriated the New Hampshire Democrats. The suspicion, later confirmed, that Webster stood behind the appointment, made them even angrier. Mason campaigned for Adams in southeastern New Hampshire with conspicuous success. Although

10. Clark, *Memoir of Mason*, pp. 314–315; House Report no. 460, p. 443; *Register of Debates* (1832), p. 1067.

11. House Report no. 460, p. 442; Clark, *Memoir of Mason*, p. 315; *Register of Debates* (1832), p. 1067. Biddle said losses were $112,000; Hill estimated them at $70,000 to $100,000.

12. Webster to Mason, Aug. 1, 1828, Clark, *Memoir of Mason*, p. 313; Webster to Biddle, Aug. 9, 1828, Smith Collection, Morristown, N.J., Biddle to Webster, Aug. 14, 1828, Nicholas Biddle Papers, LC; Biddle to Ingham, July 18, 1829, House Report no. 460, p. 441.

Portsmouth went for Jackson, the vote was close, and only three other towns of the sixteen in the Portsmouth area voted Democratic. Hill alleged later that the branch "was made a party engine previous to the last presidential election—its directors were exclusively of one political party—its favors were dispensed with a view to affect that election; and it was the principal instrument" to give the election to Adams. Once again Hill was indulging in rhetoric. The board was National Republican, and Mason had worked for Adams; but there is no evidence that the branch used its loans to influence politics.[13]

Mason's new lending policy angered Hill and the Democrats as much as his politics did. As soon as he took office, Mason abruptly halted the accommodation loans, "tradition" or not. Instead of allowing debtors to repay 10 percent every four months, he now required them to pay 20 percent every two months. In addition, he stopped lending money to persons in the interior so that within a year such loans had dropped, according to his estimate, from about $85,000 to $49,000. Woodbury charged later that Mason's policies favored manufacturers over both the merchants of Portsmouth and the farmers of the interior. He accused the branch president of refusing good loans in Portsmouth, while advancing money to manufacturers in Boston as well as in New Hampshire. Mason, Woodbury pointed out, had investments in manufacturing companies. Mason conceded that he had made new loans to "business" firms.[14]

Those in debt to the Bank, including Hill, felt the pinch. The Bank gave Hill no additional advance and called part of his original loan of $1,000. Hill later complained that Mason's contraction policy had "accelerate[d] the absolute ruin of many persons." He added that the effects were "likewise felt in the ruin of men of moderate property in the interior, whose estates

13. Webster to Mason, Mar. 20, 1828, Clark, *Memoir of Mason,* pp. 310–316; *Register of Debates* (1832), p. 1062.
14. Clark, *Memoir of Mason,* pp. 315–316; Woodbury to Biddle, July 3, 1829, Woodbury Papers, LC. Woodbury said "country" loans were down to $20,000; Mason admitted that he had advanced only $14,000 to the interior in a year.

were sacrificed at the sheriff's sales for one-third or one-fourth of their value." In Portsmouth angry citizens hanged Mason in effigy in front of his house and burned the dummy. He came to the window, but quickly retired and put out the lights when, in Hill's words, he saw "the awful sight." The Jacksonians felt that Mason's policies had led to a regional and economic crisis in New Hampshire.[15]

Biddle interpreted events differently. A "man of the first rate character and ability," he wrote, was needed to change policy in Portsmouth. Mason had "saved the bank from great losses" by "securing old bad debts and preventing new ones." Within a year he had reduced the shaky "old accommodation loans" by $80,000, while increasing the sounder "general loans" by $100,000. "This operation," Biddle commented, was "not a pleasant one" and had "raised against Mr. Mason a number of enemies," who complained loudly. "Such complaints," said Biddle, were "generally ill-founded."[16]

Although the Jacksonians and Biddle disagreed on the wisdom and necessity of the change in policy, they agreed on one point: the branch in Portsmouth had drastically reduced loans to the interior. Farmers and small businessmen in the hills had at least $50,000 less credit at the Bank of the United States in 1829 than they had in 1828. The size of the reduction, the abruptness, the poor timing (coming during the election of 1828), and the fact

15. Hill to Woodbury, Aug. 4, 1828, Woodbury Papers, LC. The first Hill quotation is in the *Register of Debates* (1832), p. 1067. Hill repeated his charges against the Portsmouth branch in three other speeches in the Senate. Two were speeches on the removal of the deposits: *Congressional Globe*, 23rd Congress, 1st Session (Feb. 17, 1834), pp. 178–179; Isaac Hill, *Speech on the Subject of the Removal of the Deposits from the Bank of the United States in the Senate, Mar. 3–4, 1834* (Washington, D.C., 1834). The third was a speech on the censure of President Jackson: *Congressional Globe*, 24th Congress, 1st Session (May 27, 1836), pp. 406–417. The description of the effigy was in the final speech and also in the *Daily Globe*, Dec. 14, 1833.

16. Biddle to Robert Lenox, July 6, 1829, Lenox to Biddle, July 7, 1829, Biddle Papers, LC; Biddle to Ingham, July 18, 1829, House Report no. 460, pp. 442–443. Accommodation loans dropped from about $280,000 to $200,000; ordinary loans increased from about $22,000 to $122,000.

that Mason was a Federalist convinced Democrats that the branch was waging war on the farmers of New Hampshire. The arrogant Mason admitted that he had reduced "country" loans.[17]

Mason's arrogance came at an inopportune time. Flushed with new-found power, Woodbury and Hill returned to Concord in June 1829 to attend the legislative and party meetings. After agreeing on a legislative program and after nominating Matthew Harvey for governor, the Regency turned to the Bank. Hill and Woodbury encouraged and heard complaints about Mason and about Timothy Upham, the former Federalist who was on the board of directors of the branch, and who would run against Harvey the following March. The party had already taken care of Upham; Jackson had removed him as port collector. Mason was next in line.[18]

The machine moved efficiently. On June 15 Woodbury told the directors of the Bank that Mason had caused "great dissatisfaction" because he was "partial, harsh, and injurious." Aware that the central bank would select a president and directors of the Portsmouth branch in July, Woodbury requested officers better acquainted with Portsmouth. On June 27 he complained directly to Biddle about the Portsmouth branch. Biddle promised to investigate, but asked Woodbury to ascertain the origins of the complaints. The New Hampshire Senator replied with a straight

17. What actually took place is difficult to establish. Mason said country loans were down $36,000; Woodbury said the reduction was at least $60,000; Biddle said "accommodation loans" (many of them, but not all, country loans) were down $81,000. The official report of the Bank of the United States recorded a drop in bills discounted on personal security (which included the "accommodation loans") of about $88,000 between June 1828 and June 1829. The same report recorded an increase of $87,000 in ordinary domestic loans during the same period. Since the terminology varied and since no one was talking about exactly the same period of time, there is no reason to expect consistency. Mason and Biddle would tend to underestimate the reduction in "country loans," and Woodbury would overestimate. When everything is taken into consideration, $50,000 is the best estimate of the reduction. House Document no. 147 (1832), pp. 8–9.

18. Anticipating the June meetings, Hill wrote Woodbury in April that he would see him in Concord in June. Hill to Woodbury, April 2, 1829, Woodbury Papers, LC.

face that Mason was "by no means acceptable as a politician to a majority" in Portsmouth, but that the charges originated with Mason's own *"political* friends."[19]

On the same day that he first wrote Biddle, Woodbury also protested to Secretary Ingham that Mason was "a particular friend of Mr. Webster," who had arranged his appointment. Woodbury said that "commercial men" and "the people of the interior," who had formerly been "accommodated" at the branch, all desired Mason's removal. According to Woodbury, both groups objected to Mason's lack of "conciliatory manners." They also disliked his "fluctuating policy" on loans and collections, "together with the partiality and harshness" that accompanied them Woodbury wrote to Ingham asking him to help obtain changes in the president and directors of the branch.[20]

Within forty-eight hours of the writing of that letter, Woodbury and Hill drew up two petitions addressed to the directors of the Bank of the United States. The first, dated June 27 and signed by fifty-eight citizens, representing both parties in Portsmouth, used language similar to Woodbury's in his letter to Ingham. It accused Mason of policies that were "partial, harsh, . . . vacillating," and asked for his removal. Two days later another petition, signed by fifty-six members of the New Hampshire legislature, made similar complaints and demands. The branch, it said, had been "oppressive" in denying "loans to the business men" of the interior, while lending "large sums . . . out of the State." It concluded that "the conduct of the head of the Board" had been "destructive to the business of Portsmouth, and offensive to the whole community." The petition closed by recommending ten men for the new board at Portsmouth. Hill said that the list included six Adams men and four Jackson men, but that was not the case. Only one, Joseph W. Haven, editor of

19. Woodbury to Directors of the Bank of the United States, June 15, 1829, Biddle to Woodbury, Mar. 19, 1829, Woodbury to Biddle, June 27, 1829, Biddle to Woodbury, June 30, 1829, Woodbury to Biddle, July 3, 1829, Woodbury Papers, LC.
20. Woodbury to Ingham, June 27, 1829, House Report no. 460, pp. 439–440.

the *Portsmouth Journal,* was a prominent National Republican, while six were well-known Democrats: John Harvey of Northwood, John H. Jenness of Portsmouth, Samuel Cushman, briefly United States Attorney for New Hampshire and later Congressman, Richard H. Ayer of Concord, Hill's brother-in-law and naval storekeeper in Portsmouth, William Pickering of Concord, later port collector in Portsmouth, and Isaac Waldron, a Democratic elector in 1836. Waldron and Jenness were directors of the Commercial Bank of Portsmouth, one of the pet banks that received federal deposits after they were removed from the Bank of the United States, Hill and the petitioners were demanding a new board of directors at Portsmouth with Jacksonians, partly from the interior, replacing some of the seacoast Federalist-National Republicans.[21]

Hill sent the two petitions with a covering letter, dated July 17, to J. N. Barker and John Pemberton, Philadelphia lawyers, asking them to deliver the package to the Bank. Typical of Hill, the letter was aggressive, partisan, and without evidence. He called "Mason's conduct partial and oppressive," designed "to disgust and disaffect the principal business men." He insisted that "no measure short" of Mason's removal would do. Turning to politics, he added: "The friends of General Jackson in New Hampshire have had but too much reason to complain of the management of the branch at Portsmouth. All they now ask is, that this institution in that state may not continue to be an engine of political oppression by any party. The Board has, I believe, invariably and exclusively consisted of individuals opposed to the General Government." His final thrust was regional: "The advantage of having two reputable men on the Board . . . out of Portsmouth, must be obvious." Hill was fighting for himself, for his region, and for his party.[22]

In another effort to benefit all three, Hill tried to force the

21. House Report no. 460, pp. 473–474.
22. Hill to J. N. Barker and John Pemberton, July 17, 1829, House Report no. 460, p. 472.

War Department to transfer United States pension agency funds from the branch to his own bank, the Merrimack County Bank, in Concord. Hill got members of the legislature to sign a petition to the Secretary of the Treasury urging the transfer on the grounds that Concord was more central than Portsmouth. Mason protested to Philadelphia that Hill's real motive was to benefit his bank. Since the pensions amounted to $80,000 a year, Mason felt the removal "would lessen our means of circulation, and,... be very injurious to this office." Secretary of War John Eaton ordered the shift on August 3, but the Bank refused, maintaining that the law required the government to keep such funds in the branches of the Bank of the United States. There the matter stood until 1831.[23]

Secretary Ingham revealed his hostility to the Bank soon after he received Woodbury's letter of June 27. He forwarded it to Biddle with his own letter pointing out the Bank's power: "You cannot be insensible, that the power possessed by extensive moneyed institutions to distribute favors or inflict injuries... must ever be an object of serious and deserved jealousy." The Jackson administration, he observed, would "learn with . . . regret . . . that any supposed political relationship . . . had operated within the bank or any of its branches." Ingham was warning Biddle that he had better not play politics.

Biddle replied to Ingham in two letters, both written July 18. Since he had not received the letter and petitions from Hill and had not learned of the attempt to remove the pension money from Portsmouth, he was not much alarmed. He denied that Webster had suggested Mason's appointment, defended Mason's political behavior, and praised his skill in ridding the branch of many of the old accommodation loans. "Obviously," he said,

23. Hill's effort to shift the pension agency is similar to Thomas W. Olcott's partially and temporarily successful attempt to move the agency from the New York branch to the Mechanics and Farmers Bank of Albany. Frank Otto Gatell, "Spoils of the Bank War: Political Bias in the Selection of Pet Banks," *American Historical Review,* 70 (Oct. 1964), 48; House Report no. 460, pp. 475–479.

"no political feeling" influenced Mason's policies. In the second
letter Biddle showed mild irritation at Ingham's suggestion that
the Bank was involved in politics. Biddle wrote that there were
not "in the whole country, any five hundred persons of equal
intelligence so abstracted from public affairs, as the five hundred"
who were "administering the bank." He repeated that the Bank
owed "allegiance to no party" and warned that it would "submit
to none." In the past, he concluded pointedly, the government
had "uniformly and scrupulously forborne from all interference
with the concerns of the bank."[24]

The arrival of the letter and petitions from Hill a few days
later destroyed Biddle's serenity. Confronted with letters from a
New Hampshire Senator and from two high-ranking officials in
the Treasury Department and with two petitions from New
Hampshire, Biddle decided he had better go to Portsmouth.
Since the report of the pension "grab" reached Philadelphia
after he had started the trip north, he was unaware of the
attempt until he reached New Hampshire.

When Biddle arrived in Portsmouth on August 20, the news
about the federal pensions annoyed him. He was also disappointed to find Woodbury out of town. The latter was ostensibly
attending a rural court session in Gilford, New Hampshire, but
typically, he may have been avoiding an unpleasant confronta-
tion. Mason, however, was on hand to deny all charges, accusing
his opponents of manufacturing "absurd untruths" to obtain
merchants' signatures on the petition. Biddle held up his decision
on Mason's reappointment until he could interview some of the
merchants. As Webster later described it, Biddle heard conflicting reports: "They came; and some said that they had signed
the petition because they had been asked to do so; some said that

24. At the same time, the secretary was unaware of Hill's letter and petitions. On October 5 Ingham wrote Biddle: "The communication made to the
Bank of the United States by Mr. Isaac Hill accompanying two memorials, was
wholly unknown to me, until I saw it adverted to in your letter." House
Report no. 460, p. 457. The first Ingham letter to Biddle is in *ibid.,* pp. 438–
439. The Biddle letters are in *ibid.,* pp. 440–446.

they had no knowledge of the subject; and others said that they had signed it because of the difficulties they found of getting discounts." At least eight charged Mason with being harsh, but Biddle was satisfied with his branch president's explanations. After six days in Portsmouth, two of which were spent interviewing, Biddle endorsed Mason, and left for Philadelphia.[25]

Defenders of Biddle and the Bank have described the investigation as "thorough and impartial." They have claimed that the "business opposition to Mason melted away in the face of [the] investigation." On the other side, a recent historian has described it differently. "For the sake of appearance," writes Robert Remini, "he visited the branch, [and] executed the outward motions of an investigation." The second view is closer to being correct. Two days were hardly enough to investigate charges that covered a year of banking. And Biddle only interviewed Portsmouth borrowers. To find out why the farmers of the interior were angry he should have followed Woodbury north to his court session and then visited Hill in Concord. But Biddle's journey to Portsmouth was more than perfunctory. It was, first of all, a long, hard trip, which he did not take simply for pleasure. Second, an investigation that turned up eight complaints of harshness in two days was reasonably intensive. Biddle worked hard enough at the job.[26]

On board a steamboat off Point Judith, Rhode Island, on August 28, Biddle wrote a long, revealing letter to the acting president of the Bank Thomas Cadwalader. Both men were contemptuous of the New Hampshire Jacksonians. In an earlier

25. Biddle to Woodbury, Aug. 20, 1829, Woodbury Papers, LC; Mason to Biddle, July 31, 1829, House Report no. 460, p. 475; Webster in the Senate, Feb. 20, 1838, *Congressional Globe*, 25th Congress, 2nd Session, p. 192; Catterall, *Second Bank*, p. 178; Govan, *Biddle*, p. 117; Biddle to Ingham, Oct. 9, 1829, House Report no. 460, p. 470; Biddle to Cadwalader, Aug. 21, 1829, Biddle Papers, LC.

26. Biddle promised to be thorough. Biddle to Cadwalader, Aug. 6, 1829, Biddle Papers, LC. The "thorough and impartial" quotation is from Govan, *Biddle*, p. 117; the "melted away" quotation from Catterall, *Second Bank*, p. 178; the "sake of appearance" and "outward motions" quotation is from Remini, *Bank War*, pp. 53–54.

letter Cadwalader had called them "dabblers...in small politics." He said that the local Democrats were so "absorbed in a
sort of dirty *strategie*" that they assumed that the Bank officials
were behaving the way they would behave if they had "a power
so mighty." Now on the steamboat, Biddle summed up the whole
affair as "a paltry intrigue got up by a combination of small
bankrupts and Demagogues." The two letters showed that the
Bank leaders were proud and powerful, scornful of their lower-
class opposition.

But in the same letter Biddle proposed changes in the
Portsmouth board. Though retaining Mason as president and
keeping some of the other board members, Biddle would replace
certain National Republicans with Jacksonians. He proposed
John Harvey of Northwood—"the only unexceptionable Jackson
man in the state"—and Abner Greenleaf—"a worthy & independent man...against Hill." Biddle thought it "well to take
[them] so as not to seem exclusive in our choice." By proposing
Harvey, Biddle met Hill's complaint that the interior was unrep-
resented, and by choosing Greenleaf he cleverly picked the
one important Jacksonian in New Hampshire who was hostile
to Hill. Three names on Biddle's list, Thomas W. Penhallow
and Joseph Haven as well as Harvey, were among the ten men
proposed in the legislative petition on June 29. Biddle was
making a concession.[27]

He also gave way on policy. In a letter the next day he told
Mason tactfully not to make "the loan" to a certain "manufacturing company." To a degree Biddle was recognizing Woodbury's complaint that the branch under Mason had favored
manufacturers over merchants and farmers. With the proposed
shifts he tacitly admitted that some complaint was justified. The
Portsmouth episode was an important struggle, and the Jacksonians had forced Biddle to make important changes.[28]

27. Cadwalader to Biddle, Aug. 4, 1829, Biddle to Cadwalader, Aug. 28, 1829,
Biddle Papers, LC.
28. Biddle to Mason, Aug. 29, 1829, Biddle Papers, LC.

Back in Philadelphia Biddle found a long letter from Secretary Ingham awaiting him. Ingham had written sarcastically on July 23 that he was surprised at the "confident . . . assertion of the universal purity of the bank" that Biddle had expressed in his statement of July 18 about the men running the Bank. No "body of five hundred men, not selected by an Omniscient eye," Ingham said slyly, can "be fairly entitled" such "unqualified testimony." Perhaps there was nothing wrong in Portsmouth, he concluded, but he thought it no ordinary case when members of both parties made "common cause" against Mason. Irritated by the "very small intrigue" that had taken him to Portsmouth, Biddle was furious at Ingham's clever letter.[29]

Biddle sent a scorching reply that turned a social-political struggle in New Hampshire into a major political issue in Washington. First he reminded Ingham that the Bank of the United States had helped the inexperienced Secretary of the Treasury pay off an installment on the public debt. He then reviewed the Mason affair and concluded that he had "now disposed of the case." Accusing Ingham of trying to influence "the choice of officers of the bank," Biddle maintained that the Bank was responsible to Congress alone, not to any "executive officer . . . from the President . . . downwards. . . ." Ingham's predecessors in the Treasury, he added, "gentlemen of acknowledged intelligence and fidelity," had never claimed the right to interfere. Certainly the new Secretary of the Treasury should not. Biddle was telling Ingham and President Jackson to leave the Bank alone.[30]

Ingham recognized three features of the letter. Biddle had been patronizing; he had accused the Treasury Department of conniving with Hill and Woodbury to attack the Portsmouth branch; he had denied the right of the administration to exercise any

29. The Ingham letter is in House Report no. 460, pp. 446–448. The "intrigue" quotation is from Biddle to Asbury Dickins, Sept. 16, 1829, McGrane, *Correspondence of Biddle,* pp. 75–76.

30. Biddle to Ingham, Sept. 15, 1829, House Report no. 460, pp. 450–456.

control over the Bank. Ingham could reply to the arrogance himself, but he needed the President's help on the last two problems. Andrew Jackson told his Secretary to make it clear that he had been unaware of Hill's letter and petitions when he first wrote to Biddle. Such a statement would "relieve the executive from any [charge of] interference with the Bank." But, added Jackson, the President reserved "his constitutional powers . . . to redress all grievances complained of by the people of the interference by the branches with the local elections of the States, & all their interference with party politicks, in every section of our country." With this backing Ingham returned to his desk to compose another letter to Biddle.[31]

Ingham's statement of October 5 summed up the right of the administration to protect the people against the Bank of the United States. In many ways the letter anticipated Jackson's veto message in 1832, though lacking the vigor of that document. "The Government of this nation," he started, "is presumed to act . . . upon all who enjoy its blessings." The Bank could not "if it would, avoid the 'action of the Government'." He said that the Bank existed either "exclusively for national purposes, and for the common benefit of all" or "to strengthen the arm of wealth." Ingham and the Democratic Party would see to it that the Bank benefited all. The Secretary compared fine old-time Republicans like Alexander J. Dallas and William Lowndes, who had been on the people's side, with Federalists like Webster and Mason, who were defending the Bank. He then suggested, ever so gently, that the administration had the power to remove the federal deposits from the Bank.[32]

Biddle decided to make peace with the administration. Charges similar to those made about Portsmouth had also been brought against branches in New Orleans, the District of Columbia, Lex-

---

31. Jackson to Ingham, n.d., Jackson Papers, LC.
32. William Graham Sumner in his *Andrew Jackson* (Boston, 1882), p. 277, argued that Ingham's letters to Biddle were the key to the Bank War. Biddle wrote a short reply to Ingham Oct. 9. House Report no. 460, pp. 456–471.

ington, Kentucky, and Norfolk, Virginia. Biddle had already censured the culprit in Washington. In October he wrote to Jackson's adviser, William B. Lewis, who was friendly toward the Bank, asking him to explain the Kentucky situation to the President. Shortly afterward he sent Samuel Jaudon, the cashier at New Orleans and a son-in-law of Senator Hugh Lawson White of Tennessee, to explain the New Orleans story. Before the month was over, both of these men reported to Biddle that the President understood that there was no cause for complaints in either place. That left Norfolk and Portsmouth.[33]

Biddle himself then came to see the Old Hero. The interview was awkward on both sides. Jackson first expressed his gratitude for the Bank's help in paying off the national debt, but he suddenly changed tack and blurted out: "I think it right to be perfectly frank with you. I do not think that the power of Congress extends to charter a Bank" outside of the District of Columbia. Before Biddle could say anything, Jackson repeated his thanks for help with the debt and promised to mention the matter in his next message to Congress. Turning to the Portsmouth affair, Jackson said that Biddle had become embroiled with Ingham "thro' the foolishness—if I may use the term—of Mr. Hill." Biddle later recalled: "Observing he was a little embarrassed I said, 'Oh that has all passed now.'" Jackson shortly afterward concluded the meeting.[34]

Jackson's mild criticism of Hill meant little, for the President had decided to speak out against the Bank in his December message. He had arrived in Washington hostile to banks, but had not made up his mind to attack the Bank of the United States. After the Portsmouth affair, the President was determined to act. Lewis and Van Buren were alarmed lest the attack be so out-

33. Lewis to Biddle, Oct. 16, 1829, Biddle to Lewis, Oct. 21, 1829, Jaudon to Biddle, Oct. 26, 1829, Biddle Papers, LC; Remini, *Bank War*, pp. 57–58.

34. Biddle's memorandum of a conversation with Jackson, n.d. [c. Nov. 20, 1829], Biddle Papers, LC.

spoken that it would hurt the party and Van Buren's future. So they sent James A. Hamilton to prevail on Jackson to tone down the message. Hamilton reported later that the original paragraphs on the bank were written "at great length in a loose, newspaper, slashing style"; he felt that they came from the pen of one of the newspaper editors: Blair, Kendall, or Hill. Hamilton succeeded in shortening the statement on the Bank. At the very end of his message on December 8, Jackson simply remarked: "Both the constitutionality and the expediency of the law creating this bank are well questioned by a large portion of our fellow-citizens; and it must be admitted that it has failed in the great end of establishing a uniform and sound currency." The Portsmouth crisis had prompted Jackson to make his first public statement against the Bank.[35]

The story of the attempt to remove Mason was kept quiet until the congressional debate over recharter of the Bank in 1832. Even then the Democrats withheld the relevant documents from the House majority report on the Bank; they did not appear until John Quincy Adams published them with the minority report. As the story emerged, the National Republican *Niles' Weekly Register* cried that the affair was "a bold attempt . . . to 'reform' the Bank at Portsmouth into a POLITICAL ENGINE, by *Samuel D. Ingham and Isaac Hill.*" The *Register* added that "executive officers" tried to "control" the Bank for "party purposes" and pointed out that Jackson's first attack on the Bank came "only two months" after Ingham's final letter to Biddle. The article concluded that "Isaac Hill and Amos Kendall appear to have been the leaders in this business." The opposition press was being unfair. When Ingham first wrote Biddle, the Secretary of the Treasury knew nothing of Hill's maneuvers. As

35. Hamilton to a friend, Dec. 28, 1829, in James A. Hamilton, *Reminiscences of James A. Hamilton* (New York, 1869), pp. 149–150; James D. Richardson, ed., *Messages and Papers of the Presidents 1789–1897* (Washington, D.C., 1896–99), II, 1025.

Ralph C. Catterall has demonstrated in his study of the Second Bank of the United States, there was no Treasury Department plot in 1829.[36]

But the fact remains that between June and December of 1829 the Bank War began. What started as an attack on the Portsmouth branch became a battle of letters between Ingham and Biddle, and ended with a presidential pronouncement against the entire Bank of the United States. The contemporary press took the Portsmouth affair seriously—the *Globe* was still denying the charges about an 1829 plot in December 1833. Contemporary opinion—of men such as Webster, Clay, and John Quincy Adams—held that the Portsmouth affair brought about the Bank War. In 1860 the biographer James Parton accepted their view: "This correspondence relating to the desired removal of Jeremiah Mason was the direct and real cause of the destruction of the bank. If the bank had been complaisant enough to remove a faithful servant, General Jackson, I am convinced, would never have opposed the rechartering of the institution." In his 1882 biography of Jackson, William Graham Sumner agreed. Twentieth century historians have rejected the nineteenth century interpretation. Catterall, who was sympathetic with Biddle and the Bank, argued in 1903 that Mason simply followed good banking policies in Portsmouth and that Hill and Woodbury had no grounds for complaint. "What effect did this *contretemps* have upon Jackson?" asked Catterall. His answer: "little or none." Remini, who sides with the Jacksonians, also denies that the "Portsmouth incident" had any great significance and concludes that "it did not start the War."[37]

Parton and Sumner, to be sure, overstated the case—the Bank War did not hinge on any single event—but Catterall and

36. *Niles' Register,* 42 (1832), 273, 289–292, 314–316. The *Register* believed that "Some good jacobin in Portsmouth wanted the place of president of the bank . . . ." Catterall, *Second Bank,* pp. 172–174. Sumner subscribed to the plot thesis. Sumner, *Jackson,* p. 275.

37. *Daily Globe,* Dec. 13–14, 1833; Parton, *Jackson,* III, 260; Sumner, *Jackson,* p. 279; Catterall, *Second Bank,* pp. 172–180; Remini, *Bank War,* p. 56.

Remini have underestimated the Portsmouth affair. Until the flareup in the summer of 1829 Jackson had shown no disposition to do anything about the Bank. Under the moderating influence of Lewis, Van Buren, and Hamilton, he might conceivably have come to accept the Bank, perhaps with modifications. The Portsmouth episode helped bring the struggle against the Bank from the local to the national level and quickly involved major figures on both sides. It also forced the Old General to take a stand on the Bank long before he intended to do so. In short, the affair helped determine the scope and the timing of the Bank War.

Even more important, the events and the exchange of letters defined the nature of that war. Politically, the New Hampshire battle pitted prominent Federalists against the Democratic Party; economically, Mason's lending policies constituted an attack on the small farmers and small businessmen of New Hampshire; socially, aristocrats such as Biddle and Mason scornfully resisted the *nouveauriche* Hill. In each case, Hill and Woodbury portrayed themselves as defending the interests of the "plain people of the North" against the "vested interests" represented by the Bank of the United States and the new manufacturers. The Bank War could have been fought over the constitutional issues, but the rhetoric of Hill and Woodbury turned it into a social battle. The Ingham-Biddle correspondence in turn made the social conflict a major political issue. The Portsmouth affair trapped the Secretary of the Treasury and the president of the Bank into committing themselves deeply—too deeply. Three years later when President Jackson vetoed the bill to recharter the Bank, his language was reminiscent of Hill's and Ingham's in 1829. The battle between Hill and Mason cast its shadow on 1832.

After the Portsmouth clash, Kendall, Taney, Benton, Blair, and Hill kept after the Bank. As Nathan Sargent, who viewed the Washington scene for many years, put it, the war on the Bank was begun by "prominent members of the Jackson party who were known to exercise much influence" on the President. "If Hill had won" in 1829, he continued, "the Kitchen Cabinet would have been satisfied, but Hill lost and so the Bank must go." Many observers believed in the spring of 1830 that the Senate rejected Hill's nomination to the Treasury Department and almost rejected Kendall's because of the part they played in the Bank War. Webster was particularly delighted by Hill's defeat. On June 30 he wrote Mason that he had seen Biddle in Philadelphia, where they "had a hearty laugh at the fortunes" that had befallen Mason's "puissant accusers," especially Hill.[38]

In New Hampshire the attack on the Portsmouth branch went on. Woodbury corresponded with General Joseph Low, who had lost the postmastership in Concord, about efforts to get the branch shifted to Concord. By June 1831, seven-eighths of the legislature supported a plan to transfer both branch and pension office. As pressure mounted, even Bank officials in Philadelphia and Portsmouth seemed reconciled to the move. But as usual Woodbury held back, and without his support the plan to move the branch collapsed.[39]

Even so, the Bank War continued to influence politics in New Hampshire. The columns of the *Patriot* repeatedly accused the branch of aiding and instructing National Republicans. When Benton renewed the attack on the Bank in the Senate, the *Patriot* carried parts of his speech on the front page for three consecutive weeks. And in the months that followed, the *Patriot* spewed out Jacksonian charges that the Bank was a "monstrous monopoly" that ruined local banks; if rechartered, it would be

38. In addition to rejecting Hill, the Senate had also repudiated the nominations of John P. Decatur and Samuel Cushman, Portsmouth Democrats who had opposed the Bank. Nathan Sargent, *Public Men and Events* (Philadelphia, 1874), I, 217–218. James Parton reported that the Senate rejected Hill because of the Bank War. Parton, *Jackson*, III, 274. Webster to Mason, June 30, 1830, Clark, *Memoir of Mason*, p. 353.

39. D. S. Palmer to Woodbury, June 23, 1831, Woodbury Papers, LC.

"a more powerful enemy to the people than an invading army of half a million of men." Out of nineteen separate arguments against the Bank, nine denounced it for being privileged or undemocratic. Only four said it was unconstitutional, only four attacked it on economic grounds, and only two called it foreign-dominated. New Hampshire Jacksonians opposed the Bank of the United States primarily because it had too much power and too many privileges. When the veto message arrived in July 1832, they welcomed the news, calling it the greatest act in President Jackson's life because the battle was a "contest between the Bank and the People." To New Hampshire Democrats the Bank represented a conspiracy of the wealthy against the plain people of the country.[40]

When Biddle decided to apply for recharter in January, 1832, and asked his subordinates to get up petitions supporting the Bank, Mason reported that he could not get petitions from the public because the Jackson Party was so well organized. At best, he concluded, the Bank would get "a divided majority in property and reputability," but would be beaten in numbers. Support from banks was another matter. Mason told Biddle that he could depend on favorable petitions from fourteen or fifteen of the twenty-two commercial banks in the state and that only five were definitely hostile. In the end ten New Hampshire banks sent in petitions, all supporting recharter. The one from the Farmers' Bank in Amherst was typical. If the Bank of the United States were destroyed, it argued, then state banks would be "immediately multiplied," and would endanger the "soundness of the

---

40. From June 1829 to June 1832, the same charges were leveled against the Bank: it was a dangerous undemocratic monopoly. *Gazette,* Oct. 19, 1830, Aug. 31, 1832; *Patriot,* Jan. 31, Mar. 28, April 4, 11, Dec. 12, 19, 1831, Jan. 23, Feb. 6, 13, July 23, Sept. 3, 9, 1832. The *Patriot* warned that if the Bank were rechartered, "we shall in fact have no liberties only as the Bank Directors shall see fit to grant us." *Ibid.,* Feb. 13, 1832. The statement about the contest between the Bank and the people was in a letter from Congressman Thomas Chandler to John Weeks, Aug. 8, 1832, Weeks Papers, NHHS.

common currency." The petition insisted that the "present monied system" worked "admirably well."[41]

The location of the petitioning banks, however, is instructive: seven of the twelve commercial banks in the southeast sent petitions, but only three of the ten banks located elsewhere did so. Three prominent banks that refused to send petitions—the Commercial and Portsmouth banks in Portsmouth and the Merrimack County Bank in Concord—later received federal deposits as pet banks. One historian has argued that the Bank was popular among the state banks. In New Hampshire it is true that many banks supported the Bank in 1832, but this support was concentrated on the seacoast. Banks in the interior and a majority of the people opposed the Bank.[42]

In the cabinet, Woodbury's position on the Bank was not entirely clear. When Jackson was preparing his Bank statement for the 1831 annual message, Roger B. Taney was the only cabinet member wholeheartedly anti-Bank. Woodbury was so careful that Churchill C. Cambreleng of New York warned Van Buren that Woodbury kept "snug" and played "out of all the corners of his eyes." At the same time, Biddle received conflicting reports on Woodbury's position. Above all, Woodbury wanted the government to control the Bank. He confided in William Plumer that the Bank would have to become "an incidental instrument of the *government,* like the Army, Navy, and Customs House establishment." Jackson had faith in his Secretary of the Navy,

---

41. The Mason quotation is from Mason's letter to Biddle, Jan. 23, 1832, Biddle Papers, LC. See also Mason to Biddle, Feb. 10, 1832, Simon Gratz Collection, Historical Society of Pennsylvania; *Memorial of the Farmers' Bank in Amherst, N.H., Executive Documents* (House), 22nd Congress, 1st Session (1832), Doc. no. 110; Jean Wilburn, *Biddle's Bank: The Crucial Years* (New York, 1967), pp. 67–70; *Globe,* Sept. 29, 1832.

42. Four of six Portsmouth banks sent petitions, but none of the two Concord banks. Wilburn, *Biddle's Bank,* p. 68. For the names of the banks sending memorials see *House Journal,* 22nd Congress, 1st Session, pp. 286, 293, 330, 385, 413, 444. For pet banks see Gatell, "Spoils of the Bank War," pp. 35–58. See also Smith, "Banking in New Hampshire," p. 161.

and by June Woodbury had committed himself against the bill.[43]

The other New Hampshire Jacksonians were less equivocal, for Senator Hill and all the Congressmen voted against recharter. Aside from the Maine Congressmen, they were the only members of Congress from New England to oppose the Bank. On June 9, 1832, two days before the Senate voted, Hill presented his case. He started by dismissing the economic importance of the Bank. "Strike this bank out of existence," he proclaimed, "and the means for preserving a sound currency...exist precisely the same." Before long he turned to politics. "Does any one doubt," he asked rhetorically, "that the agents of the bank have made use of the money power of the bank to influence the elections...?" In spite of public opinion, he continued, Biddle had chosen Mason for the Portsmouth branch and had insisted on keeping him in office. Biddle wanted the people of the state, "weak alone against his power," to "feel the giant monopoly." Hill reviewed the events of 1828 and 1829 to prove that Congress must not recharter the Bank. His speech defined the Bank War just as he and Ingham had defined it in 1829.[44]

In spite of Hill, Congress voted to recharter the Bank, and Jackson prepared to veto the bill. For almost a week several men labored over the message. Kendall wrote the first draft, and Taney spent three days on the final version. Woodbury came in

43. Jackson wrote Van Buren in June 1832 that Taney and Woodbury were the only cabinet members he could count on against the Bank. Jackson to Van Buren, June 14, 1832, Bassett, *Correspondence of Jackson,* IV, 448. John Randolph, a steady opponent of the Bank, wrote Jackson December 19, 1831, that "Mr. Taney and Mr. Woodbury I have confidence in." Randolph to Jackson, *ibid.,* IV, 387; Robert Gibbes to Biddle, Dec. 11, 1831, Cadwalader to Biddle, Dec. 21, 1831, Charles J. Ingersoll to Biddle, Feb. 21, 1832, McGrane, *Correspondence of Biddle,* pp. 139, 150, 183. The Cambreleng quotation is in a letter from Cambreleng to Van Buren, Jan. 4, 1832, Van Buren Papers, LC. Woodbury to Plumer, Jan. 6, 1832, Miscellaneous Woodbury Papers, New-York Historical Society; Roger B. Taney, "Explanation of His Relations to the United States Bank . . .," pp. 73, 119–120, Taney Papers, LC; Swisher, *Taney,* p. 177; Wheaton, "Woodbury," p. 42.

44. Benton, *Thirty Years' View,* I, 205, 250–251; *Register of Debates,* 22nd Congress, 1st Session (June 8, 1832), pp. 1056–1068.

on the second day and stayed on the job until it was finished. Jackson himself added words and phrases. The message the President sent to Congress on July 10 was a powerful social-economic-political document that denounced the Bank as a "monopoly" with "exclusive privileges." Laws such as the act rechartering the Bank, said Jackson, made "the rich richer and the potent more powerful." As a result, "the humbler members of society, the farmers, mechanics, and laborers . . . have a right to complain of the injustice of their government." Jackson concluded that he would "take a stand against all new grants of monopolies and exclusive privileges, against any prostitution of our government to the advancement of the few at the expense of the many." It was an effective message.[45]

The Portsmouth branch war and the ideas of the New Hampshire Jacksonians had their effect on the veto message. Jackson could have attacked the Bank in many ways. He chose to attack it in the same terms as those used by Hill, Woodbury, and Ingham in the 1829 affair. Just a few days before the veto, Hill had gone over the same ground in his Senate speech. In his wording Kendall reflected Hill's views, and Hill undoubtedly had direct influence on the message. Woodbury likewise brought his New Hampshire experiences and assumptions to bear on the veto.[46]

The next spring when Jackson asked his cabinet for their views on removing federal deposits from the Bank, Woodbury refused

45. [Washington, D.C.] *The Daily Madisonian*, April 27, 1843; Taney, "United States Bank," p. 126; Van Buren, *Autobiography*, p. 625; Richardson, *Messages of the Presidents*, II, 1139–1154. Lynn Marshall in "The Authorship of Jackson's Bank Veto Message," *Mississippi Valley Historical Review*, 50 (1963), 466–477, argues convincingly that Amos Kendall was the principal author.

46. Arthur B. Darling in *Political Changes in Massachusetts, 1824–1848: A Study of Liberal Movements in Politics* (New Haven, Conn., 1925), p. 136, note 13, argues that David Henshaw of Massachusetts influenced the message. Woodbury and Hill both knew Henshaw well. John S. Bassett contends that Hill and Kendall were responsible for the opening and closing sections of the message, where the political charges against monopoly and privilege are expressed, while Taney wrote the constitutional arguments in the middle. John S. Bassett, *The Life of Andrew Jackson* (Garden City, N.Y., 1911), p. 619.

to take a definite position, but urged the President to delay removal for a year. In hesitating over deposit removal, Woodbury followed a course parallel to Van Buren's. Ever since 1826 he and Van Buren had tried to maintain a middle position, holding as many factions of the party together as possible. Thus both had been cautious about the Bank, and Van Buren had been anxious to conciliate South Carolina after nullification. The two had not always worked closely, but by 1833 they had formed an alliance that would last until President Van Buren and Secretary of the Treasury Woodbury both left office in 1841. In the summer of 1833 they both decided to support removal of the deposits. Biddle complained in August that Woodbury had said: "We are not against a bank, but against the Bank. . . . We want to scramble for the Stock and to have the Offices." When Biddle asked him about the constitutional question, he supposedly retorted: "Poh, that we can use to suit ourselves." Although the statement is second-hand and sounds far more forthright than Woodbury ordinarily did, it does demonstrate that he favored deposit removal.[47]

When Jackson called the cabinet together on September 18, 1833, to support removal, Woodbury had one final moment of hesitation. Secretary of State Louis McLane, who spoke first, opposed taking the deposits from the Bank. After Secretary of the Treasury William J. Duane, who was against removal, passed, and after Secretary of War Lewis Cass repeated his opposition, the President turned to Woodbury. Jackson, who had counted on his support, must have been annoyed as the Secretary of the Navy hemmed and hawed through a long discourse. First he declared that the deposits were perfectly safe in the Bank. The President had the constitutional "right" to shift the funds, but he should make the decision on the basis of "expediency." He finally concluded lamely that since Jackson had more information on the subject than he did, he would go along with him

47. Parton, *Jackson*, III, 526–527; Biddle to Cooper, Aug. 16, 1833, McGrane, *Correspondence of Biddle*, p. 215.

in favor of removing the deposits. Since the word "expedient" or "expediency" appears in his notes four times, it is apparent that Woodbury considered deposit removal far from a crusade.[48]

Crusade or not, from that cabinet meeting on, Woodbury was swept up in the removal of the deposits. On September 26 he received a letter from acting Secretary of the Treasury Taney that he and Kendall, who was assisting him, wanted Woodbury's help in selecting the pet banks. Safe Levi Woodbury was just the man to supervise the distribution of the federal funds. The Metropolis Bank of Washington, D.C., in which he had investments, became one of the first pet banks. When the Senate in June 1834 refused to confirm Taney as Secretary of the Treasury, Woodbury advanced to that office.[49]

In New Hampshire the *Patriot* had been urging the removal of the deposits all through the summer of 1833, and the Jackson banks in Portsmouth had been maneuvering to receive the funds. In August 1833, both the cashier of the Piscataqua Bank and Isaac Waldron, a director at the Commercial Bank, wrote Kendall offering their banks as depositories. The Portsmouth Bank also made a bid. On October 5, 1833, Hill urged Woodbury to give the deposits to the Commercial Bank because it had "done more to accommodate businessmen than any other" bank in the town. Here was a dilemma for Woodbury. He had money invested in both the Piscataqua and Portsmouth banks, but Hill was sup-

48. Bassett, *Jackson*, pp. 634, 644–645; Stickney, *Autobiography of Kendall*, pp. 376-378; William J. Duane, *Narrative and Correspondence concerning the Removal of the Deposits* ... (Philadelphia, 1838), p. 6; Van Buren, *Autobiography*, pp. 598–604; Woodbury, notes on cabinet meeting of Sept. 18, 1833, Woodbury Papers, LC; Catterall, *Second Bank*, p. 295; Remini, *Bank War*, pp. 112–119.

49. Senate Document no. 16, 23rd Congress, 1st Session (1833–1834), p. 262; Hammond, *Banks and Politics*, p. 342. Woodbury's appointment was confirmed June 27, 1834. *Senate Executive Journal*, 4 (1829–1837), 433. In his "Intimate Memoranda," Woodbury claimed that he would have been appointed Secretary of the Treasury ahead of Duane if Van Buren and Louis McLane had not stood in the way. Ari Hoogenboom and Herbert Ershkowitz, "Levi Woodbury's 'Intimate Memoranda' of the Jackson Administration," *Pennsylvania Magazine of History and Biography*, 92 (Oct. 1968), 510.

porting the Commercial. When Woodbury decided in favor of the Commercial, he pleased Hill, who had no money invested there, and Franklin Pierce, who did. The opposition *Portsmouth Journal* remarked accurately that the Commercial won because it had a Jackson man as president.

The choice of the Commercial Bank underscored the socioeconomic conflict involved in the Bank War. Not only was the Commercial the smallest bank in Portsmouth, but it was a bank in which many persons of moderate means had investments. Woodbury later gave federal funds to the Portsmouth, Piscataqua, and New Hampshire banks in Portsmouth. All were Jacksonian banks, and like the Commercial, the Piscataqua had many small investors. When the Piscataqua finally closed, in 1844, it announced that 485 shares were held by farmers and laborers, 104 by mechanics, only 332 by merchants, and just 62 by lawyers.[50]

In his October letter Hill also asked Woodbury to transfer the pension funds from the Bank branch to the Merrimack County Bank in Concord, the bank of which he was a director. In renewing the transfer attempt of 1829, Hill promised that his bank would pay the pensions without charging any fee, but neglected to add that his bank would thereby get a large sum of money

---

50. Gatell, "Spoils of the Bank War," pp. 52–53. Asa Clapp's Maine Bank also received deposits. Even the *Journal* reported that the Commercial had many small investors. *Portsmouth Journal*, Aug. 31, Sept. 7, Oct. 26, 1833; *Patriot*, Sept. 30, Oct. 2, 21, 1833; *Gazette*, Aug. 4, 1829, Aug. 27, Sept. 3, Oct. 1, 8, 15, 1833, Jan. 14, 1834; Isaac Waldron to Kendall, Aug. 24, 1833, Louis M. Frederick to Secretary of the Treasury, Oct. 10, 1833, Waldron to Roger B. Taney, Oct. 15, 1833, Samuel Lord to Woodbury, Aug. 13, 1833, Letters from Banks, Treasury Department, National Archives; Hill to Woodbury, Oct. 5, 1833, Hill Papers. Franklin Pierce said that the Commercial Bank in Portsmouth was called "Woodbury's special pet." D. W. Bartlett, *The Life of Gen. Franklin Pierce* (Buffalo, N.Y., 1852), p. 55. Woodbury had no money invested in the Commercial Bank in 1833, but he did by 1836. Waldron to Woodbury, July 11, 1836, Woodbury Papers, LC. Two Portsmouth banks received no deposits: the New Hampshire Union Bank, which owned shares in the Bank of the United States, and the Rockingham Bank, a National Republican bank. Total shares in the Piscataqua Bank in 1844 numbered 2,888. *Hill's New Hampshire Patriot*, May 14, 1846.

interest free. At first the pension money went to the Commercial Bank in Portsmouth along with the federal deposits, but starting in 1836 pensions were distributed out of the Merrimack County Bank.[51]

Concord, all the while, had no pet bank. The Deposit Act of 1836, however, which limited the amount of deposits in any one bank, opened the way for more pet banks. When the Mechanics' Bank and the Merrimack County Bank—both Democratic banks in which Hill and Woodbury had investments—applied for federal deposits in 1836, the Secretary of the Treasury hesitated. He wrote Peter Renton in Concord that due to "motives of personal delicacy, arising from my pecuniary interest in two of the banks at Concord," he was turning the matter over to the President. Before long, both banks had federal deposits. Hill's decade-long effort to make more capital available for small investors of the interior had finally met success.[52]

In 1834, on the heels of the removal of the deposits, a business recession hit the United States. In New Hampshire, factories in Newmarket, Pembroke, Dunstable, Great Falls, and Dover shut down in March; Portsmouth and Somersworth also suffered. As elsewhere, Democrats blamed the difficulties on the contraction in loans started by the Bank of the United States in the fall of 1833. But in the spring of 1834 Senator Samuel Bell presented a memorial from merchants in Portsmouth blaming the removal of the deposits. Hill rose angrily to rebut. The branch bank, he said, had plenty of money for loans but was holding back to make the depression worse. After the government transferred the deposits to the Commercial Bank, the branch held on to as many Commercial bills as possible in order to embarrass the Commercial by demanding specie at inopportune moments. He charged that those who signed the memorial were permanent

51. Hill to Woodbury, Oct. 5, 1833, Hill Papers; *Portsmouth Journal*, Mar. 8, 1834; Isaac Waldron to Woodbury, July 11, 1836, Woodbury Papers, LC.

52. Gatell, "Spoils of the Bank War," p. 36; Woodbury to President of Mechanics' Bank, Concord, N.H., July 23, 1836, Sept. 5, 21, 1836, Treasury Department, National Archives.

debtors to the Bank of the United States under the thumb of the branch. None of them were Democrats. Bell defended the memorial and the Bank, but admitted that the branch might have acted improperly. In Portsmouth the *Gazette* identified thirty-four of the memorialists as chronic debtors of the Bank.[53]

During the dark year 1834, as the struggle between Bank and Administration went on, worried Democrats wrote Hill for assurance. "If the President does not stand firm," warned one, the United States would soon be "at the feet of the money Aristocracy." Another, afraid that "yielding" would end in "loss of liberty," concluded that the war was between the "great industrious class" and the "monopolist whose aim is to live on the labor of other men." In a letter to John Weeks, Joseph Harper showed more confidence. The "desperate Bank men," who wanted to "perpetuate the monster," would fail because "Old Hickory" was "as firm as a rock." The letters revealed again the emotions and rhetoric of the Bank War.[54]

Jackson was indeed as firm as a rock, and with the help of his Secretary of the Treasury he finished off the Bank the next year. First Woodbury issued an order prohibiting the receipt of branch drafts in payment of government dues; then he ordered receivers of public money not to take notes of the Bank. As early as the summer of 1835 branch offices of the Bank were closing across the country even though the Bank charter had almost a year to go.[55]

The Panic of 1837, which followed the Bank War, was as painful for Hill and Woodbury as it was for all Jacksonians. Hill wrote his old ally in March 1837 complaining that deposits at the

53. *Gazette*, Feb. 4, Mar. 10, 1834; *Patriot*, Mar. 3, May 12, 1834; *Congressional Globe*, 23rd Congress, 1st Session (1833–1834), pp. 178–179. Hill's information came from a letter from a constituent in Portsmouth, who claimed that the branch had $50,000 in specie and $30,000 in local bills that it was holding back. The letter also charged that the memorialists represented three-quarters of the debts owed the branch. See also Philip A. Grant, "The Bank Controversy and New Hampshire Politics, 1834–1835," *Historical New Hampshire*, 23 (Autumn 1968), 21–23.

54. Cyrus Ware to Hill, Feb. 25, 1834, Samuel Allen to Hill, May 24, 1834, Hill Papers; Joseph Harper to Weeks, July 24, 1834, Weeks Papers, NHHS.

55. Catterall, *Second Bank*, p. 452; *Patriot*, June 27, 1836. The first order was on January 1, 1835; the second was in 1836.

Merrimack County Bank were down to $24,000 and were threatening to go lower. Could Woodbury keep federal deposits at the Merrimack up to $50,000? The secretary at first promised little, but on May 17 he sent Hill's bank $10,000. Later in 1837 Hill became president of the Mechanics' Bank in Concord and before long was asking Woodbury to help his new venture. And in Charlestown, New Hampshire, another Jacksonian, Henry Hubbard, pleaded with Woodbury in 1839 to send his bank $20,000 in Treasury notes. Politics and banking were as closely related in 1839 as they had been in 1829 and in 1800.[56]

Hill's motives in the Bank War were complex. Bray Hammond was only partly correct in contending that Hill joined the fray because he was a rival banker who stood to gain from crushing the Bank. A self-made man, he was worth perhaps $50,000 by 1829, and some of his investments were in banking. He also needed bank loans to pay off the debts he had accumulated. The Bank, for example, loaned Hill $3,700. Money was tight in interior New Hampshire, and Hill profited when federal funds were transferred to his bank in Concord. But he did not profit much, since his bank received nothing until 1836, the Panic hit a year later, and Hill was in financial distress in 1839.[57]

56. Hill to Woodbury, Feb. 13, 23, Mar. 20, May 12, 15, Sept. 6, Nov. 7, 1837, Nov. 2, 1839, Woodbury to Hill, Mar. 27, May 17, 1837, Hubbard to Woodbury, May 22, 1837, Oct. 30, 1839, Woodbury to Hubbard, Nov. 4, 1839, Woodbury Papers, LC.

57. The opposition press made amusingly exaggerated charges about Hill's wealth. It accused him of controlling thirteen banks, thirteen newspapers, and thirteen mail contracts and said that he had made "five times $70,000 since General Jackson came into power." *Gazette,* Sept. 29, 1834; *Patriot,* Feb. 27, 1832; *Sentinel,* Jan. 7, 1836. Hill's own statement of his worth can be found in his letter to his uncle Nathaniel Russell, Sept. 16, 1830, Hill Papers, and in his letter to Woodbury, Nov. 1, 1839, Woodbury Papers, LC. See also Bradley, *Hill,* p. 142. Hammond's description of Hill is in Hammond, *Banks and Politics,* pp. 330–331. Hill's debts are discussed in Hill to Robinson and Lord, Sept. 18, and Dec. 4, 1826, and Hill to Luther Roby, Dec. 11, 1834, Hill Papers, NHHS. Robinson, "Hill," pp. 28, 38, 188, discusses Hill's economic successes and failures. The relationship between Hill and the Bank of the United States is covered in McGrane, *Correspondence of Biddle,* p. 357; *The Present State of the Times* (Portsmouth, 1838), p. 6.

To argue that Hill attacked the Bank simply because he hoped to benefit financially is to close one's eyes to his personality. Once poor, chronically lame, and socially insecure, he delighted in beating upper-class opponents. The Bank War enabled him to battle "aristocrats" like Mason and Biddle and to attack a "privileged monopoly" like the Bank of the United States. Hill convinced New Hampshire farmers that bankers threatened them, then led them in a war against the Bank.

Hill also fought for political reasons. For years he had been fighting Webster, Mason, and other "Federalists"; the Bank War continued that fight. Hill was never able to prove his charges that the Bank had used its powers illegally to sway votes, but he knew that Bank people tended to be National Republicans. For Hill that was a good enough reason to stage a war.

The New Hampshire Bank War was partly an entrepreneur's war, for Democratic bankers had something to gain from defeating the Bank. The war, however, was far more than simply "the Rise of Liberal Capitalism." In part the fight was psychological—the reaction of insecure people against an imagined banking conspiracy. In part it was personal—Hill against Mason, Jackson against Biddle. It was certainly political—Democrats were against the Bank. Finally, it was a social war in which aspiring common people fought to destroy a bank that they thought hampered their upward progress.[58]

In New Hampshire the social and political reasons for the Bank War outweighed the entrepreneurial. The bitter struggle stemmed essentially from long-range regional and social differences in the state. It was a particularly important struggle because it had such an impact on the Bank War in Washington. The New Hampshire story suggests that Schlesinger was closer to being correct than Hammond; but it also suggests that the Bank War was more complex than many historians have allowed.

58. The phrase "the Rise of Liberal Capitalism" is part of a chapter title in Richard Hofstadter, *The American Political Tradition and the Men Who Made It* (New York, 1948), p. 44.

VI

The Presidential
Election of 1832

In August 1832, Isaac Hill returned to Concord to attend the dinner in his honor at the Eagle Coffee House. After the meal he rose to give the fiery speech in which he kicked off the presidential campaign. The issue, he said, was Henry Clay and the aristocracy against Andrew Jackson and the people. Clay's speeches revealed "the arts of the demagogue," but Jackson, fortunately, stood "in the way of ambitious demagogues who would cheat the people of their rights, [and] in the way of monopolies." In Boston the *Courier* said that there were no "distinguished" persons at the dinner, but the *Patriot* had the usual answer for that. Only "the people—the vulgar Democrats"— were there, "farmers and mechanics," who were distinguished only for their "patriotism."[1]

Hill and the *Patriot* had set the keynote for the campaign, since the personality of Jackson and the issue of democracy and the common man were central to the election. The opposition *Statesman,* for example, carried frequent references to "King Andrew," to "Jacksonism," and to "Jacksonians." The *Patriot*

1. This chapter is a revised and expanded version of an article in *Historical New Hampshire* and is published with the permission of that journal. Donald B. Cole, "The Presidential Election of 1832 in New Hampshire," *Historical New Hampshire,* 21 (Winter 1966), 32–50. *Proceedings at Dinner to Hill.* Hill's speech is reprinted in Bradley, *Hill,* pp. 194–200. *Patriot,* Sept. 24, 1832.

insisted that only Democrats could represent the common man. There were other issues, too, including Federalism and the Bank of the United States. Democrats continued to talk as if they were running against the Federalist Party. In a letter to the *Patriot,* "Veritas" wrote: "While the federalists are marshalling their corps..., we should be ready to meet and counteract every deception." Above all, campaigners focused on the Bank War. Hill accused the Bank's officials of "betting the Bank's money" on the election and of "scattering its thousands" in New Hampshire. Since Jacksonians interpreted the struggle over the Bank in democratic terms, the issue of the Bank served to bring out the issue of the common man.[2]

With his reputation as a spoilsman, his contributions to the Bank War, and his well-known hostility to Henry Clay, Hill himself was an issue in the campaign. During the election months the Washington *Globe* published few speeches in full, but one of them was Hill's Concord speech in August. The opposition *Niles' Register* quoted liberally and disdainfully from the same speech. The *Patriot* was much in demand partly because it revived the old "bargain" story against Clay. During the campaign Hill radiated confidence, as when he told his wealthy gambling friend Thomas Green of Boston not to "let the Bank braggarts bully" him. He advised Green to take all the bets he could get "on New York, Pennsylvania, and Ohio for Jackson." "Don't be weak!" he exhorted, "Take everything in sight." Green and Jesse Hoyt of New York each supposedly won $50,000 on the election; Hill also made a tidy sum.[3]

Even though Democrat Samuel Dinsmoor had won the March election by almost 10,000 votes, Democrats expected the campaign to be spirited and the election close. Deposed postmaster Joseph Low, for example, said privately that he would join

2. *Patriot,* Sept. 24, 1832; *Statesman,* July 7, 21, Aug. 4, Sept. 1, Oct. 13, 1832; Hill to Thomas Green, Oct. 8, 1832, quoted in Buell, *Jackson,* II, 271; Hill to Jesse Hoyt, Oct. 15, 1832, quoted in William L. Mackenzie, *The Life and Times of Martin Van Buren* (Boston, 1846), p. 239.
3. Bowers, *Party Battles,* pp. 248–251; Hill to Green, Oct. 8, 1832, quoted in Buell, *Jackson,* II, 271; *Niles' Register,* 43 (1832), 10; *Globe,* Aug. 18, 1832.

anyone to defeat Andrew Jackson. Both sides soon resorted to filth. When the *Patriot* stated that Clay did not deserve to be President because he was known to have patronized brothels, National Republicans replied with a circular that started:

OPEN PROFLIGACY AND DESPICABLE INTRIGUES

EVIL, DISGRACE OR DANGER

IGNORANCE AND QUACKERY

PARTISAN POLITICIAN

Niles' Register accurately reported that in New Hampshire "much warmth" was shown by both parties.[4]

Since Freemasonry was closely identified with the Democratic Party, Anti Masonry entered the campaign. John Parker Hale reported in December 1831 that if the Anti-Masons set up a newspaper in Concord, they would carry the state for their candidate William Wirt. No newspaper appeared, and the Anti-Masons, who won in Vermont in 1832, were unable to get organized in New Hampshire. When they belatedly tried to line up a slate of electors, old William Plumer refused to run. It was "obvious," he said, "that if the National Republicans and Anti-Masons" each had "separate lists of . . . electors, neither of them" could succeed. He urged those opposed to Freemasonry to vote for Clay. When John Prentiss of the National Republican *Sentinel* tried to attract Anti-Mason votes, the *Patriot* pointed out that Prentiss was actually a Mason himself and a "Federalist" at that. Such were the obstacles for Anti-Masonry in New Hampshire. Gideon Welles reported that Anti-Masons and National Republicans were united against Democrats in Connecticut, but that Democratic prospects were good in New Hampshire.[5]

---

4. *New Hampshire Manual 1891*, p. 153; Low to Samuel Bell, May 7, 1832, Bell Papers; *Patriot*, Mar. 19, 1832, Sept. 25, Oct. 1, 1832; *Niles' Register*, 43 (1832), 133.

5. Heald, "Thirty-nine Governors Were Freemasons." Plumer's statement appeared in *Niles' Register*, 43 (1832), 170. *Patriot*, Oct. 22, Nov. 5, 1832; Hale to John W. Taylor, Dec. 26, 1831, John W. Taylor Papers, New-York Historical Society; Welles to Woodbury, Oct. 26, 1832, Woodbury Papers, LC.

In a bid to win the election, the opposition brought Daniel Webster back to New Hampshire on the eve of the election, but he had been out of the state for sixteen years, and it was too late. Jackson carried the state 26,269–19,627. The President received a smaller percentage of the vote than Dinsmoor in the gubernatorial election because many of the opposition, who had stayed away from the polls in March, returned in November. With Jackson and the Bank veto at stake, National Republicans and old Federalists came out to vote against the Old General. As in 1828, the issues and personalities of Jacksonian Democracy brought out the voters. Throughout the land the President's program stimulated considerable voter resentment, and Jackson is the only incumbent President to be reelected with a smaller percentage of the popular vote in his second election than in his first. Nonetheless, he won by a substantial margin. In New Hampshire, where he no longer faced the well-known New Englander John Quincy Adams, he won a decisive victory (Table 3). Where he had lost six of eight counties in 1828, he carried seven of eight in 1832; an Adams majority of 3,202 changed to a Jackson majority of 6,642.[6]

Table 3. Votes Cast in New Hampshire Elections, 1828–1832

	1828 Presidential election	1830 Gubernatorial election	1832 Gubernatorial election	1832 Presidential election
For the Democratic candidate	20,922	23,214	24,167	26,269
Democratic candidate's percent of total vote	46	55	62	57
For the opposition candidate	24,124	19,040	14,920	19,627
Total vote cast	45,046	42,441	39,233	45,978
Percent of adult males voting	76	71	64	75

Source: Journal of the House of Representatives of New Hampshire, passim; New Hampshire Manual 1891, pp. 153, 159.

6. For Webster's visit, see *Patriot*, Nov. 12, 1832. See Chapter III for an analysis of the 1828 election. McCormick, "New Perspectives," p. 292; Remini, *Bank War*, p. 106. For additional documentation see Table 3.

The results of the New Hampshire election provide an opportunity to analyze the nature of Jacksonian Democracy. Historians have long been concerned with identifying eastern Jacksonian Democrats. In 1935 Frederick Jackson Turner argued that they "found their rural following among the less prosperous towns." He concluded that the eastern Democracy was strongest "among the poorer people," especially the farmers in the "hilly and mountainous districts" and the factory workers in the cities. A decade later Arthur M. Schlesinger, Jr., described Jacksonian Democracy in terms of class conflict and called particular attention to the urban worker wing of the party.[7]

In the 1950's and 1960's these views of Jacksonian Democracy came under attack, as consensus historians denied that issues or classes made much difference. Lee Benson in particular rejected the "traditional" Turner and Schlesinger interpretations. By studying the presidential vote in New York State in 1844, he contended that the rank order of Democratic vote in cities as well as in towns did not coincide with a ranking of economic status. The very poorest communities were not necessarily those with the strongest Democratic vote. Benson went on to discard the entire concept

7. Turner concluded that the "Democratic strongholds of Maine and New Hampshire were in the counties where farm lands had a relatively low value, and the same general trend appeared in southern New England." Frederick Jackson Turner, *The United States 1830–1850: The Nation and Its Sections* (New York, 1935), p. 66. He added later, "In general in the Middle Atlantic States, the hilly and mountainous districts (including the 'northern tier' of counties in Pennsylvania, and at times, adjacent counties of New York) tended to be Democratic ... On the whole the better farm lands, the lines of communication, the areas settled by New Englanders, tended to vote the Whig ticket." *Ibid.*, pp. 116–117. Schlesinger demonstrated that radical Jacksonians supported labor programs but was less concerned with proving that labor voted Democratic. He contented himself with statements such as: "During the Bank War, laboring men began slowly to turn to Jackson as their leader, and his party as their party." Schlesinger, *Age of Jackson*, pp. 143, 505. Turner was more direct: "the urban labor classes [in New England] ... were Democratic." Turner, *United States 1830–1850*, p. 66. In his analysis of New York state politics Dixon Ryan Fox subscribed to the same economic interpretation. "Where mechanics made their home," he argued, "Democratic candidates generally were certain of election." Fox, *Decline of Aristocracy in the Politics of New York*, pp. 430–437, quotation on p. 437.

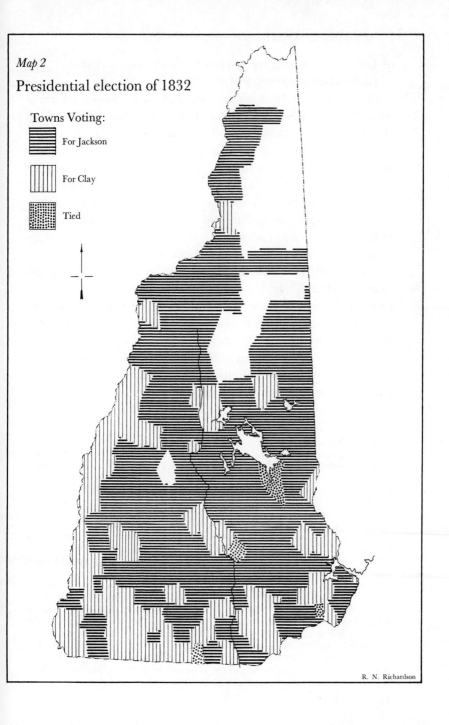

Map 2

Presidential election of 1832

Towns Voting:

For Jackson

For Clay

Tied

R. N. Richardson

of Jacksonian Democracy, preferring to call the period the "Age of Egalitarianism" instead of the "Age of Jackson."[8]

The election of 1832 and the state of New Hampshire are a good time and place to test the Turner and Schlesinger theses about Jacksonian Democracy. The year 1832 marks the apogee of the Jackson movement while Jackson was President and the Bank War was hot. It is surely a better time to study Jacksonian Democracy than 1844, when the Old General was close to death and the election hinged on slavery and expansion. And although New Hampshire was not one of the most important states in 1832, its combination of agriculture, manufacturing, and shipping made it reasonably typical of the North.[9]

The 45,978 New Hampshire votes in 1832 were cast in 209 towns, of which 63, or 30 percent, voted for Clay, 142 or 68 percent voted for Jackson, and 4 were tied. The towns were located in seven geographic regions (see Map 3). In the south, reading roughly from east to west, were the southeast lowlands (the seacoast), the southeast uplands, the Merrimack Valley, the southwest uplands, and the Connecticut Valley; in the north were the Lake Winnipesaukee region and the mountain region. Population was most dense along the seacoast and in the two river valleys.[10]

---

8. New York State voting data appear in Benson, *Concept of Jacksonian Democracy*, pp. 140–164. Regarding Turner's interpretation of voting behavior, Benson stated: "traditional claims about Democratic strength among the urban lower classes rest upon spurious relationships." *Ibid.*, p. 146. He added, "for the rural areas, where the great bulk of the electorate lived, it [the traditional interpretation] simply lacks the factual basis." *Ibid.*, p. 147. For Benson's concept of "the Age of Egalitarianism," see *ibid.*, p. 336.

9. For details on the New Hampshire economy see Chapter I.

10. Detailed tables supporting the findings in this chapter are collected in the Appendix. Results for Danbury, Milan, Berlin, and Waterville were not available. Since the total for those towns was at the most 150 votes, the omission is of no importance. Detailed results for the remaining 209 towns are available in *Patriot*, Nov. 12, 19, 1832. The state total can be found in *Journal of the House of Representatives of the State of New Hampshire, at Their Session . . . Commencing Wednesday, Nov. 21, 1832* (Nov. 23, 1832), p. 19. The results are conveniently tabulated in *New Hampshire Manual 1891*, p. 159. I also used Petersen, *History of Elections*, p. 143. The division into seven geographic regions is taken from Margery D. Howarth, *New Hampshire: A Study of Its Cities and Towns in Relation to Their Physical Background* (Concord, N.H., 1936), p. 7. I have modified the regions in the Howarth book. See Appendix, Table A.

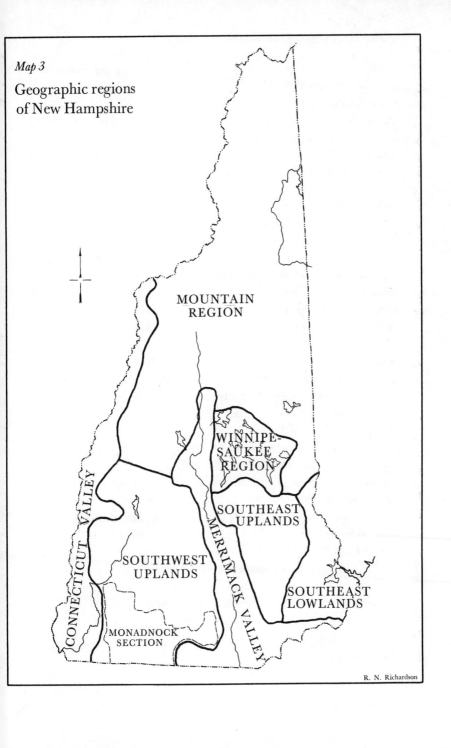

Map 3

Geographic regions
of New Hampshire

MOUNTAIN
REGION

WINNIPE-
SAUKEE
REGION

SOUTHEAST
UPLANDS

CONNECTICUT VALLEY

MERRIMACK VALLEY

SOUTHWEST
UPLANDS

SOUTHEAST
LOWLANDS

MONADNOCK
SECTION

R. N. Richardson

In the election, the towns divided partly according to whether they were located in the three low regions (seacoast and river valleys) or in the four high regions (upland, lake, and mountain districts). The high regions were decidedly for Jackson, giving him four towns out of five, and the low regions divided evenly. Similarly, 70 percent of Jackson's strength came from the high towns, while 62 percent of Clay's support came from low towns.

Over half of the communities in the high areas gave two-thirds or more of their vote to Jackson, but only one-seventh of those in the low areas did so. Among the 79 towns that voted two-thirds or more for Jackson, 86 percent were in the high regions. Almost every town in the southeastern hills, the lake district, and the White Mountains voted for Jackson. The Connecticut Valley, on the other hand, was just as solidly National Republican, for only seven of the twenty-three communities supported Jackson, and six of those were on high land on the outer fringes of the valley.

These statistics help prove the continuity in New Hampshire politics. In most elections going back to 1800 the Connecticut and Merrimack valleys had supported first Federalism and then the National Republican Party. Even an exception to the high-low pattern shows the continuity. In the Monadnock section of the southwest uplands, almost all of the towns surprisingly voted for Clay. In those earlier elections this section had been the one upland area voting Federalist-National Republican. Otherwise, hill and mountain regions were consistently Republican-Democratic from 1800 to 1832. The statistics also supported what Hill kept saying, that upland farmers were ordinarily Democratic. In 1832 Jackson had 30 percent of towns in the Connecticut Valley, 55 percent of those in the Merrimack Valley, and 91 percent of those in the upland and mountain regions of the interior, with the Monadnock section excluded.[11]

11. For a summary of earlier voting patterns see Table 2. See also Appendix, Tables B, C, D.

Geological and agricultural surveys make it possible to distinguish between the good and the poor farmland in the state and to generalize about the economic basis of Jacksonian Democracy. Farmland was rated relatively good or poor depending on elevation, rainfall, the type of soil, the length of the growing season, and the flatness of the land. On this basis, it appears that farmers in the poor areas (generally less prosperous farmers) were more likely to vote for Jackson than for Clay. Throughout the state Jackson carried 68 percent of the towns, but in the poor agricultural regions he did even better, carrying 78 percent. Over half of those towns gave him two-thirds or more of their votes. In the good areas Clay did much better, limiting Jackson to 58 percent of those towns. Similarly, 68 percent of Clay towns were in good regions, while almost 56 percent of the Jackson towns were in poor regions. Once again the data supported Hill's claim that the poor farmers working rocky upland soil were the most loyal Democrats.[12]

The figures on arable land give Hill's interpretation additional backing. Towns with a large number of acres of arable land per 100 eligible voters would probably have had larger, more prosperous farms; according to Hill they should have been for Clay. Hill was correct. Though Clay lost the state by a wide margin, he carried over half of the communities with the largest farms, while Democrats carried three-quarters of the rest. Furthermore, only one of the towns with the smallest farms gave two-thirds of its votes to Clay, while ten gave two-thirds to Jackson. Only 8 percent of the towns for Jackson were those with large farms, compared to 25 percent of those for Clay. No matter how

12. The division of towns into good and poor agricultural areas was taken from New Hampshire Agricultural Experiment Station, *Types of Farming Areas in New Hampshire,* Circular 53, 1936–1937. See Appendix, Tables E, F. See also Charles H. Hitchcock, *The Geology of New Hampshire* (Concord, N.H., 1874), vol. I. I have been assured by the Agricultural Experiment Station personnel that natural soil conditions in New Hampshire were essentially the same in 1832 as they were when the station made its survey in 1936–1937.

the figures are arranged, towns with small farms tended to be Democratic.[13]

The best way, however, to separate the prosperous towns from the poor towns is to study the tax records. Every four years the legislature determined the value of property in each town and assessed state taxes accordingly. It assigned each town a certain apportionment of every $1,000 of taxes to be raised by the state. This apportionment or tax rate adjusted for the population of the town provides an index for the prosperity of the particular town. Farmers in towns with a high rate were presumably better off than those in towns with a low rate. Table 4 divides the towns according to the taxes they paid in the year 1832–33 for every $1,000 of state taxes to be raised and for every 1,000 in town population. Hampton Falls, for example, on rich farmland, had the highest tax rate in the state—$3.26 for $1,000 in state taxes. Since the population of Hampton Falls was only 582, the rate adjusted for 1,000 in population was $5.60. Nearby Newcastle, a poor fishing harbor, was next to the bottom, with a rate of $1.41 for 850 people or $1.66 for 1,000.

Again, the percentage of poorer towns for Jackson is seen to be much higher than that of more prosperous towns. As the tax apportionment climbs (Table 4), the percentage for Jackson drops, Among the thirty-five towns in the lowest bracket, twenty-nine voted for Jackson, and nineteen of them gave Jackson two-thirds or more of their vote. Conversely, among the twenty-six towns in the highest group, Clay carried fifteen, and two were tied. When the same figures were arranged according to party, they showed that 44 percent of the Clay towns had a tax rate of $4.00 or better, compared to 21 percent of the Jackson towns.

Although villages with small farms on poor upland soil were generally the Jacksonian strongholds, one part of New Hamp-

13. The figures on arable land are taken from Farmer, *New Hampshire Register 1829*. See Appendix, Table G. Among the twenty-six towns with the smallest farms (0–50 acres of arable land per 100 eligible voters) six voted for Clay, nineteen for Jackson, and one was tied.

shire—the Monadnock section in the southwest running from Sullivan east to Amherst—failed to fit that pattern. These small, upland villages on poor soil with small farms "should" have voted for Jackson, and yet fourteen of the sixteen voted for Clay, and twelve gave Clay at least two-thirds of their vote.

Table 4. Voting Results Arranged by Tax Rate[a]

Tax rate	Towns voting for Clay		Towns voting for Jackson		Tied		Total number
	Number	Percent	Number	Percent	Number	Percent	
Below $3.00	5	14	29	83	1	3	35
$3.00–$3.49	13	23	44	77	0	0	57
$3.50–$3.99	17	32	35	66	1	2	53
$4.00–$4.49	13	39	20	61	0	0	33
$4.50 and over	15	58	9	25	2	7	26
Total[b]	63	30	142	68	4	2	209

Source: tax rate—*Laws of New Hampshire* (Concord, N.H., 1922), 10 (1829–1835), 412–418; population—*Patriot,* April 11, 1831.

[a]Tax rate was a town's apportionment of every $1,000 in taxes to be raised by the state, adjusted per 1,000 population. It was based on assessed value of property.

[b]Five Jackson towns with no tax figures available are included in the total column, but not in the other columns.

See also Appendix, Tables H, I.

In part these towns violated the patterns because of their Federalist background. But they also did so because they fitted the tax rate pattern. To vote for Clay, they "should" have been prosperous towns paying a proportionately high tax rate. That proved to be the case. Seven of the fourteen towns for Clay in the section had a rate over $4.00, and six more had a rate between $3.50 and $3.99. Thus 50 percent of these towns had a rate over $4.00; this high percentage was comparable to the 44 percent of all Clay towns in the state that paid such a high rate. The similarity of the percentages suggests that tax rate is a more valid key to the nature of the Jackson movement than elevation of land or size of farms. It also suggests that the traditional view that poor farmers were Jacksonians is correct.[14]

Both Turner and Schlesinger held that factory workers also were Democrats. Since Schlesinger presented no statistical evidence, rival scholars attacked this part of his thesis. It is still not clear how urban workers voted. In New Hampshire there are several ways to approach the relationship between labor and the Democratic Party: one, by analyzing the larger communities (which were ordinarily the manufacturing towns), another, by studying the manufacturing towns themselves.[15]

The statistics clearly support the *Patriot*'s claim that the villages were Jacksonian while the larger communities were often National Republican. Whereas Jackson took 70 percent of the towns under 2,000 in population, he could capture but 54 percent of the twenty-eight towns with 2,000 inhabitants or more. At the same time a greater proportion of Clay towns than Jackson towns were large: 21 percent of those for Clay had more than 2,000 people, compared to only 11 percent of those for Jackson.[16]

By isolating the twenty-five leading manufacturing towns, it is possible to make a better estimate of how labor voted. Unlike

14. The sixteen towns were: Sullivan, Roxbury, Marlborough, Troy, Fitzwilliam, Nelson, Dublin, Jaffrey, Rindge, Peterborough, Sharon, New Ipswich, Temple, Wilton, Milford, Amherst. All gave two-thirds or more of their vote to Clay, except Peterborough and Amherst, which gave 51–66 percent to Clay, Wilton, 51–66 percent to Jackson, and Sharon, over two-thirds for Jackson. See Appendix, Table J. See also Map 3.

15. Schlesinger agued that the Democratic Party had a pro-labor platform, particularly during the locofoco years after 1835, but he did not flatly state that laborers voted Democratic. Schlesinger, *Age of Jackson,* pp. 143, 339–346. William Sullivan demonstrated that labor in Philadelphia voted against Jackson. Edward Pessen was less successful in doing the same for Boston. Walter Hugins showed that "labor" in New York meant more than merely factory workers. William Sullivan, "Did Labor Support Andrew Jackson?" *Political Science Quarterly,* 62 (1947), 569–580; Edward Pessen, "Did Labor Support Jackson?: The Boston Story," *ibid.,* 64 (1949), 262–274; Robert T. Bower, "Note on 'Did Labor Support Jackson?: The Boston Story'," *ibid.,* 65 (1950), 441–444; Walter Hugins, *Jacksonian Democracy and the Working Class: a Study of the New York Workingmen's Movement 1829–1837* (Stanford, Calif., 1960); Benson, *Concept of Jacksonian Democracy,* pp. 142–147.

16. See Appendix, Table K.

the state as a whole, which was decidedly for Jackson, the manufacturing towns divided almost evenly, and the largest manufacturing centers went for Clay. Of the twenty-five manufacturing towns, twelve, or 48 percent, were for Clay, while of the eight largest, seven, or 88 percent, voted for Clay. The evidence is limited, of course, for the number of workers was small and many were women, who could not vote; but the available data indicate that workers were likely to vote National Republican. Hill and the *Patriot* gave negative evidence that such was the case, for they ignored workingmen and their problems. A Democrat in Newmarket, a town with three large cotton mills, reported that in his town and in "every town in the state where the manufacturing influence prevail[ed], . . . the cause of Aristocracy and federalism predominate[d]." "The strength of democracy," he concluded, "rest[ed] with the hardy sons of the soil." In 1832 Newmarket voted 180–124 for Clay. Contrary to the interpretation of Turner and Schlesinger, labor in New Hampshire did not vote Democratic.[17]

In addition to geography and economics, population growth and religion appear to have had an influence on voting. New Hampshire was not a fast-growing state: between 1820 and 1830 the population had gone up only 11 percent compared to 18 percent in all of New England and 30 percent in the nation. But adults had grown up in a state with a population of some 180,000 in 1800 and had seen the total swell to about 270,000 by 1832. An increase of 90,000, or 50 percent, in a third of a century

17. The twenty-five manufacturing towns were as follows: Rockingham County: Portsmouth, Exeter, Newmarket; Strafford County: Durham, Dover, Somersworth, Rochester, Gilmanton, Sanbornton, Center Harbor; Merrimack County: Concord, Pittsfield, Hooksett; Hillsborough County: Hillsborough, Goffstown, New Boston, Antrim, Peterborough, Nashua (Dunstable); Cheshire County: Walpole, Keene, Dublin, Winchester; Sullivan County: Claremont; Grafton County: Lisbon. The eight largest manufacturing towns: Exeter, Newmarket, Dover, Somersworth, Concord, Pittsfield, Peterborough, Nashua. Salmon C. Bulkeley to Gideon Welles, June 1, 1840, Welles Papers, Connecticut Historical Society. Farmer and Moore, *Gazeteer of New Hampshire 1823;* United States Census Office, *Compendium of the Sixth Census,* pp. 360–364.

may have seemed like rapid growth to them and may have influenced their voting.[18]

Towns and counties that voted for Jackson seem to have grown more rapidly than those for Clay. The correlation by counties (Table 5) is particularly noticeable. The four leading Jackson counties included three of the four that were growing most rapidly, while the four leading Clay counties embraced three of the slowest-growing counties. The difference between Coos County, which gave Jackson almost 80 percent of its votes and gained 70 percent in population, and Cheshire, which voted 37 percent for Jackson and actually lost population, is most startling.

Table 5. Population Change and Vote for Jackson in New Hampshire Counties, 1832

County	Population change, 1820–1830, percent	Vote for Jackson, percent
Coos	+70 (1)[a]	78 (1)
Merrimack	+ 6 (5)	66 (2)
Grafton	+28 (2)	59 (3)
Strafford	+14 (3)	59 (4)
Hillsborough	+ 6 (5)	58 (5)
Rockingham	+11 (4)	55 (6)
Sullivan	+ 6 (5)	54 (7)
Cheshire	− 3 (8)	37 (8)

Source: Concord Directory 1830, p. 153.
[a]The population rank for each county is in parentheses.

Almost as interesting is the correlation between population change and voting for the twenty-five leading Jackson towns and the twenty-five leading Clay towns. The median growth for the Jackson towns was 19 percent, considerably higher than that of the state as a whole; while the median growth of the Clay towns

18. United States population in 1820 was 9,618,000; in 1830, 12,901,000. New England population in 1820 was 1,660,071; in 1830 1,954,717. New Hampshire population in 1800 was 183,858; in 1820 244,161; in 1830 269,328. *Statistical History*, pp. 7–13.

was only 2 percent. In fact, nine of the Clay towns lost population, compared to only three of the Jackson towns.[19]

Clay towns apparently were more settled communities that had achieved their growth earlier in the century, but Jackson towns were undergoing the strains of swelling population. There is one important exception. The eight leading manufacturing towns had all, of course, grown rapidly in the 1820's, and seven of the eight voted for Clay. Otherwise, the evidence suggests that sluggish communities were National Republican and that dynamic towns were for Jackson. If so, the generalization strengthens the impression that there were important continuities from the first party system to the second. As several historians have demonstrated for New Hampshire and elsewhere, Federalists at the turn of the century tended to be from slow-growing, stable areas, Republicans from fast-growing, dynamic regions.[20]

In Protestant New Hampshire, religion was another key to party affiliation. Ever since Hill began to form the Democratic Party, he had linked Congregationalism with the opposition. The evidence in the election of 1832 confirmed his rhetoric. In the twenty-five towns that gave two-thirds or more of their vote to Clay, there were twenty-four Congregational churches, or 9.6 for every ten towns; in the towns that were 51–66 percent for Clay, there were 8.9 Congregational churches for every ten towns. Compare this with the 7.1 per ten towns that voted 51–66 percent for Jackson and the meager 4.7 per ten towns that gave two-thirds or more of their vote to Jackson. In Coos County, furthermore, where 78 percent of the vote went to Jackson, only 36 percent of the churches were Congregational, while in Cheshire, 64 percent for Clay, 60 percent were Con-

19. Population changes were taken from *Concord Directory 1830*, pp. 147–152.

20. Fischer, *Revolution of American Conservatism*, Appendix I; Kaplanoff, "Social and Economic Bases," pp. 35–37, 39–49, 54–72, 82–98.

gregational. The Democratic way was not the Congregational way.[21]

Democrats, then, did better in the poorer towns than in the prosperous ones; they fared better also in non-Congregational towns than in towns with Congregational churches. It remains to determine the relative importance of the economic and religious factors. It is possible, for example, that Democrats did well in poor towns only because they were non-Congregational towns. Such, however, was not the case, for the pull of economics was slightly stronger than the pull of religion. Tax rate was somewhat more important than Congregationalism in determining whether towns voted Democratic (Table 6). Even though they had Congregational churches, thirty-two towns with low tax rates voted for Jackson.

Table 6. Voting Results Arranged by Religion and Tax Rate

Church category	Number of towns for Jackson	Percent of towns in category for Jackson
Non-Congregational: tax rate under $3.50	41	89
Congregational: tax rate under $3.50	32	71
Non-Congregational: tax rate $3.50 and over	19	68
Congregational: tax rate $3.50 and over	45	56
All towns in state[a]	142	68

[a]The number of towns in the four categories does not total 142 because there was no tax rate for some towns.

21. The pattern is not infallible, because Strafford and Hillsborough, which gave Jackson approximately the same support (59 percent and 58 percent), had very different Congregational percentages (28 percent in Strafford, and 50 percent in Hillsborough). Generally, however, the percentage of Congregational churches decreases as the Jackson percentage rises. In the thirty-eight towns voting 51–66 percent for Clay, there were thirty-four Congregational churches. The sixty-three towns voting 51–66 percent for Jackson had forty-five Congregational churches. The seventy-nine towns giving two-thirds or more of their vote to Jackson had only thirty-seven Congregational churches. John Farmer, *New Hampshire Annual Register and United States Calendar, 1828* (Concord, N.H., 1827), pp. 88–93. See Appendix, Table L.

A comparison of the twenty-five leading Jackson towns with the twenty-five leading Clay towns confirms the patterns already established. It has already been shown that the Jackson towns were growing much more rapidly. They were also much poorer towns. When the top Jackson towns were matched with the twenty-five towns with the lowest tax apportionment, ten names appeared on both lists. The correlation of the top twenty-five Clay towns was less exact—only five were on the list of the twenty-five most prosperous towns. The correlation was better, however, when deviations were studied. None of the leading Jackson communities ranked among the twenty-five leaders in apportionment; in fact, the highest was Lee, which ranked 66th. Nor did any of the top Clay communities rank in the bottom group in apportionment. Furthermore, the median tax apportionment for the Jackson group was low ($2.93), the Clay median higher ($3.92).[22]

The religious correlation of the twenty-five leading Jackson and Clay towns was also strong. Only one of the Clay towns had no church, compared to eight of the Jackson towns. Conversely, five Clay towns had three or four churches; while only one Jackson town had so many. The Clay towns had a total of forty-eight churches; those for Jackson only twenty-seven. Whereas the Clay towns had twenty-four Congregational churches and four Freewill Baptist or Methodist churches, the Jackson towns had five Congregational churches and fourteen of the latter sects. In short, the Democratic Party flourished in towns that either had no churches or had the less "aristocratic" churches, such as the Freewill Baptist. The National Republicans were strongest in communities with several churches including a Congregational church. Congregational, upper-class towns went to Henry Clay.

The leading Jackson towns differed markedly from the leading Clay towns in almost every other category that has been analyzed in this chapter, as shown in the following tabulation.

22. For details see Cole, "Election of 1832," p. 50.

	Number of:	
	Leading Clay towns	*Leading Jackson towns*
Towns on high land	13	21
Towns on poor farmland	11	17
Towns with population under 1,000	10	19
Towns with 0-50 acres of arable land per 100 eligible voters	1	5
Manufacturing towns	5	0

As might have been expected, the leading Clay communities had more textile mills and larger farms than the leading Jackson communities; many were losing population. Predictably, those for Jackson were small towns on high land with poor soil. Many were rapidly gaining population. As noted earlier, twelve of the ranking Clay towns were among the fourteen in the Monadnock section which failed to fit into most of the prevailing patterns. Democratic influence radiating from Concord had never been strong in the southwest, where the National Republican *New Hampshire Sentinel* dominated politics. Farmers on small but often prosperous farms in the Monadnock section voted against Jackson partly because they were in the habit of opposing the Democratic machine in Concord.

This upland Clay area was also close to the Massachusetts border and thus much more accessible by roads than the rest of the hilly region, which generally went to Jackson. Accessibility was more important than elevation in distinguishing Clay towns from Jackson towns. Almost all of those strongest for Clay were south of a line drawn from Exeter to Sullivan, barely twenty miles north of the Massachusetts border, whereas almost all of the ranking Jackson towns were north of the line. Practically every leading Clay town was on a main road, but fifteen of the twenty-five leading Jackson towns were on back roads. Eleven of the Clay group were communication centers: Exeter, Chester,

Keene, Milton, Jaffrey, Claremont, New Ipswich, Rindge, Winchester, Fitzwilliam, and Marlborough; only Barnstead of the Jackson group was a center. Each of the six main highways entering New Hampshire from Massachusetts went through several of the Clay communities. The road to Exeter continued on to Brentwood on its way to Concord; the road to Derry passed through Windham and Chester; the road to Dunstable went on to Milford, Temple, and Dublin; they were all leading Clay towns. And so it went: the leading Clay towns were in the swim of things; the leading Jackson towns were not.

A typical Jackson community was Jackson, New Hampshire. With a population of 515, Jackson lay far to the north, tucked under the mass of Mount Washington. Although a road of sorts ran from Lake Winnipesaukee north to Jackson, travel was light; and during the winter months Jackson was isolated. Farms were small; the soil was rocky. With an apportionment of only $2.62 (only fifteen units were lower), it was poor. Few homes or buildings of distinction marked the center of Jackson: the sole church was Freewill Baptist. Jackson, or Adams as it was once called, had voted for the Republicans and against the Federalists in the past. When the votes were counted in 1832, the record read: Jackson 85–Clay 0.

Exeter, typically National Republican, was another world from Jackson. Settled in 1638, it had always been one of the leading communities in New Hampshire. The hub of Revolutionary activity, it became the first state capital. The center of New Hampshire Federalism, it had dominated politics at the end of the eighteenth century. Its stately Congregational Church gave it a link with the past; the Exeter Manufacturing Company looked to the future. Elegant federal homes and graceful elms lined Main, Water, Court, and High streets. Exeter had over 3,000 people, boasted two Congregational Churches, and paid a tax rate of $4.14. Busy roads led to Portsmouth, Concord, and Boston. Ships sailed for Portsmouth and the Atlantic by way of

Great Bay. The *Exeter News-Letter* kept its citizens informed. Barely a dozen miles from the ocean, Exeter lay on low, fertile meadows. The 1832 vote read: Clay 307–Jackson 140.

But New Hampshire did not divide neatly into Jacksons and Exeters, even though those examples suggest the major distinctions between Democratic towns and National Republican towns. A final step is to construct an overall correlation between economic data and voting results. To do so, the towns were ranked politically according to percentage of the vote cast for Jackson and economically according to the tax apportionment. Then the towns were divided both politically and economically into ten groups. Group 1 in the political data was made up of the twenty leading Jackson towns, Group 2 the next twenty, and so forth; Group 1 in the economic data consisted of the twenty towns with the lowest tax apportionment, Group 2 the next twenty, and so forth. The evidence already presented suggests that strong Jackson towns should have ranked low in apportionment and strong Clay towns should have ranked high. If the correlation had been perfect, towns in Group 1 politically would have been in Group 1 economically, and so on down the line. In that unlikely case there would have been no deviations. If a town were in Group 1 in one category and Group 2 in the other—still a good correlation— there would have been a deviation of one group. As it turned out, twenty-seven towns showed no deviation, forty-seven deviated by one group, thirty-six by two, thirty-one by three, nineteen by four, and forty-one by five or more. The median town showed a deviation of two groups.[23]

The fact that a majority of the towns deviated by no more than two groups indicates that there was a valid correlation between the political and economic data, but the large number of towns with a deviation of over four weakens the correlation. Ten towns had a deviation of seven or eight: Atkinson, South Hampton, Deering, and Wentworth were high-ranking Jackson

23. See Appendix, Table M.

towns with a high tax apportionment; while Milton, Hinsdale, Mason, Orange, Seabrook, and Windham were Clay towns with a low tax apportionment.

Location seemed to be the most important reason for the deviation. Among the four Jackson towns, Deering and Wentworth were in the hilly or mountainous regions; while among the Clay towns, Hinsdale, Mason, Seabrook, and Windham were on the Massachusetts border. The remaining towns were more anomalous: Milton was on a main road on the Maine border, and that may account for the strong National Republican vote; South Hampton had a Baptist Church, and Baptists were often Democratic. Atkinson and Orange simply attest that people are not always predictable.

But despite deviations it is again evident that people in the poorer towns showed a strong tendency to vote for Jackson; those in the richer towns showed a similar tendency for Clay. This correlation was apparent when the towns were divided into quartiles according to tax apportionment. Whereas Jackson carried 82 percent of the fifty-one towns in the bottom quartile, he had 71 percent of those in the middle two quartiles and only 45 percent of those in the top quartile.[24]

This evidence and the evidence of the twenty-five leading towns (both in taxation and in voting) reveal that where towns had either a very high tax apportionment or a very low one, a strong correlation appeared: the very poor towns for Jackson; and the very rich for Clay. The record of the towns in the top and bottom quartiles confirms the Turner and Schlesinger interpretations.

A final test of the relationship between the economic and political data is to determine the coefficient of correlation. According to the Pearson scale the coefficient of correlation is a

24. In the lowest tax quartile Jackson carried forty-two towns, Clay eight, and one was tied. In the middle two quartiles Jackson carried eighty-two towns, Clay twenty-nine, and one was tied. In the highest quartile, Jackson carried twenty-three towns, Clay twenty-six, and two were tied.

number ranging from zero (indicating absolutely no correlation) to plus or minus one (indicating a perfect correlation). In this case it was determined by first computing the mean percentage of the vote for Jackson in the towns and the mean apportionment rate in the towns. After establishing the deviation of each town from the norm in each of the two categories, the Pearson formula was then employed to determine the coefficient of correlation. If the deviation from the norms had been extremely consistent, then the correlation would have been high (over 0.50); if it had been extremely inconsistent, then the coefficient would have approached zero. In the case of New Hampshire towns, the coefficient of correlation was −0.31, indicating a definite correlation. The Pearson formula thus produced the same result as other arrangements of the data: there was correlation between voting and economic status, but with deviations. If only the more extreme towns had been studied (the bottom and top tax and voting quartiles), then a very much higher coefficient figure would have appeared.[25]

The 45,978 votes cast in New Hampshire that November day in 1832 say much about Jacksonian Democracy. The strongest Democratic towns consistently revealed common characteristics: they were hilly, poor, and small; they had few industries and few Congregational churches; they were growing rapidly, but they were not yet on the main lines of communication; in the past they had opposed Federalism. In New Hampshire Turner was correct when he argued that the "Democracy found its strength among the poorer people," especially the farmers in the "hilly mountainous districts." He and Schlesinger were not correct, however, in their view that workers in manufacturing towns voted Democratic.

25. For an explanation of the Pearson formula for determining coefficients of correlation, see T. G. Connolly and W. Sluckin, *An Introduction to Statistics for the Social Sciences* (London, 1953), particularly p. 132. Mr. Leslie Koepplin, a graduate student at the University of California at Los Angeles, and Martin Carmichael III, a student at the Phillips Exeter Academy, helped me compute the coefficients of correlation throughout this study.

Men voted for Jackson for many reasons. The economic interpretation is particularly valid when the poorest and richest towns are studied, but an exact economic-political correlation did not exist. It is difficult to explain why Orange voted for Clay and Atkinson for Jackson. But no one should expect exact correlations. The existence of deviant cases does not destroy an interpretation unless a more convincing one appears. In New Hampshire and perhaps throughout the North, the best available keys to explain Jacksonian voting patterns are economic status and geography. For rural areas, Turner's interpretation of Jacksonian Democracy is still sound.[26]

26. Turner, *United States 1830–1850,* pp. 66, 116–117. Although Fox's voting analysis in his *Decline of Aristocracy in the Politics of New York* is simplistic and old fashioned, his economic interpretation is still a valid guide to politics in the Empire State, despite the efforts of Lee Benson. The latter uses hard data insufficiently in his *Concept of Jacksonian Democracy,* and when he does, the results are inconclusive. On pp. 148–149, for example, he points out deviations from the Fox interpretation in Delaware County. Franklin, one of the most prosperous towns, voted for the Democrats in 1844, while Hamden, one of the poorer towns, voted Whig. By dividing the sixteen towns in halves, according to both Democratic voting percentage and property valuation, I found that in twelve of the cases, high Democratic voting matched low property assessment, or low Democratic voting matched high assessment. When the Pearson formula was applied, a coefficient of correlation of -0.29 was revealed. Benson, *Concept of Jacksonian Democracy,* p. 149. Frank Otto Gatell has demonstrated that, contrary to Benson, the wealthy in New York City were overwhelmingly Whig. Frank Otto Gatell, "Money and Party in Jacksonian America: A Quantitative Look at New York City's Men of Quality." *Political Science Quarterly,* 82 (June 1967), 235–252. More work needs to be done on New York politics, but until then the Fox interpretation, with all its loopholes, still stands.

VII

The Jacksonian
Commonwealth in the 1830's

A few months after the election of 1832, Isaac Hill invited President Jackson to visit Concord while he was on his northern tour. In his gracious acceptance the President remarked that American "freedom and independence" rested on the institutions of New Hampshire and he predicted that those institutions would be "as durable as her own granite hills." To Woodbury the Old General is supposed to have confided less pompously that he simply wanted "to see if Ike Hill behaved better at home than he did in Washington." [1]

Early in June Jackson set forth with Van Buren, Donelson, Lewis Cass, Hill, Woodbury, and others. When they reached New England, they visited Cambridge, where Harvard awarded the Old Hero the degree of Doctor of Laws. After inspecting the factories at Lowell, the party followed the Merrimack River north to the town line separating Bow and Concord. At noon on Friday, June 28, members of the town committee and eight companies of the militia spied the dust that signaled the arrival of the President. Greetings over, the town fathers and Andrew Jackson, straight and tall on his horse, led the way back to town. The

1. Hill to Andrew J. Donelson, April 3, 1833, Hill Papers; *Patriot*, June 24, 1833. Jackson's statement to Woodbury, which is probably apocryphal, is in Buell, *Jackson*, II, 307.

long column passed the state house, turned west at the north end, and doubled back to the Eagle Hotel, where Henry Hubbard introduced Jackson to the throng.

The next day large crowds gathered as the President and Governor Dinsmoor reviewed the troops on State Street, after which Jackson shook hands with the legislators and with members of the city and state governments. Hill then held a luncheon for the President's party and the few remaining New Hampshire veterans of the Revolution. He had gone to considerable difficulty and expense to bring them to Concord because he knew how much the memories of the Revolution meant to Jackson. The oldest was Jonathan Welles of Amoskeag, who had served on the *Ranger* with John Paul Jones. When Welles was introduced to the President, he supposedly remarked that Jackson and Jones had given "them English the two d---dest lickings they ever got!" Jackson, who was touched by the comparison, unbent and chatted gaily with the soldiers and sailors. That evening he met the people in a formal reception at Doric Hall in the state house. By the time the Old General had shaken hands with all who filed by, he was utterly exhausted.

Sunday was no easier because the Committee had arranged three special church services. In the morning Jackson attended the Congregational Church, in the early afternoon the Unitarian Church, and before supper the Baptist Church. For years Hill and the *Patriot* had drawn the image of Jackson as the man of prayer; so the President took pains to be just that. But the frantic pace began to tell. Ill and weak from loss of blood after many lancings, Jackson had eaten little but bread and milk since his arrival. After the last prayer was said and the last hymn sung, he made his way back to the Eagle, passing the word that his party would start back for Washington the next morning instead of going on to Portland, Maine.[2]

2. John McClintock, *History of New Hampshire* (Boston, 1888), pp. 565–566; *Patriot*, July 1, 8, 1833; Robinson, "Hill," p. 104. Buell is also the source for Welles' remarks to Jackson. Buell, *Jackson*, II, 308.

Jackson had found New Hampshire firmly in Democratic control. Four-fifths of the legislators were Jacksonians; Governor Dinsmoor had had practically no opposition in the March election. In the next presidential election Van Buren would carry the state by a three-to-one margin over William Henry Harrison. Hill had created a powerful machine that would continue to win for years to come. In the quarter century after 1829, a democratic governor ruled the state every year but one. The Concord Regency ranked with Martin Van Buren's Albany Regency and Thomas Ritchie's Richmond Junto as one of the three strongest Democratic machines in the land. New Hampshire was the firmest Democratic state in New England, and Hill's machine had influence in Washington far beyond what the size of the state warranted. The New Hampshire Democratic Party offers a good case study of Jacksonianism.[3]

During the 1830's about two dozen men made up the core of the party. Next to Hill and Woodbury were governors Matthew Harvey, Samuel Dinsmoor, and William Badger, and Congressmen Henry Hubbard and Franklin Pierce. A wide reader, young Harvey graduated from Dartmouth in 1806 and then took up a law career in Hopkinton. His patience, good nature, and fund of salty stories made him a success in politics. Dinsmoor, who also went to Dartmouth, had vainly opposed Woodbury for governor in the 1820's. Badger, who had a genial disposition, followed his father and grandfather into politics. Hubbard, another Dartmouth graduate, was a Federalist until 1815 and an Adams man until May of 1828. When he finally announced that he was for Jackson, the *Gazette* called him a

---

3. Coolidge and Mansfield, *New Hampshire*, pp. 705, 708. New Hampshire had more Democratic Senators than any other New England state, 1829–1849. During those twenty years each state had forty senator-years. The number of Democratic senator-years was New Hampshire thirty-two, Maine twenty-eight, Connecticut twenty-four, Rhode Island ten, Vermont and Massachusetts zero. In 1830, of course, New Hampshire was more populous in comparison to the rest of the United States than, say, in 1960. New Hampshire had six Representatives in 1830 and only two in 1960.

"notorious changeling." Pierce was speaker of the state House of Representatives before he was elected to Congress in 1833.[4]

The twenty-five Jacksonian leaders were rather old men. Their median birth date was 1783; all but six were born before 1790. In 1833 at the start of Jackson's second administration they had a median age of fifty. Like many other Jacksonians—Van Buren, Benton, Jackson, and Kendall were all born between 1767 and 1782—they grew up in the Revolutionary era. As adults they were strongly moved by the second war against Great Britain. Even a young Jacksonian such as Franklin Pierce was raised on tales of the Revolution. At least eight of the twenty-five served in some military capacity, from Benjamin Pierce in the Revolution and John Weeks in the War of 1812 to Franklin Pierce in the Mexican War. As a group they were old men of the Revolution.

They believed in and practiced the theories of rotation in office and the common man in government. Steadily involved in politics, they started with lowly jobs and gradually worked their way up, using the Democratic machine as a means of personal success. Congressman Benning Bean, for example, who was born the year after the battle of Yorktown, entered politics at the age of

4. Biographical information for the Jacksonians can be found as follows: Governor Benjamin Pierce—*New Hampshire Manual 1957*, p. 186; Governor Matthew Harvey—William L. Foster, *Matthew Harvey* (Concord, N.H., 1867); George W. Nesmith, "Matthew Harvey," *Memorials of Judges Recently Deceased, Graduates of Dartmouth College, 1880* (Concord, N.H., 1881), pp. 31–40; Governor Joseph M. Harper—Stackpole, *History*, III, 322; Governor Samuel Dinsmoor—*ibid.*, p. 91; Governor William Badger—Badger to Samuel Bell, Nov. 17, 1827, Bell Papers; Congressmen Jonathan Harvey, John Weeks, Henry Hubbard—Stackpole, *History*, III, 33, 117–118, 322; *Gazette*, May 20, 1828; *Patriot*, Dec. 27, 1824, June 20, 1825; Nichols, *Pierce*, p. 65. Congressmen John M. Brodhead, Joseph Hammons, Thomas Chandler—Stackpole, *History*, III, 314–315, 322; Brodhead to Weeks, Oct. 29, 1830, Weeks Papers, NHHS; *Statesman*, April 15, 1839; Congressmen Samuel Cushman, Tristram Shaw, James Farrington, Ira Eastman, Charles G. Atherton—Stackpole, *History*, III, 316, 318, 329; Congressman Franklin Pierce—Nichols, *Pierce;* Congressmen Joseph Weeks, Edmund Burke, John Page, Jared Williams, Robert Burns, Benning M. Bean—Stackpole, *History*, III, 114, 147–148, 312, 314, 333; *Biographical Directory of the American Congress* (Washington, D.C., 1961).

twenty-nine, the year before the War of 1812. Selectman of Moultonboro, justice of the peace, speaker of the House, president of the Senate, a member of the governor's council, Bean touched all the bases before he was elected to the United States Congress. Franklin Pierce was justice of the peace, moderator, state representative, speaker of the House, Congressman, Senator, and finally President. He and Bean earned the right to speak for their fellow citizens.

The Jacksonians came from small towns in farming areas. Only four of the twenty-five grew up in towns of more than 2,000. Since it was necessary to choose representatives from all parts of the state, a number of the Jacksonians came from the Connecticut Valley and the seacoast—regions not generally associated with the party; but most of them had been born in interior areas more typically Jacksonian. James Farrington, for example, represented Rochester on the seacoast but started life in Conway in the mountains.

The movement of these Jacksonians from town to town indicates the high degree of mobility during the early nineteenth century. Seventeen of the twenty-five moved at least once before settling into a career; and eight came from another state. Hill, who shifted from a farm in Massachusetts to a tiny town in southern New Hampshire and finally made his living in Concord and Washington, was typical.

The twenty-five Jacksonian leaders did not make fortunes, but they did make good. Though often of lowly birth, nine went to college, ten became lawyers, and many invested prudently. Hill's progress from farm boy to successful publisher was not unusual. Democratic Congressmen and governors represented farmers who were often poor, but they were not poor themselves. Some of them were leading citizens in their communities—examples of deference politics. It is not surprising, however, that they were moderately prosperous, for political parties in America have ordinarily nominated well-to-do candidates. The crucial point is whether they were less well off than their Whig opponents.

They probably were. A study of nineteen National Republican-Whig candidates for Congress or for governor in the 1830's reveals that they differed from the Democrats (Table 7). While the Jacksonians were likely to be farmers, Whigs were more often engaged in business. Eight Democrats farmed for a living and others farmed as an avocation; but only one Whig was a farmer. Five Whigs were businessmen, compared to only two Democrats. A higher proportion of Whigs attended college, studied law, grew up and lived in large towns, and engaged in trade and manufacturing. Democrats and Whigs were about the same age, and both moved frequently before settling down; but otherwise their differences outweighed their similarities. Historians have argued recently that Whig politicians were no more affluent than Democrats. The evidence in this study is too limited to be conclusive, but it suggests that in New Hampshire Whig leaders ranked economically ahead of Democratic leaders.[5]

To attract young politicians Hill's machine offered rewards in the form of jobs, patronage, and money. In 1828, John Parker Hale, twenty-two, who had just graduated from Bowdoin, was training for the law and considering a political career. One of his friends wrote: "I hear you are writing history and turned politician!! Shocking!!!! . . . Woe to the liberties of this country if you have espoused the cause of Jackson . . . Look forward to the miseries we shall suffer if your influence should assist to raise to the supreme chair a man or demon who without remorse will cut our throats from ear to ear." But Hale enlisted with the Democrats. He was a member of the state legislature in 1832; shortly after that Jackson appointed him United States Attorney

---

5. In comparing the congressional slates in 1829, the *Patriot* said that the Democrats had three farmers and three professional men, while the National Republicans put forward five professional men. *Patriot,* Jan. 26, 1829. My position on the economic status of Democratic and Whig leadership differs from that of Lee Benson, who finds Democratic leaders at least as well off as Whigs in New York. Benson, *Concept of Jacksonian Democracy,* pp. 64–85. It is less significant to compare political leadership than to compare voters. In Chapter VI I demonstrated that Democrats ranked lower economically than National Republicans.

Table 7. Social Profile of Political Leaders in New Hampshire
in the 1830's

Profile	Democrats, percent of total	National Republicans or Whigs, percent of total
Moved from one town to another	68	64
Grew up in large towns	16	27
Lived as adults in large towns	44	67
Attended college	36	56
Occupation		
Business	8	28
Farming	32	6
Law	40	55
Medicine	16	11
Clergy	4	0

Source: For the data on Democrats see note 4 of this chapter. The data on National Republicans and Whigs are taken from *Exeter News-Letter,* Mar. 12, 1833, Feb. 10, 1835, Feb. 26, 1839; Stackpole, *History,* III, 14, 33, 70, 86, 87, 123–126, 312; Charles H. Bell, *Bench and Bar of New Hampshire* (Boston, 1893); *Biographical Directory of Congress.*

in New Hampshire. Later Hale served as a Democratic Congressman before becoming a Free Soil Senator and presidential candidate. With the election of Jackson, Hill and Woodbury controlled hundreds of jobs. Federal and state printing contracts and federal mail contracts balanced the budgets of Democratic newspapers. Federal deposits later strengthened Democratic banks.[6]

The machine attracted others who simply enjoyed politics, for in nineteenth-century New Hampshire, politics was a form of recreation, part of a way of life. Once the intensive haying, harvesting, cider-making, and wood-cutting were done, and as winter with its ice and snow closed in, farmers turned to politics. It was no trick at all to get 100 farmers to a town caucus or 1,000 to a state convention. The *Patriot* recorded dozens of local meetings every January as the party prepared for the town meetings in March.

6. James Perham to Hale, Jan. 2, 1828, Hale Papers, NHHS; Reid, "Doe's World"; Richard H. Sewell, *John P. Hale and the Politics of Abolition* (Cambridge, Mass., 1965), pp. 7–8.

The constitutional and other political arrangements in New Hampshire favored a two-party system. Presidential electors and Congressmen were elected on a statewide ticket, which meant that every voter in the state had a chance to vote for all six Congressional candidates. This "winner-take-all" system stimulated party activity. The Democratic committee of correspondence and the Democratic central committee strengthened the power of the party. Since printed ballots were used in all elections, each party provided ballots listing its candidates. The Democrats enhanced party discipline by replacing the legislative caucus with a party convention. After 1831, delegates gathered every June in Concord to nominate the Democratic candidates.[7]

Hill, who ran the machine, set up party headquarters in his office building just south of the state house—the "Dictator's Palace," the opposition called it. Every June he returned from Washington to preside over secret meetings in the room next door to the *Patriot* office. Hill also kept the party treasury full. In August 1828, in the heat of the presidential campaign, he gave Woodbury a detailed financial statement. Hill had printed and distributed free 6,200 copies of the proceedings at the June Democratic meeting in Concord, 4,000 copies of his own *Sketch of Jackson,* 3,500 copies of speeches at Democratic Fourth of July celebrations, and 1,700 copies of his January 8th speech in Concord. The cost was $300, but he had collected only $130 from party members. In spite of his real estate, bank and factory stock, and profitable printing business, he had exhausted his credit and wanted Woodbury to arrange a $2,000 loan.[8]

Democratic newspapers aided the Democratic machine. In 1830 there were about 600 newspapers in the United States, and of these New Hampshire had 17, well more than its share. Hill

7. McCormick, *Second American Party System,* p. 55; for later references to the Democratic machine in operation: *Niles' Register,* 48 (1835), 310; 52 (1837), 386; 54 (1838), 273, 289. There had been a convention in 1828, but the Democrats used the legislative caucus in 1829 and 1830.

8. McCormick, *Second American Party System,* p. 61; Hill to Woodbury, Aug. 4, 1828, Woodbury Papers, LC; Nichols, *Pierce,* pp. 46–47.

organized and used the newspapers effectively. Within forty-eight hours of a party meeting at Ela's Tavern in Dover in 1828, for example, copies of the resolutions appeared in five Jackson newspapers. The Democratic press formed a ring about the state with Concord in the center. Under Gideon Beck and then Abner Greenleaf, the *New Hampshire Gazette* in Portsmouth was a powerful Democratic voice, but it backed Woodbury more than Hill. The Newport *New Hampshire Spectator,* renamed the *New Hampshire Argus and Spectator,* became under Edmund Burke the Democratic spokesman of the Connecticut Valley. To the north in Haverhill, James Madison Rix made the *Democratic Republican* a force to reckon with. But throughout the 1830's the *New-Hampshire Patriot* of Concord, which Hill had sold to his brother Horatio and to Cyrus Barton, was the supreme Democratic organ in New Hampshire. It spoke for Hill, and many considered it the leading Democratic newspaper in New England.[9]

Hill's machine had out-of-state connections. Hill had sent his brother George and his crony William Masters to edit newspapers in Bellows Falls and Montpelier, Vermont, and he had newspaper contacts in Maine as well. Articles flowed back and forth from the *Patriot* to other Democratic newspapers—to Amos Kendall's *Argus of Western America,* to Thomas Ritchie's *Richmond Enquirer,* to Mordecai Noah's *New York Enquirer,* and to Francis Blair's Washington *Globe.* As chairman of the New Hampshire committee of correspondence, Hill kept in close contact with the national Democratic committee.[10]

---

9. Charles E. Perry, "The New Hampshire Press in the Election of 1828," *The Granite Monthly,* 61 (1929), 454–458; *Patriot,* April 14, 1828, June 13, 1829; Jacob B. Moore, "History of Newspapers Published in New Hampshire from 1756 to 1840," *American Quarterly Register,* 13 (1840), 170–181. Other Democratic newspapers were the *Dover Gazette,* the Keene *Farmer's Museum,* and the Charlestown *Sullivan Mercury.*

10. Robinson, "Hill," p. 38; Reid, "Doe's World"; Remini, *Election,* pp. 94–95. Some said that Hill got the material for the Jackson biography from Kendall's *Argus.*

New Hampshire Democrats had a powerful message. They looked to the past by extolling the old rural values and by recalling the spirit of 1776, 1798, and 1812. They appealed to "yeomen" farmers, small businessmen, "artisans," and "mechanics," that is, the "plain people of the North." They claimed to speak for lower social and economic classes against those who held power and privilege. Above all, they believed in democracy. To gain power, they based their party on the common man; and once in power, they established the spoils system and rotation in office. New Hampshire in the 1830's was a democratic place: any adult male could vote and 75 percent frequently did. Hill spoke often about the glories of democracy, but no Jacksonian expressed his faith in popular rule more clearly than Woodbury. America was a secure place, he once maintained, because Americans had been "participating" in government for 200 years. "The great mass of society," he said on another occasion, was "very sagacious about its interests and rights and, though liable to be misled for a time," soon used "judgment" to "place the ship of State in the right track to ensure *the greatest good for the greatest number.*" [11]

Andrew Jackson embodied all the appeals. He was a military hero from the past, a defender of the common man, and an opponent of privilege. As John W. Ward has explained, Jackson provided a symbol for democracy and for an age. Some historians have denied the validity of the concept of "Jacksonian Democracy," but it had specific meaning in New Hampshire. From the news of New Orleans in 1815 until his death in 1845, the name and image of the Old Hero dominated politics. According to Hill, "Old Hickory" was "completely identified" with the Democratic Party. New Hampshire Democrats saw in him what they

---

11. For Hill and the *Patriot* on democracy, see *Patriot,* Dec. 24, 1821, Oct. 2, 1826. In his "The Strange Stillbirth of the Whig Party," *American Historical Review,* 72 (Jan., 1967), 445–468, Lynn Marshall portrays the spoils system as an explicit democratic political philosophy. It was nowhere more explicit than in New Hampshire. For Woodbury on democracy, see Woodbury to Francis Lieber, Feb. 27, 1831, Oct. 24, 1832 (HM LI 4631, 4634), Francis Lieber Papers, the Huntington Library, San Marino, Calif.

liked to see in themselves. In his biography of Jackson, Hill portrayed the Old General as a New Hampshire farmer, but in heroic form. The *Patriot* summed up the attitude of New Hampshire Democrats: "No man, probably, ever possessed the confidence of the American people in a greater degree, than Gen. Jackson—and no man ever better deserved his [*sic*] confidence." On the Fourth of July, 1829, Democrats in the little mountain town of Adams demonstrated their confidence by renaming their community Jackson.[12]

Jacksonian Democracy was more Jacksonian than Democratic, for the term "Democrat" appeared infrequently in New Hampshire until well into the 1830's. After Plumer and Hill had beaten the Federalists in 1816, most politicians called themselves Republicans. Reverence for Jefferson, which died hard, made it difficult for Hill and his followers to drop the name "Republican." Their hero was Jackson, but their ideal was Jefferson. As late as 1833 the *Patriot* said that the principles of the Democratic Party were "the same as in Mr. Jefferson's time." When opponents first called them "Democrats," the Jacksonians insisted on the term "Republican," but settled for "Democratic Republican," which was in vogue through the election of 1832. Not until 1835 when the *Patriot* bragged about a great "Democratic" victory did the Jacksonians accept the name "Democrats." The movement was "Jacksonian Democracy," rather than "Democracy," for the image of Andrew Jackson united the party.[13]

During the 1830's New Hampshire Democrats had the opportunity to back up their rhetoric and put their theories into prac-

12. *Gazette,* Sept. 30, 1828; Ward, *Jackson;* Hill, *Sketch of Jackson;* Hill to Flagg, July 19, 1830, Azariah Flagg Papers, New York Public Library; the *Patriot* quotation was reprinted in the Washington *Globe,* July 19, 1831. The renaming of Adams is in *Laws of New Hampshire,* 10 (1829–1835), 87.

13. The reference to Jefferson was in *Patriot,* Jan. 28, 1833; opposition use of the term "Democrat" was first mentioned in *ibid.,* May 30, 1825; the *Patriot* called Hill's followers "Democratic Republicans" in *ibid.,* June 26, 1826. Even in 1828 the *Patriot* referred to the "Republican cause," *ibid.,* Jan. 7, 1828. Election of 1832, *ibid.,* Oct. 29, Nov. 5, 1832. In 1832 the *Patriot* used the term "Republican" nominations, *ibid.,* Mar. 3, 1832. The term "Democratic" appears in the *Patriot* frequently after 1834. *Ibid.,* Mar. 16, 23, 1835, May 8, 1837.

tice. Like other Jacksonians they had followed a negative course in Washington, but they regarded their state in a much more positive way. Ever since the War of 1812, for example, the Hill Republicans had fought for a state university and had often supported state expenditures for roads and canals. They had favored reforms such as the Toleration Act of 1819 and the abolition of imprisonment for debt. In the 1830's the Jacksonians turned their attention to a wide spectrum of social evils. They favored better treatment for debtors, murderers, and the insane; they believed in religious freedom and in tolerance for immigrants; they urged democratic reforms; and they persisted in efforts to establish a state university. But they were moderate pragmatic reformers. They opposed the movement to abolish slavery for practical political reasons, and they chartered dozens of new corporations to further the economy of the state. In short, Jacksonians in New Hampshire envisioned a positive commonwealth, in which they would seek the common good within political and economic limits.[14]

In his first inaugural address in 1830 Governor Matthew Harvey concentrated on prisons and the plight of the debtors. The state in 1827 had let debtors out of jail, confining them, however, to the boundaries of their town. Harvey asked the legislature to go even further—to abolish imprisonment for debt entirely. He furthermore suggested enlarging the state prison so that each prisoner could have a private cell and not be corrupted by the old prisoners. Prodded further by Governors Dinsmoor, Hill, and John Page, the legislature finally outlawed imprisonment for debt in 1840.[15]

14. My interpretation in the succeeding pages differs from that in Benson, *Concept of Jacksonian Democracy,* pp. 39, 44–46. Benson argues that "the Jackson Party in New York was out of sympathy with the social and humanitarian reforms ... which have been treated as integral components of Jacksonian Democracy." Jacksonians in New Hampshire were not New Dealers, but they were humanitarians.

15. Harvey also asked the state to give a small sum of money to each discharged prisoner. Matthew Harvey, *A Message to Both Branches of the Legis-*

The Jacksonian governors also pressed for the end of capital punishment. The case of Abraham Prescott, an insane man who murdered a woman while she was picking berries, led to two trials before he was convicted. Governor Badger bravely postponed the date of execution for several weeks, but finally on a cold January day Prescott was hanged before a gigantic crowd. The legislature reduced the number of types of murder punishable by death from nine to two. At the end of the decade Governor Page once again denounced all capital punishment, but no legislation followed.[16]

The *Patriot* kept the subject of the insane before the people with many articles proposing an insane asylum, including one moving account of a mad Revolutionary war hero found wandering about in the snow. A striking letter to the *Patriot,* which cried "Remember the Insane," urged the state to break the "shackles" of some 300 insane prisoners by relieving them from "their dungeons, from filthy cages, and loathsome jails." Governor Dinsmoor made the first official recommendation for an asylum, and Democrat Charles Peaslee chaired the committee that drew up the bill. The final result in 1838 was not a state insane asylum but a charitable home chartered by the state.[17]

---

lature, June 4, 1830 (Concord, N.H., 1830); Samuel Dinsmoor, *Message to the Legislature of New Hampshire, June Session, 1831* (Concord, N.H., 1831); Samuel Dinsmoor, *Message to Both Houses of the Legislature, June Session, 1832* (Concord, N.H., 1832); Samuel Dinsmoor, *Message to Both Branches of the Legislature, November Session* (Concord, N.H., 1832); Isaac Hill, *Message to Both Houses of the Legislature,* June Session, 1836 (Concord, N.H., 1836); John Page, *Message to Both Houses of the Legislature, June Session, 1839* (Concord, N.H., 1839); John Page, *Message to the Legislature, June 1840* (Concord, N.H., 1840); *Patriot,* Jan. 1, 1841.

16. The legislature did enlarge the state prison and spent $50 to buy books for prisoners. In 1842 the *Patriot* had to admit that the issue of capital punishment was "dead." Amos Hadley, "New Hampshire in the Fourth Decade of the Passing Century," *Proceedings of the New Hampshire Historical Society,* 3 (1895–1896), 20, 56–57; *Patriot,* June 8, Nov. 2, 1835; Jan. 27, 1842; *Gazette,* May 25, 1830; Page, *Message, 1839.*

17. *Patriot,* May 18, 25, 1835, Feb. 29, Mar. 7, 21, April 18, 25, Aug. 9, Oct. 17, Nov. 5, 1836, July 9, Dec. 31, 1838; Hadley, "New Hampshire in Fourth Decade," pp. 57–60; "Charles Hazen Peaslee," New England Historic Genealogical Society, *Memorial Biographies,* VI (1864–1871), 187–191.

Democrats were at first uninterested in the temperance movement. When John Parker Hale brought a resolution to the
legislature to investigate failure to enforce the 1827 license law,
there was little response. Franklin Pierce laughed at Hale's
attempts to reduce the sale of liquor, and the *Patriot* announced
that temperance societies went "too far." But while he was governor in 1834 and 1835, William Badger was also president of
the New Hampshire State Temperance Society. And under
Governor Hill in 1838, the state passed its strongest temperance
law, one calling for a $25–$50 fine for the nonlicensed sale of
spirits.[18]

The *Patriot* persistently called for democratic reforms in the
state government. Letters signed appropriately "Jefferson" and
"Langdon" condemned life tenure for judges and demanded
instead a five-year limit. In addition, the *Patriot* proposed increasing the size of the Senate, eliminating the Governor's Council, and reducing the term for registrar of probate. It also
suggested reducing the size of the House in order to make it
more effective. The registrar of probate's term was soon dropped
from life to five years. New Hampshire was already a democratic
state when the Jacksonians took over, but they sought ways to
make it even more so.[19]

Hill's followers continued the old fight for a state university
with mixed motives. Some really wanted a university; others
merely sought political mileage attacking Dartmouth College and
Congregationalism. According to the *Patriot,* Dartmouth in the
1830's was "sectarian," its faculty considered "all liberal Chris-
tians infidels and heretics," and its students were mostly Federalists. When Dartmouth boys unfurled banners painted with devils
in a spring prank, the *Patriot* snorted that the scene represented

18. Five years later Hill turned against temperance because he considered
the movement a cover-up for opposition to the Democratic Party. Nichols,
Pierce, p. 57; *Patriot,* Aug. 19, 1833; Hadley, "New Hampshire in Fourth
Decade," p. 55; *Hill's Patriot,* May 11, 1843; *Statesman,* June 6, 1835.
19. *Patriot,* Jan. 30, 1832, Jan. 14, Feb. 18, Oct. 9, 1833, Jan. 27, Feb. 17, 24,
1834, Aug. 7, 1837.

the true character of the college, which acknowledged no "responsibility to the State authority" and which took every opportunity to "ridicule our republican institutions." In spite of the demands for a state university, New Hampshire did not get one until Republicans passed the Morrill Land Grant Act during the Civil War.[20]

Democrats were much concerned about religious freedom. The *Patriot* defended the delivery of mail on Sunday, arguing that otherwise there would be a union of church and state, and quoted large parts of United States Senator Richard M. Johnson's statement on the subject. When Universalist preacher Abner Kneeland was tried for supposedly blasphemous newspaper articles in Boston, the *Patriot* defended him too. It also suggested that the state abandon the provision requiring members of the state government to be Protestants, saying that the Catholic religion was "no more intolerant" than "some Protestant creeds." Democratic pressure brought about this particular reform at the Constitutional Convention of 1850.[21]

The *Patriot* frequently reminded its readers to be tolerant. It was disappointed when nativists drove Irish Catholic workers out of Concord in 1834, for the laborers were "honest, industrious," and far from "depraved." The *Patriot* also repudiated a mob attack on a nunnery in Pennsylvania. After Maria Monk published her *Awful Disclosures* of lust in a Montreal convent, the *Patriot* correctly labeled the book a fabrication.[22]

Toleration was linked with politics. Many articles appeared defending Shakers, Methodists, Baptists, Freewill Baptists, and Universalists, who were often under attack and who frequently voted Democratic. The *Patriot* had less tolerance for Anti-Masonry, which was strongest in the old Federalist strongholds of Rockingham and Cheshire counties. Aware that Anti-Masons were often anti-Democrats, the *Patriot* linked them with Federal-

20. *Ibid.*, June 3, 1833, Aug. 24, 1835, April 18, 1836.
21. *Ibid.*, Nov. 30, 1829, Jan. 18, Dec. 28, 1830, Jan. 3, 1831, Jan. 30, 1832, Feb. 3, June 16, 1834.
22. *Ibid.*, Aug. 24, 1835, May 30, 1836.

ists and Congregationalists and warned that the "inquisition and rack" might soon appear in the state.[23]

National Republicans and Whigs showed less enthusiasm for reform than did Democrats. Since Jacksonians dominated all branches of the state government, their opponents could not be expected to have much influence over legislation, but they could be expected to speak out for reforms in the press and in their party statements. In this regard the leading opposition newspaper, the *New Hampshire Statesman,* was particularly disappointing. Instead of favoring reform, the *Statesman* ridiculed the "beautiful theory of reform," and was silent or negative on reform issues. When Democrats proposed changes in the state prisons, the *Statesman* complained about the waste of money. Late in 1832 the *Statesman* mentioned the establishment of a committee to investigate an insane asylum but passed up the opportunity to speak in its favor. While Democrats were trying to turn Dartmouth into a state university, the *Statesman* was defending Dartmouth students. The newspaper calmly described the extreme crowding of the Irish in Lowell tenements but showed no sympathy for immigrants. The formal addresses of the National Republican and Whig central committees were equally disappointing, for they carried few references to reform. There is not enough evidence to "prove" that National Republicans and Whigs were against reform, but there is enough to suggest that Democrats outstripped them as reformers.[24]

In their attitude toward abolitionists, even Democrats were far from reformers. Most Democrats, to be sure, were opposed to slavery, but many were willing to ignore it or even defend it for political reasons. They had sided with the South during the

23. Defense of Protestant groups in *ibid.,* June 15, July 29, 1833, June 15, 1835, June 4, July 18, 1836. On Anti-Masonry see *ibid.,* Oct. 10, 1831, Oct. 22, Nov. 5, 1832, Feb. 4, Mar. 25, Aug. 26, 1833.

24. *Statesman,* 1832–1838, *passim,* especially June 16, 23, 30, July 7, Aug. 25, Sept. 15, Nov. 3, 17, Dec. 29, 1832, Jan. 12, 1833, Jan. 4, July 12, 26, 1834, Aug. 1, 1835.

Missouri and Panama debates; they did so again over abolition-ism. The *Patriot* warned that Federalists were exploiting the abolition movement just as they had used Anti-Masonry. Hill compared the situation with the Missouri crisis, for in both instances, he said, Federalists were trying to organize a northern party at the expense of the Democracy. Hill pointed out that the same Congregationalists who had defended the Cherokees in Georgia were interfering with Negro slaves in the South. As usual, Hill saw a Congregationalist-Federalist plot.[25]

Democrats feared that the abolitionist "plot" endangered both their party and the Union itself. Hill stressed the "obligations which the non-slaveholding States owe[d] to the slaveholding States by the compact of the confederation." Abolitionist trouble-makers, he said, would only cause conflict between North and South. In Democratic Barnstead, the town meeting resolved that the "pathetic appeals" of the abolitionists were "sapping the foundation" of American liberty. Convinced that their party depended on a delicate North-South balance to survive as a national organization, Democrats stood against anything that fomented sectional conflict.[26]

In speeches and in articles, Democrats settled upon the term "fanatic" to describe the abolitionists. At the first session of the Twenty-fourth Congress, Senator Hill blamed the antislavery trouble on "misguided fanatics"; Senator Henry Hubbard blamed it on the "spirit of fanaticism"; and Congressman Franklin Pierce blamed it on the "misguided and fanatical zeal of a few." The *Patriot* denounced "such miserable fanatics as Garrison"; while the *Dover Gazette* called the abolitionists the "deluded fanatics of hypocritical philanthropy." And in New York United States Senator Silas Wright borrowed an overworked word when he said that "these fanatics" were even trying "to agitate the public mind

25. *Patriot*, Feb. 23, June 15, Aug. 10, 1835, Mar. 28, 1836; *Congressional Globe*, 24th Congress, 1st Session (1835–1836), Appendix, pp. 89–90.

26. *Congressional Globe*, 24th Congress, 1st Session (1835–1836), Appendix, pp. 90–91; *Patriot*, May 2, 23, 1836.

as to the evil of slavery in the abstract."[27]

Since the Democratic stance reflected the public will, abolitionists found it difficult to speak in New Hampshire. When John Greenleaf Whittier tried to hold an antislavery meeting in Concord in 1835, the selectmen closed the town hall and courthouse to him, but the very same day they allowed Hill to address an anti-abolition assembly. The antislavery *Herald of Freedom* of Concord cried that "drunks" drove Whittier away from Concord, but the *Patriot* retorted that "respectable citizens" had merely spattered a "little dirt" on the poet. The British antislavery reformer George Thompson reported that he "narrowly escaped" losing his life in Concord. After he had sneaked out of town dressed as a woman, the local citizenry burned him in effigy amid "some hundred discharges of artillery." The Reverend George Storrs, who represented the New Hampshire Anti-Slavery Society, had a difficult time in both Dover and Exeter. During a lecture at the Dover Methodist church, Storrs faced an unruly crowd and spoke amid shuffling feet. Afterward, John Parker Hale, who turned antislavery a decade later, arose and gave a spirited talk against abolitionism. In nearby Exeter a mob drove Storrs out of town with a fire hose. Still another abolitionist, Abigail Folsom, in 1840 demanded the right to speak before the legislature. When ruled out of order, she screamed that she would not leave until God told her to do so. Not waiting for God, three strong men hustled her out of the hall.[28]

27. For the Hill and Hubbard quotations see *Congressional Globe*, 1st Session (1835–1836), Appendix, pp. 89, 169; for Pierce's use of the term *see ibid.*, p. 33. See also *Patriot*, July 22, 1833; *Dover Gazette*, Aug. 25, 1835. Wright's statement is in *Niles' Register*, 52 (1837), 239. The circumstances surrounding the *Gazette* quotation are discussed in Sewell, *Hale*, p. 32. Gerald S. Henig refers to several of these quotations as well as to many more in his perceptive article "The Jacksonian Attitude toward Abolitionism in the 1830's," *Tennessee Historical Quarterly*, 28 (Spring 1969), pp. 42–56.

28. The *Patriot* said that less than 5 out of 100 adults in the state were abolitionists and that none of these were Democrats. *Patriot*, Sept. 21, 1835, Mar. 28, April 11, Aug. 15, 1836, June 11, 1840; *Congressional Globe*, 24th Congress, 1st Session (1835–1836), Appendix, p. 90; Sewell, *Hale*, p. 32. Benton, *Thirty Years' View*, I, p. 618.

In addition to opposing abolitionism, Democrats revealed deep-set prejudices against blacks. The *New Hampshire Gazette* was content to speak out against the "amalgamation of Blacks and Whites," but the town meeting in Barnstead went much further. "We despise," the resolution began, "no human being for the form of his features, or the color of his skin; but in our opinion of the African race their intellect is too feeble, their passions too strong, and their dispositions too irritable, to encourage their immediate emancipation in this country." In his Dover response to Reverend Storrs, Hale described blacks as "beasts in human shape, not fit to live free."[29]

Democrats shared the common fear that Negroes might be sexually attractive to white girls. J. B. Wiggin wrote Tristram Shaw: "A *nigger* has been lecturing in this town . . . He is admitted into the most respectable abolition families, and it is said, that some of the fair sex are *really* in *love* with him!" A letter to the *Patriot* signed "Nancy Squeak" accused abolitionists of being predominantly women who wanted to "take up with 'niggers'." The *Patriot* wrote hopefully that "nothing can operate a revolution in the chaste and delicate feelings of the highly polished females of our country, which shall make them regard the African as a suitable companion for the nuptial couch."[30]

At times Democrats adopted the argument that slavery was a positive good. A Democratic Sullivan county convention declared that antislavery sentiment was "based upon an ignorance of the true condition of the slave." The *Patriot* said that the living conditions of the slaves were good. In his 1836 inaugural address, Governor Isaac Hill maintained that since the "colored race"

29. *Gazette*, Sept. 16, 1834; *Congressional Globe*, 24th Congress, 1st Session (1835–1836), Appendix, p. 91; *ibid.*, 31st Congress, 1st Session (1849–1850), Appendix, p. 800; Sewell, *Hale*, p. 32; Henig, "Jacksonian Attitude toward Abolitionism," pp. 50–51.

30. The sexual overtones in white anti-Negro sentiment are discussed at length in Winthrop Jordan, *White over Black: American Attitudes toward the Negro, 1550–1812* (Chapel Hill, N.C., 1968). J. B. Wiggin to Tristram Shaw, Jan. 11, 1840, Tristram Shaw Papers, NHHS; *Patriot*, Aug. 3, 1835, Aug. 14, 1837.

was "unaccustomed to take charge of their [sic] own conduct, it was fit only for servitude"; slaves, therefore, were better off than free blacks. But Henry Hubbard made the most forthright statement defending the South's peculiar institution. After visiting plantations in Maryland and Virginia, he described the "warmth of feeling," the "ardency of attachment" that he had observed between master and slave. The slaves were "well fed, well clothed, well taken care of in sickness and in health"; there were "no instances of cruel and barbarous treatment." In contrast, the free blacks were "more debased, more degraded, more desperate, and more abandoned, than the slaves themselves."[31]

Assumptions of black inferiority were widespread in New Hampshire and not restricted to Democrats. The state had abolished slavery, to be sure, and was one of only four states to allow its free adult male Negroes the right to vote on an equal basis with whites. But blacks did not share all rights with whites. Only white citizens, for example, could enlist in the state militia. And since there were only 607 blacks in New Hampshire out of a total population of almost 270,000 in 1830, the suffrage concession was meaningless. Barely 125 Negroes would have been eligible to vote, and there is no evidence that they did.[32]

An episode at Canaan showed how unwilling whites were to see the number of blacks in New Hampshire increase. When Noyes Academy, which opened in Canaan in March 1835, admitted both black and white students, it won the praise of *The Liberator* but the disdain of Canaanites. Since some of the fourteen Negro students came from outside the state, the citizens

31. *Patriot,* April 18, 1836; *Congressional Globe,* 24th Congress, 1st Session (1835–1836), Appendix, pp. 91, 168; Hill, *Message 1836.*

32. Slavery was abolished in New Hampshire by an interpretation of the bill of rights of the state constitution, which declared: "All men are born equally free and independent," 1784 Constitution, Stackpole, *History,* III, 355; Leon F. Litwack, *North of Slavery: The Negro in the Free States, 1790–1860* (Chicago, 1961), pp. 3, 60, 75. There were, inexplicably, still five slaves in New Hampshire in 1830. There were 279 free colored males, of which I estimate 125 were twenty-one and over. United States Census Office, *Abstract of the Returns of the Fifth Census,* pp. 4, 48.

feared that before long their town would be a magnet for hundreds of fugitive slaves. They were also uneasy about boarding Negro students in white homes. After several mobs had failed to close the academy, the town voted in July to abolish the school. On a hot August day a crowd of 300 gathered, full, as the *Patriot* put it, "of the spirit of '75." They lined up 100 yoke of oxen, dragged one school building into a swamp, and dumped the other on the village common. The *Patriot* applauded "such mild and peaceable measures." Hill remarked later that the trouble had started when an attempt was made to "mingle these colored persons as equals in a community of persons exclusively white." The episode, he concluded, showed the state's hostility to "slave agitation." It also revealed that like other northerners, especially in the old Northwest, New Hampshiremen would use violence to keep free blacks out.[33]

New Hampshire Jacksonians in Washington reflected the attitudes of their constituents back home. When the Concord branch of the Society of Friends in 1836 petitioned Congress to end slavery in the District of Columbia, the request proved embarrassing for Hill, Hubbard, and Pierce. Although John C. Calhoun moved that the Senate refuse to accept the petition, Hill suggested receiving it and tabling it. Abolitionists in New Hampshire, he said, were mostly clergymen who had been unpatriotic in the War of 1812. There were so few abolitionists that Congress should leave them alone and let the movement "burn out." Tabling, he argued, would prevent a bitter discussion between North and South such as the one that arose over nullification. Hill should have sat down at this point, but he plunged on to add that the 1832 affair had ended in "deep disgrace" for South Carolina.

Calhoun knew that Hill opposed both abolition and the petitions, but he could not allow a northerner to connect South

33. *The Liberator,* Oct. 25, 1834, Aug. 8, Sept. 5, Oct. 3, 1835; *Patriot,* Aug. 17, 1835; *Congressional Globe,* 24th Congress, 1st Session (1835–1836), Appendix, pp. 90–91; Litwack, *North of Slavery,* pp. 72–74, 117–120.

Carolina with "deep disgrace." Using the *Herald of Freedom* as evidence, he protested that abolition was much stronger in Hill's state than the Senator would admit. Before Henry Hubbard in the chair could gavel him to silence, Calhoun spoke of his "disgust and contempt" for Hill and taunted him by branding Van Buren Democrats in New Hampshire as mostly abolitionists. Hubbard, seeing that his chief was in trouble, came to his rescue. Calhoun, he said, should not have read from the *Herald of Freedom;* he was the one out of order. Hill had every right to make a "descriptive" statement about the 1832 crisis and was not impugning the motives of anyone. Hill, again on his feet, denied that Van Buren's supporters were abolitionists and lashed back that Calhoun's feelings "could not exceed the contempt and disgust felt for that Senator in the State of New Hampshire, and in all the nation."

Hill concluded by defending Franklin Pierce, who had also been attacked by Calhoun. Pierce had stated in the House that almost everyone in New Hampshire respected the rights of the South. Abolition, he had added, was the cause of simply "a few," and the petitions had been signed mostly by women and children. Hill said Calhoun's remarks called Pierce a liar. At that moment Pierce came into the Senate chamber and went directly to Thomas Hart Benton. After a few whispers Benton pointed out that the *Herald of Freedom* had misled Calhoun by exaggerating the number of abolitionists in New Hampshire. Senator William R. King of Alabama then asked logically: why did Calhoun attack a northerner who was actually defending slavery? Reminding Calhoun that debate would only help the abolitionists, Hubbard urged that the petition be tabled.[34]

Calhoun's motion not to receive the petitions was defeated 35-10, with Hill and Hubbard leading all New England Senators against it. As Benton and King could see, the New Hampshire

---

34. Benton, *Thirty Years' View,* I, 614–617; *Congressional Globe,* 24th Congress, 1st Session (1835–1836), 185–186, 230, 258, Appendix, pp. 89–93; *Patriot,* Feb. 15, April 4, 1836; Nichols, *Pierce,* pp. 82–86.

formula provided a way to avoid a battle over slavery, a way to preserve the unity of the Democratic Party and the nation. It was a simple formula: defend slavery, fight the abolitionists at home, but let no battle reach the national level. From the spring of 1836 on, the Senate followed a policy of receiving antislavery petitions and then rejecting them; while the House laid such petitions on the table. Charles G. Atherton, freshman Democratic Congressman from New Hampshire, reflected the proslavery attitude of many New Hampshire Democrats when in 1838 he introduced one of the annual "gag rules" into the House. During the next two decades the Democratic Party followed this policy of trying to sweep the slavery issue under the rug.[35]

Franklin Pierce, said the *Herald of Freedom* in 1836, was "a doughface." John Randolph coined the term "doughface" in 1819 to describe northerners who voted against the Tallmadge Amendment to prevent the further introduction of slavery into Missouri. Since that time Democrats in New Hampshire deserved the epithet because, at home and in the nation's capital, they had defended the institution of slavery and had shown their contempt for black Americans. As believers in democracy they opposed slavery; but as loyal Democrats they hated the abolitionists; and as white men they looked down upon Negroes.[36]

While Jacksonians were righting wrongs and attacking abolitionists, they were also building up the economy of New Hampshire. From 1829, when they took over the state, until the end of the 1830's, Democratic legislators chartered 188 corporations (Table 8). The average of seventeen per year far exceeded the average of twelve between 1820 and 1828. Had it not been for the Portsmouth financial panic of 1828 and the national panic of 1837, the numbers in the thirties would have been even higher. In the two years following each panic, the Jacksonians granted

35. Benton, *Thirty Years' View,* I, 619; *Patriot,* June 27, 1836.
36. Nichols, *Pierce,* p. 85; *Dictionary of American History* (New York, 1940), II, 163. For a summary of the abolition movement in New Hampshire, see Harland Skinner, "Slavery and Abolition in New Hampshire," thesis, University of New Hampshire, 1948.

few charters. Between 1831 and 1837 they averaged twenty-two corporations per year. Although over half of the total consisted of mills and manufacturing companies, there was also a substantial number of banks, railroads, bridges, and canals. Jacksonian reform included no attack on free enterprise.

Table 8. Acts of Incorporation in New Hampshire, 1820–1839

Year	Number of incorporations[a]	Year	Number of incorporations
1820	10	1830	7
1821	5	1831	20
1822	14	1832	26
1823	25	1833	16
1824	21	1834	16
1825	14	1835	24
1826	11	1836	34
1827	8	1837	21
1828	11	1838	9
1829	3	1839	12

Period	Mill or manufacturing company	Bank	Railroad	Road, bridge, canal, navigation, or aqueduct	Other	Total
1820–1828						
Total	46	17	0	47	9	119
Annual Average	5	2	0	5	1	12
1829–1839						
Total	105	15	10	40	16	188
Annual Average	10	1	1	4	1	17

Source: Laws of New Hampshire, passim.
[a]All figures include charter renewals.

Far more positive at home than in Washington, New Hampshire Jacksonians were both moderate reformers and enterprising capitalists. Although they were not the uncompromising radicals portrayed by Schlesinger in *The Age of Jackson,* they were more interested in reform than their opponents were, and certainly more humanitarian than the New York Democrats in Benson's

The Concept of Jacksonian Democracy. Like most northerners, they disliked slavery, but they were anti-Negro, and they fought the abolition' movement. Good Jeffersonians, New Hampshire Democrats would reform their state, not the nation.[37]

37. Schlesinger, *Age of Jackson, passim;* Benson, *Concept of Jacksonian Democracy,* pp. 39, 44–46.

VIII

Radical Democracy, 1836-1846

One day in early June 1836, companies of the state militia and a delegation of government officials awaited Isaac Hill at the Concord-Bow line just as they had stood there three years before to greet Andrew Jackson. When Hill arrived, they escorted him to the center of Concord, where the townspeople cheered their newly elected governor. Hill had given up his final year as Senator to return to New Hampshire. As he prepared his inaugural address, New Hampshire was entering its radical, or locofoco, period.[1]

Locofocoism began in 1835 as a reform movement within the Democratic Party in New York City. The reformers were given the name "locofocos" after they used "locofoco" matches to light one of their meetings. They were also called "radicals" because they demanded radical changes in the American economy and society, including a ten-hour work day, free public schools, and restraints on building railroads and chartering banks. At times the term "locofoco" was applied to all Democrats.

Historians have debated the role of the locofocos. In *The Age of Jackson* Arthur Schlesinger contended that many Jacksonians, particularly the eastern locofocos, waged an effective class war against "capitalist domination." The "tradition ... of Jackson," he wrote, was a "movement on the part of other sections of

1. *Patriot,* June 13, 1836.

society to restrain the power of the business community." In short, the locofocos were radicals in an anticapitalist sense. Entrepreneurial historians responded that locofocos were far from radical and that most Democrats welcomed the rise of industry and sought to share in its rewards. In his essay, "The Locofocos: Urban 'Agrarians'," Carl Degler argued that locofocos were city boys with country ideas and were conservatives at heart. The debate is important, for just as the Bank War helps explain the early stages of Jacksonian Democracy so the locofoco struggle helps clarify the later period.[2]

New Hampshire is a good place to study the locofocos because the battle between conservative and radical Democrats dominated the history of the state between 1836 and 1846. Since Democrats greatly outnumbered Whigs in New Hampshire, the intraparty battle largely determined state policy. New Hampshire, furthermore, had become sufficiently industrial by 1840 so that a strong business interest was able to combat the powerful agrarian interest. The census for 1840 listed the state ninth among the thirty states and territories in capital invested in manufacturing.[3]

Democrats disagreed on how to respond to the new industrial society. Those interested in business wanted the state to help manufacturing, encourage banks, and support railroads. Those primarily concerned with farming would use the state to prevent factories, banks, and railroads from exploiting them. In the debates, politicians and newspaper editors used the term "conservative" to describe Democrats who supported business interests, and "radical," or occasionally "locofoco," for those who opposed business expansion. The words were used

2. Schlesinger, *Age of Jackson,* pp. 339, 505; Carl Degler, "The Locofocos: Urban 'Agrarians'," *Journal of Economic History,* 16 (1956), 322–333.

3. In 1840 New Hampshire had $9,252,448 invested in manufacturing out of a national total of $267,726,579. United States Census Office, *Compendium of the Sixth Census,* p. 364.

loosely and did not carry the same connotations that they have today. The word "radical" carried no present-day Marxist overtones.[4]

During the ten-year battle, older Democrats led by Isaac Hill generally took the conservative side and younger ones, led by Edmund Burke of Newport and Thomas Treadwell of Portsmouth, held the radical position. Both sides sought the backing of leading Democrats Henry Hubbard, Levi Woodbury, and Franklin Pierce, who were in between. Between 1836 and 1839 the conservatives won most of the fights, but from 1840 to 1844, as the middle-of-the-roaders became more radical, the locofocos succeeded in passing laws against railroads and banks that severely hampered the business interest.[5]

In his three-hour inaugural address in 1836, Hill started with national matters that did not directly involve locofocoism. Since he supported state rights and strict construction of the Constitution, he opposed high federal expenditures, especially those for internal improvements. He blamed the Bank of the United States for the national Panic of 1819 and the New Hampshire panic of 1828. He defended the institution of slavery, warning that antislavery "agitation" would lead to trouble between the sections. These were standard Jacksonian views.

4. Few words have plagued historians more than "conservative" and "radical." "Radical" farmers who opposed the railroad in New Hampshire were often "conservative" in defending their property against the corporation and in opposing the changes brought by industrialization. They feared that the railroad might change their way of life because new transportation threatened the horse business and state loans to railroads meant higher taxes. In this chapter I use the terms exactly as they were used in New Hampshire at the time. References to "radicals" and "conservatives" and a variety of other epithets are scattered throughout the New Hampshire newspapers between 1836 and 1846, particularly in the *Patriot, Hill's Patriot,* and the *Statesman.*

5. Edmund Burke, who was born in 1809, was a lawyer in Colebrook, New Hampshire, before he became editor of the *Argus and Spectator.* With his big sharp nose and long hair hanging about his ears, he was an unforgettable figure. He was elected to Congress in 1839 and served until 1845. Stackpole, *History,* III, 314; Henry H. Metcalf, *Franklin Pierce and Edmund Burke: A President and a President-Maker* (Concord, N.H., 1930).

On state matters he tried to take a moderate position, but leaned toward the conservative side. He called for transportation projects financed by the state or by private enterprise. Otherwise he wanted no unnecessary state expenses. He was particularly proud that outsiders laughed at the low pay given New Hampshire officials, proud that the pay of a "mere boy in the navy" was equal to that of the highest judge in the state. He did ask for a few reforms—the end of imprisonment for debt and increased care for the insane—but they would cost little and had been proposed many times before. There was little in the speech to appeal to the radicals.[6]

During the legislative session that followed Hill's inauguration, radicals fought conservatives over the issue of the railroad. The first railroad in America was built in Quincy, Massachusetts, in 1827, and interest in rail transportation spread north. As early as 1830 a railroad meeting in Concord had sparked a lively debate that demonstrated the plight of many Democrats. When the opposition *Statesman* remarked that "Jacksonianism was averse" to a railroad through Concord, the *Patriot,* not prepared to take a stand, called the statement a libel; but concluded lamely that since New Hampshire already had plenty of good roads, it was not "ready yet" for railroads. No one really knew, said the *Patriot,* whether railroads were suited for a "frosty climate."[7] Only one railroad was chartered in New Hampshire before 1835.

After some hesitation, the legislature granted charters to six additional railroads in 1835 and 1836. One was to run from Boston to Exeter, another from Boston to Keene, and a third, the Concord Railroad, extended the Lowell-Nashua line to Concord. In each case conservatives in the legislature were able to grant the line the right of eminent domain to secure unlimited amounts of land for tracks, stone, and gravel. By granting this right, the legislature was only keeping pace with other states, for everywhere state legislatures were generous in giving privileges to

6. Hill, *Message 1836.*
7. *Statesman,* April 10, 1830; *Patriot,* April 19, 1830, April 11, 1831.

railroads. Radicals, who were unhappy, managed to pass a law in January 1837 restricting railroad land to six rods along the tracks; but they were not satisfied. They argued that if the state could take land for a railroad, then it would soon be confiscating private property for factories. But the *Patriot,* now firmly conservative, replied that a railroad, a bridge, or a turnpike differed from a factory because they had public use.[8]

Hill, who was a director of the Concord Railroad, sought ways to raise money. In September, presiding over a meeting of the railroad, he announced that Boston financiers had bought 5,000 shares, 3,000 more had been sold in Concord, but 2,000 remained unsold. All Concord, he concluded, would benefit from the railroad. At a special town meeting that followed, the town voted to invest $40,000 of school and parsonage funds—$30,000 borrowed—in 800 shares.[9]

With the town won over, Hill then turned to the legislature. When that body held its quadrennial fall session in November, the most pressing issue was the use of the some $900,000 to be received as the state's share of the federal surplus. Hill started his address with a look to the past, a nostalgic picture of New Hampshire farm life. But he then shifted abruptly to the future and proposed that the state lend the $900,000 at low interest rates to four railroads: lines to Portsmouth, Exeter, and the Connecticut River, and, "most important," the one to Concord. Governor Hill, who

8. Democratic Congressman John W. Weeks, who represented the north country, strongly supported a federal survey for a line to Canada. Engineering Department of the War Department to John Weeks, May 8, 1830, Harry Hibbard Papers, II, NHHS; *Patriot,* July 20, Aug. 24, Sept. 21, Oct. 5, 1835, June 16, Oct. 3, 1836; *Laws of New Hampshire,* 10 (1829–1835), 382, 644, 680–681, 688, 717; *Gazette,* Sept. 1, 1835; *Laws of New Hampshire,* Nov. 1836, 248–252. For a discussion of the way in which other state legislatures treated railroads, see George Rogers Taylor, *The Transportation Revolution, 1815–1860* (New York, 1951), pp. 75, 89; Louis Hartz, *Economic Policy and Democratic Thought: Pennsylvania 1776–1860* (Cambridge, Mass., 1948); Oscar Handlin and Mary Flug Handlin, *Commonwealth: A Study of the Role of Government in the American Economy: Massachusetts, 1774–1861* (New York, 1947), pp. 189, 222, 239–242.

9. *Patriot,* Sept. 12, 26, Oct. 3, 17, 1836; Bouton, *History of Concord,* p. 425.

was fighting for federal deposits and pension funds at his bank in Concord, also wanted federal money for his railroad.[10]

The New Hampshire press treated Hill more gently than might have been expected in an open case of conflict of interest, and criticism was more regional than political or philosophical. The Democratic Portsmouth *New Hampshire Gazette* derided him for "dwell[ing]" on the Concord railroad, while barely mentioning the Exeter and Portsmouth lines. In Keene the Whig *Sentinel* criticized him for neglecting a Nashua-Keene line. Both major Concord newspapers, the Whig *Statesman* and the Democratic *Patriot,* backed the railroad plan, but the Democratic *Argus and Spectator* in the Connecticut Valley opposed it.[11]

The debate over the disposition of the federal surplus funds also split radicals and conservatives. Radicals like Treadwell of Portsmouth and the editors of the *New Hampshire Gazette* fought to have the state refuse the money. Hill's railroad schemes, said the *Gazette,* would exhaust the resources of the state for the next ten centuries and would hurt the poor to help the rich. The *Argus and Spectator* favored accepting the federal funds but opposed using them to build the property of a few railroad stockholders. To this the *Patriot* replied that such "newfangled democracy . . . would cary us back to a state of barbarism, and reduce us to the glorious equality of roaming through forests and over rivers the common property of all." In contrast the *Patriot* was "in favor of improving the facilities of communication as well as the soil, and of availing ourselves of all our natural advantages."[12]

In an attempt to break the deadlock, Hill held an elegant Christmas party for legislators in both parties, but he was unable to get his way. The legislature finally voted for a compromise plan whereby the state accepted federal money but distributed it

10. Robinson, "Hill," p. 170; *Patriot,* Nov. 28, 1836.
11. *Gazette,* Nov. 29, 1836; *Sentinel,* Dec. 1, 1836; *Statesman,* Dec. 3, 1836; *Patriot,* Dec. 2, 1837; *Argus and Spectator,* Dec. 3, 1836.
12. *Gazette,* Oct. 11, Nov. 29, 1836; Hadley, "New Hampshire in Fourth Decade," pp. 42–43; *Patriot,* Dec. 19, 1836, Jan. 2, 1837; *Argus and Spectator,* Nov. 26, 1836.

to the towns instead of to the railroads. Radicals opposed a plan to allocate the funds according to what towns paid in state taxes because the richer towns would have received the most money. Burke, editor of the *Argus and Spectator,* called it "robbing the poor for the benefit of the rich." The money finally went to the towns on the basis of both taxation and population.[13]

After blocking state aid to railroads, the radicals won several other victories. First, the legislature passed a resolution opposing the protective tariff, internal improvements at federal expense, and distribution of proceeds from the sale of land. Another resolution threatened monopolies by supporting an 1835 law that gave the state the right to amend any charter. But Treadwell's extreme proposal to deprive corporations of the right to limited liability failed.[14]

The break between the two wings of the Democratic Party widened during the campaign of 1837 even though Hill had no real opponent. The *Gazette* accused Hill of growing wealthy through patronage and attacked Senator Henry Hubbard, who temporarily sided with Hill and the conservatives. Franklin Pierce was surprised by the *Gazette*'s attack on Governor Hill. "Who would have expected," he laughed, "to hear Isaac Hill's democracy in question . . .?" As usual Woodbury failed to make his position clear, but the *Patriot* denied that he was with his old "*Gazette* crowd." Although the *Gazette* backed the slate of Democratic Congressmen, it would not support Hill and left the space for governor blank. The old Concord-Portsmouth rift had turned into a conservative-radical split.[15]

Concord Democrats also faced a challenge from the Connecticut Valley, where Burke's *Argus and Spectator* was as radical as the *Gazette.* When Burke suggested shifting the registry of deeds

13. New Hampshire received $892,115.71. *Argus and Spectator,* Dec. 31, 1836, Jan. 14, 28, 1837; *Patriot,* Jan. 2, 16, Feb. 20, 1837.
14. *Patriot,* Jan. 2, 16, 1837; *Argus and Spectator,* Jan. 28, 31, 1837; Hadley, "New Hampshire in Fourth Decade," pp. 38–39.
15. *Gazette,* Feb. 7, Mar. 7, 1837; *Patriot,* Jan. 23, Feb. 20, 27, 1837; Pierce to McNeil, Jan. 15, 1837, Pierce Papers, NHHS.

from the county to the towns, the *Patriot* sneered that before long the *Argus* would want all state offices including that of governor turned over to the towns. The *Argus* approved when the legislature took life tenure away from the registrar of probate and made the office of sheriff elective. This was more democracy than Hill wanted. When the *Argus* turned against Hill, the *Patriot* charged that Burke was a sorehead who had never been successful in politics. As the cry "Concord dictation" was heard again, Hill was back where he had been in the 1820's—leading the interior against Portsmouth and the Connecticut Valley.[16]

In spite of the rupture in the party, Hill was easily reelected in March. The opposition, however, carried the senate seat in the Concord area, a seat that Hill had normally in his pocket. In Portsmouth he received only 126 votes to 464 for various opponents. If Whigs had united with dissident Democrats, they might have threatened Hill. But Whigs, who were conservative on economic issues, had little in common with radical Democrats.[17]

When the legislature met in June 1837, locofocos sought comprehensive bank reform. They had earlier proposed a bill chartering a bank without limited liability. Since the bill would have made all stockholders individually liable for the debts of the bank, a risk few were willing to take, it would have blocked banking expansion in New Hampshire. Postponed in 1835, it passed the House in 1836, only to be postponed in the Senate by a margin of one vote. Throughout the debate the radical *Argus and Spectator* insisted that no bank should have the benefit of unlimited liability. To prevent banks from making "fictitious money," the state should allow no bills under ten dollars and should require each bank to maintain a high specie reserve to back its own notes.[18]

---

16. *Argus and Spectator,* Jan. 28, Feb. 6, 18, Aug. 5, Dec. 18, 1837; *Patriot,* Dec. 26, 1836, Mar. 20, 1837.

17. *Patriot,* Mar. 20, 1837.

18. *Ibid.,* June 29, 1835; Hadley, "New Hampshire in Fourth Decade," p. 39; *Argus and Spectator,* June 24, 1837.

Even conservatives were willing to back some banking reform. In January of 1837 the legislature passed an act stating that no bank could issue notes under twenty dollars or import such notes from outside the state, but the act was suspended for half a dozen years. New Hampshire bankers hoped that note restriction would help free them from dependence on Boston banks. Deeply in debt to Boston and short of hard money, the local banks were hard put when Boston demanded repayment. As the depression of 1837 worsened, the *Patriot* called for a new state banking system whereby every New Hampshire bank would accept the notes of the others and monthly reports would be made to a state banking commission. "Why," said the *Patriot,* should the banks of the state ... remain in eternal vassalage" to Boston? In his inaugural address Isaac Hill also proposed banking changes.[19]

The legislature compromised. The banking act of July 5, 1837, allowed banks to circulate notes only up to four-fifths of their capital stock and prevented banks that suspended specie payments from paying dividends. A commission was established with the power to examine any bank without notice and to recommend lifting the charter of those that were "unsafe." The act did not destroy paper money, but it did provide additional regulation. Like the New York banking act of 1838 it set up a commission, but unlike New York, New Hampshire did not allow banks to be incorporated without a special legislative charter. Locofoco newspapers criticized the act for not cutting notes in circulation to one-half of a bank's capital and for not giving the commission sufficient power.[20]

Content with a compromise over banking, conservatives were delighted with the corporation act passed the very next day. Not

19. *The Revised Statutes of the State of New Hampshire, ... 1842 ...* (Concord, N.H., 1843), p. 264; *Laws of New Hampshire,* Nov. 1836, pp. 272–273, June 1838, pp. 337–338, June 1840, pp. 444–445, June 1842, pp. 589–590. *Patriot,* May 22, 29, June 12, 26, July 24, 1837.

20. *Laws of New Hampshire,* 1837, pp. 291–297. The act also allowed persons indebted to banks to suspend specie payments when the bank did. *Patriot,* July 17, Aug. 21, 1837. The *Argus and Spectator* called the bill a "mockery" for not requiring a certain amount of specie behind bank notes. *Argus and Spectator,* July 1, 29, 1837; *Gazette,* June 27, 1837.

only did they block radical efforts to prevent limited liability but they passed an act that granted corporations the privilege on a general basis. Early in the nineteenth century, American businessmen had shown little interest in the concept of limited liability. But when New Hampshire and Connecticut began to grant the privilege on an individual basis in the 1820's, entrepreneurs were encouraged to build textile mills in those two states rather than in Massachusetts. In the 1830's Massachusetts and most other states began to grant limited liability, but still on an individual basis. The New Hampshire Act of 1837 made shareholders in manufacturing companies automatically immune from future liability after the entire capital stock of the corporation had been paid in for its debts.[21]

For the next two years radicals continued to be unable to pass reform laws, but the Panic of 1837 succeeded in checking business expansion where radicals had failed. The number of corporations chartered dropped from thirty-four in 1836 to nine in 1838. The state chartered only two railroads in 1838 and 1839; by 1840 it had only thirty-five miles of track.[22]

The combination of a business depression, radical complaints, and Whig opposition meant that Governor Hill and conservative Democrats faced hard times in the election of 1838. Whigs attacked Hill, who was United States pension agent, for keeping the pension funds in his Mechanics' Bank, and tried to prove

21. For the early history of limited liability in America see Oscar Handlin *Journal of Economic History*, 5 (1945), 17, and Shaw Livermore, "Unlimited and Mary Flug Handlin, "The Origins of the American Business Corporation," Liability in Early American Corporations," *Journal of Political Economy*, 43 (1935), 774–786. The ratio of cotton factories erected in Massachusetts, New Hampshire, and Connecticut was 5–1–2 before 1817 and 2–1–2 between 1817 and 1830, the period in which the two smaller states granted limited liability and Massachusetts did not. Edwin M. Dodd, *American Business Corporations until 1860 with Special Reference to Massachusetts* (Cambridge, Mass., 1954), pp. 400–403. For the corporation act, see *Laws of New Hampshire*, 1837, pp. 297–303.

22. *Laws of New Hampshire, passim;* Edward C. Kirkland, *Men, Cities, and Transportation: A Study in New England History* (Cambridge, Mass., 1948), I, 284. The number of manufacturing companies chartered fell from forty in the years 1836–1837 to nine in the years 1838–1839.

that there was an illicit connection between the bank and Democrat David Henshaw's Commonwealth Bank in Boston. They charged that Hill owed the Commonwealth Bank a large sum and had received advance notice that the bank was about to close. Hill did owe the Commonwealth $5,000. As elsewhere, Whigs in New Hampshire grew bolder. In Hillsborough County a Whig resolution blamed Jackson and Van Buren for all the ills of the country, and in Portsmouth a rumor spread that Whig owners of an iron factory threatened to discharge anyone who voted Democratic.[23]

The election of 1838 restored the two-party system to New Hampshire. The *Patriot* grew so alarmed that for the first time in several years it carried a large election advertisement; once again the newspaper tried to convince voters that the opponents were former Federalists. Hill barely defeated the exciting Whig candidate, James Wilson, who had commanded the Keene Light Infantry, by some 3,000 votes. The 54,570 who cast ballots numbered nearly 9,000 more than in any previous election; they also represented 87 percent of those eligible to vote, far above the former highs of 78 percent in 1814 and 76 percent in 1828. Richard McCormick has pointed out that the presidential election of 1840 brought a far greater outpouring of voters than the elections of 1828 or 1832. In New Hampshire and presumably elsewhere the great interest in politics began with the depression of 1837 and the state election of 1838.[24]

Democrats gave assorted reasons for the close election that brought their majority in the House down to twenty-five. They cited Federalism, imported votes, the Boston press, the depression, the retirement of popular Democrats, and Whig success in the large towns. But one Democrat correctly concluded that the

23. *Patriot*, Aug. 15, Oct. 3, 1836, Jan. 16, June 19, Aug. 14, Sept. 25, Nov. 20, 1837, Jan. 8, 22, Mar. 5, 1838.
24. *Ibid.*, Mar. 5, 1838. The vote was Hill 28,697, Wilson 25,675. *New Hampshire Manual 1891*, p. 154. The largest vote before 1838 was 45,978 in the 1832 presidential election. For relevant statistics see Tables 2 and 3. See McCormick, "New Perspectives," pp. 292, 296.

unpopularity of Isaac Hill was an important reason. With any other candidate, he decided, the winning margin would have been much greater.

Hill was unpopular because he was out of date. Since he faced the dual challenge of locofocos within the party and Whigs without, the burden was on him to offer a new program; and his final message of June 1838 showed that he had none. In a traditional speech Hill summed up twenty years of Republican-Democratic rhetoric. He called for limited state and federal governments; opposed internal improvements, the Bank, the protective tariff, and abolition; and urged the same old reforms—an insane asylum and the end of imprisonment for debt. Once again he asked the state to lend money to railroad companies. Another old Democrat, Vice-President Richard M. Johnson, a hero of the War of 1812, congratulated Hill for his "well-digested, well written, patriotic, sensible and sound democratic message." But the message was too well disgested and not very sensible; Hill's vigorous crusade had turned into a tired appeal to the past; the reformers of 1828 had become the conservatives of 1838.[25]

With a new candidate for governor, former Senator John Page, Democrats bucked the Whig tide and won a decisive victory in 1839. They reelected Page the next two years and carried the state for Van Buren over Harrison in 1840. Almost 90 percent of all eligible voters turned out in the presidential election that year.[26]

In 1840 at the age of fifty-two, Hill found himself ill and out of a job. His eyesight was failing, persistent catarrh made his eyes

25. There was still continuity in New Hampshire politics. The *Patriot* pointed to twenty-two solid Whig towns that had been Federalist in 1812. *Patriot*, Mar. 19, April 23, 30, May 7, 1838. In his letter commenting on Hill's unpopularity, Charles Fox said that Democratic failure to cope with the depression was another important factor. Charles Fox to Charles G. Atherton, Mar. 27, 1838, C. G. Atherton Papers, NHHS. Isaac Hill, *Message to Both Houses of the Legislature, June Session, 1838* (Concord, N.H., 1838); Johnson to Hill, June 14, 1838, Hill Papers.

26. In 1839 Page had 30,518 votes to 23,928 for Wilson. In 1840 Van Buren won over Harrison, 32,671 to 26,434. The percentage voting in the presidential election of 1840 was 89 percent. *New Hampshire Manual 1891*, pp. 154, 159.

and nose run, and the depression had nibbled away at his fortune. He wrote Levi Woodbury admitting that he could not pay what he owed the Secretary of the Treasury. With heavy losses at a factory in Hooksett and in bad land speculation, he was $8,000 in debt. He asked his old associate to help him find a job, but Woodbury failed to get him the Boston customs house. When Van Buren did make him receiver-general for the Boston subtreasury, the new Whig administration took the job away from him in 1841. At the same time the legislature elected Woodbury instead of Hill as United States Senator for the term beginning in 1841. Hill could not even resume his post as editor of the *Patriot* because he had sold the newspaper to his banker friend Cyrus Barton in 1834. When Hill filed suit to regain control of it in 1841, he was unsuccessful. Since Barton and the *Patriot* had turned locofoco, Hill decided to start a conservative newspaper, *Hill's New Hampshire Patriot,* which for the next few years spoke for the old Democracy in New Hampshire.[27]

With Hill out of office, the Democratic Party was changing. Benjamin Pierce and Samuel Dinsmoor were dead; Jonathan Harvey had retired and Judge Matthew Harvey was out of politics. Party leadership devolved more and more on moderate young Democrats who had adopted the radical line. At the head of the list was United States Senator Franklin Pierce, only thirty-six in 1840, but considered by many the most popular man in the

27. Hill to James M. Rix, Jan. 7, 1841, James M. Rix Papers, NHHS; Hill to Woodbury, Nov. 1, 1839, Woodbury Papers, LC. While he was receiver-general, Hill was accused of illegally depositing funds in a Boston bank, but nothing came of the charges. Pierce to K. Elwyn, Dec. 6, 1839, Pierce Papers, NHHS; Randall Stewart, "Hawthorne and Politics: Unpublished Letters to William B. Pike," *New England Quarterly,* 5 (1932), 249; *Hill's Patriot,* Mar. 31, May 5, 1841; *Patriot,* Feb. 16, April 13, 1843. U.S. Senator Henry Hubbard blocked Hill from the Senate by temporarily running for reelection until after the presidential election of 1840, when it was obvious that Woodbury would be interested in the Senate. *Patriot,* Dec. 5, 1840, Feb. 24, 1842. When Hill sold the *Patriot* to Cyrus Barton in 1834, Barton gave him the option to buy it back within ten years. Levi Woodbury, *Argument . . . before the Hon. Messrs. Henry Hubbard, Leonard Wilcox, and Frederick Vose, . . . in the Case of Isaac Hill versus Cyrus Barton, September 29, 1841* (Concord, N.H., 1841). Hill started his new newspaper in 1840.

state. Outside of New Hampshire Pierce had won many friends: some like Jefferson Davis and Thomas Hart Benton from the South and West, others like George Bancroft and Robert Rantoul from New England. He was so much in demand as a speaker that during the campaign of 1840 in New Hampshire he had to turn down many speaking engagements, and the *Patriot* praised his "manly, patriotic, and truly eloquent appeals." Popular in New Hampshire and not very effective in the Senate, Pierce was thinking of returning permanently to Concord. Like many Democrats he was not a doctrinaire radical. In voting against a bankruptcy bill in 1840, he wrote his siter: "Locofoco as I am, it is quite too *agrarian* for me." But committed or not, many Democrats like Barton and Pierce had gone over to the radicals by 1840.[28]

At this moment of transition, the depression showed signs of abating and pressure for railroads revived. The first railroads had just started to run in New Hampshire as trains pulled into Nashua in 1838 and into Exeter and Portsmouth in 1840. The success of the Lowell-Nashua line in particular renewed interest in rail transportation. The trains were fast—a traveler leaving Nashua at 6:45 A.M. reached Lowell at 9:00 A.M. and Boston at 11:00 A.M.; the service was regular—three trips a day; and the profits were considerable. The price of shares of stock had risen rapidly. Promoters, therefore, started the extension to Concord, claiming that the new line would "impart life and activity to every kind of business along the way." They dreamed of tapping the flow of western goods that normally went to New York City by the Erie Canal and the Hudson River. With new railroads, goods could go from Lake Ontario to Ogdensburg, New York, and thence to Burlington, Vermont, Concord, Nashua, and

28. For Pierce's early career, see the following: Nichols, *Pierce*, pp. 48–111; Nathaniel Hawthorne, *Life of Franklin Pierce* (Boston, 1852); *Dedication of a Statue of Pierce.* For references in this paragraph, see also Benton, *Thirty Years' View*, I, 617; *Patriot*, Oct. 8, 1838, Oct. 19, 1840; Pierce to Dr. William Prescott, Oct. 1, 1840, Pierce to Elizabeth McNeil, June 27, 1840, Pierce Papers, NHHS. For an estimate of Pierce in Congress see Nichols, *Pierce*, pp. 98–111.

Boston. Other entrepreneurs planned a railroad from Maine through northern New Hampshire to Canada, and others urged the extension of the line that had already reached Exeter.[29]

Both the promoters and the opponents of railroads appealed to the people. Promoters claimed that most of the stock would be held by farmers and promised that railroad transportation would help farmers get higher prices for their crops. Opponents replied that the railroads would ruin the horse business, cut off the hay market, and break down in winter anyway. When one unfortunate fellow riding on top of a railroad car stood up as the train went under a bridge, the injury to his head reminded skeptics that railroads were dangerous.[30]

Radical Democrats moved rapidly to hold back the railroad boom. They said that railroads should not have the right to take land by eminent domain. If a railroad were absolutely necessary, the state should build it and own it. They warned farmers that a railroad might get enough land to cut them off from access to the track. In February 1840, John Parker Hale urged his friends to "resist the arbitrary and tyrannical proceedings" of a railroad corporation that had acquired land through the right of eminent domain. He accused the railroad of "illegal and high handed usurpation" in taking land "by the hands of violence." Hale, like other young Democrats, had joined the radicals.[31]

On June 20, 1840, in spite of opposition from Whigs and conservative Democrats, radical Democrats passed an act checking railroad construction. The Railroad Act of 1840 allowed railroads already chartered to use the right of eminent domain but

29. Expenses on the Lowell-Nashua line were only $25,000 a mile, partly because the grade was never more than fifteen feet a mile. Kirkland, *Men, Cities, and Transportation,* I, 161–169; *Patriot,* May 20, 27, June 3, Sept. 16, Nov. 25, 1839, Feb. 3, 1840; *Hill's Patriot,* Dec. 16, 1840.

30. *Hill's Patriot,* April 7, 1841; *Patriot,* April 29, May 6, 13, 1839, Nov. 17, 1842.

31. *A Letter to a New Hampshire Land Owner upon the Constitutionality of Granting the Power of Taking Private Property to Railroad Corporations* (n.p., 1840); *Patriot,* June 8, 1840; Hale to E. W. Toppan, Feb. 14, 1840, Hale Papers, NHHS.

prevented them from building on the land until every claim for land damages had been paid. According to an amendment in November 1840, farmers could remove tracks from their land if they were not satisfied with their compensation. The act also denied the town of Concord the right to buy stock in the Concord Railroad. Most important, future railroads no longer had the right to acquire land through the use of eminent domain.[32]

Leading the locofocos in the debates were Albert Baker of Bow and Thomas Treadwell, now Chairman of the House Committee on Roads, Bridges, and Canals. Treadwell accused agents of the Boston and Maine Railroad of lying when they claimed that farmers did not mind selling their land. Other Democrats such as Moses Norris and Samuel Swasey joined in denouncing railroads. In the voting Democratic backing for the new law was almost unanimous. From Washington came support from Pierce and Burke; only Tristram Shaw of the delegation opposed the law. The *Patriot,* which had turned against railroads, charged that the Boston and Maine Railroad had taken land without paying for it. Other Democratic newspapers and numerous Democratic meetings joined in the chorus opposing railroads.[33]

During the next year Whigs and conservative Democrats fought to repeal the railroad act. Hill argued that no railroad would ever be built without eminent domain because "any speculator" who chose to "purchase for the purpose of extorting money" could block construction. Since railroads provided "public use" and were for the "public benefit," the legislature had the right to grant them property without the consent of the owner. Unlike many private manufacturing corporations, he continued, railroads were a positive good for the state. Although Hill insisted that he was fighting for the farmers who owned stock in the Concord Railroad, he was also defending his own

32. *Revised Statutes, 1842,* Laws of 1840, pp. 433, 504; *Patriot,* June 29, 1840; Kirkland, *Men, Cities, and Transportation,* I, 275.

33. *Patriot,* Jan. 1, 1840, Jan. 8, 1841, Jan. 13, 20, 1842.

investment. Despite Hill, radical Democrats defeated an effort to repeal the railroad act in June 1841. Of 148 Democrats in the lower house, 136 opposed repeal, and most Whigs supported it.[34]

The act did not completely end railroad building. When zealots tried to block construction of a railroad bridge across the Piscataqua River by restricting the number of pilings, even Treadwell and Baker opposed the motion. Unwilling to have trains fall into the river, the legislature allowed the extra pilings. The Concord Railroad made steady progress. To accommodate the Amoskeag mills, the railroad crossed to the east bank of the Merrimack River three miles below Manchester and then returned to the west bank eight miles above. By the summer of 1842 trains ran from the capital of New Hampshire to the capital of Massachusetts.[35]

Even though the Concord Railroad was completed, the act of 1840 did seriously curtail railroad construction. In the next five years only fifty-seven miles of track were laid in New Hampshire. The legislature chartered only one railroad between 1840 and the middle of 1844. Although the depression was one reason for the sluggish performance, radical Democrats were also responsible. Once the 1840 law was repealed, railroad construction went rapidly ahead.[36]

Radicals also attacked banks and industry; in a New Orleans Day address in 1839, Burke maintained that the nation Jackson saved in 1815 was now threatened by corrupt corporations, which bought elections, created "a Monied Aristocracy," and like "vampires" of old, "suck[ed] the life blood of the community." That same year, Baker, Swasey, and Treadwell secured a law

34. *Ibid.,* Jan. 13, 20, Feb. 3, 1842; *Hill's Patriot,* April 7, 1841, Jan. 14, 1842. Eighty-one Whigs voted for repeal.

35. *Patriot,* July 2, Dec. 9, 1841; *Hill's Patriot,* Nov. 30, 1841; Kirkland, *Men, Cities, and Transportation,* I, 161.

36. Between 1840 and 1845 Massachusetts built 249 miles of railroad track, Connecticut 100 miles, Maine 51 miles, Rhode Island only 4 miles. Kirkland. *Men, Cities, and Transportation,* I, 284.

granting the state the right to amend all future charters but failed to get a similar law for earlier corporations.[37]

Renewed attempts to destroy the privilege of limited corporate liability touched off a debate in 1840 between Whigs and the *Patriot*. According to the Whig *Statesman,* such a change would "destroy all corporate property and prevent any new enterprise or measure of improvement in the State." To this the *Patriot* replied that corporate privileges had been granted too freely in the past and accused monopolistic factories of building up one or two towns at the expense of the rest. In 1841 the radicals got a law limiting the right of a bank director to borrow from his own bank and a resolution granting the state the right to amend earlier corporate charters as well as future ones; but they failed to get rid of limited liability.[38]

Radicals were more successful in blocking the expansion of the textile industry. Between 1840 and 1842 the legislature refused to charter a single manufacturing corporation. As in the case of railroads, part of the reason for the denial, but only part, lay in the depression. Economic conditions in New England improved after 1840; and Massachusetts and Connecticut granted about as many charters in the years 1840–1841 as they had in the years 1838–1839. But in New Hampshire radical Democrats held manufacturing back. The Whig newspaper, the *New Hampshire Statesman,* which represented the textile interests, was so angry that it called Democrats "levelers" as well as "agrarians."[39]

37. Edmund Burke, *An Address Delivered before the Democratic Republican Citizens of Lempster, N. H., on the Eighth of January, 1839* (Newport, N.H., 1839); *Patriot,* July 8, 1839; *Laws of New Hampshire,* June 1839, pp. 414–417; *Hill's Patriot,* Oct. 21, 1840, Jan. 27, Mar. 3, June 2, 1841, Feb. 18, 1842. The *Patriot* resumed the old cry of taking over Dartmouth College. *Patriot,* May 11, 1840.

38. The bank law was aimed at directors like Hill who borrowed heavily from their banks. *Statesman,* Dec. 23, 1840; *Patriot,* Jan. 22, Feb. 26, Mar. 4, May 14, July 2, 9, Aug. 19, 26, Oct. 7, 1841; *Laws of New Hampshire,* June 1841, pp. 539–541.

39. Dodd, *American Business Corporations,* p. 403; *Statesman,* Dec. 23, 1840; *Patriot,* Jan. 22, Oct. 7, 1841, Jan. 26, Feb. 24, 1842.

Fearful of losing the state to the Whigs, Democrats sought unity at the party convention in June 1841. The *Patriot* pointed out that the Whigs had taken advantage of their presidential victory in 1840 to remove Democratic officeholders. "The Guillotine," wailed the *Patriot*, was at work in Carroll County, and hardly any Democratic postmasters were left. But the Democrats could not unite. Hill first tried vainly to prevent the nomination of Henry Hubbard for governor and then failed to block a radical resolution opposing future railroad construction. Before long, Hill and conservative Democrats were backing a splinter candidate, John H. White. The winter campaign of 1842 became a battle over economic policy.[40]

Both factions hoped to get the backing of Senator Woodbury. As Secretary of the Treasury, Woodbury had agreed with locofocos over hard money and the Independent Treasury, but no one was certain of his position on corporations. When he gave a major speech in Portsmouth before returning to the Senate in November of 1841, he came out on the radical side. Though private corporations might "be good for some purposes," especially where "the end [was] great, as well as hazardous," they were "ridiculous" for most public objects. But, he added, Democrats were not so radical as to be called "Jacobins." Using the old rhetoric, he concluded that Democrats were farmers and mechanics; Whigs were wealthy merchants and "nabob bankers."[41]

Woodbury rallied behind Hubbard, not White, in the campaign. Hubbard's position on corporations was also somewhat in doubt, but in December 1841, he spoke clearly in locofoco language. He attacked Hill's railroad for taking land without farmers' consent, supported individual liability in corporations,

40. *Patriot*, June 11, July 17, 1841; *Hill's Patriot*, Sept. 28, 1841, Jan. 28, 1842; Pierce to Henry H. Carroll, June 24, 1841, Pierce Papers, NHHS; Nichols, *Pierce*, pp. 118–119.
41. Levi Woodbury, *Speech Delivered at the Democratic Meeting in Jefferson Hall, Portsmouth (N. H.), November 18, 1841* (Alexandria, D. C., 1841).

and opposed rechartering banks with their old privileges. The *Patriot* backed Hubbard completely. Since most Democrats adopted the radical position, Hill was isolated in the party.[42]

Even in Concord, Hill's backing showed signs of slipping away as the Democrats of that town held a series of meetings in January and February to decide on party policy. First they voted for resolutions endorsing the Hubbard-*Patriot* line. Hill countered with amendments calling railroads public and urging Democrats not to support Hubbard unless he opposed the repeal of railroad charters. When compromise resolutions were offered at the third meeting, Hill was furious. For three hours he rambled on, defending his amendments and listing the wrongs done him. They were all against him, he said, the radicals, the Portsmouth crowd, the abolitionists, Burke, Hubbard, Pierce, Woodbury. Reaching into the past, he accused them of being Federalists and asserted that he alone represented Jacksonian Democracy. It was paradoxically pathetic, yet powerful. Hill gained ground, but still no action was taken.

In the end Hill had his way. At the next meeting after radicals tried in vain to stall, the Democrats voted in favor of each of Hill's fifteen amendments. They also agreed to support conservative Democrat John H. White for governor in place of Hubbard. When the radicals held a rump session a few days later, Hill and his men broke in. The chair refused to recognize Hill; so he nominated his crony Peter Renton chairman and declared him elected. Shouting to Renton that he would put him in the chair, "his countenance livid with rage," Hill tried to force the gate separating the chairman from the floor. A riot followed in which men wrestled and swore, swung clubs and canes. Hill's son William smashed the chairman's desk. The radicals retired in haste, leaving Hill in control of the Concord party.[43]

42. *Patriot*, Dec. 23, 1841; *Gazette*, Jan. 4, 25, Feb. 1, 1842; *Statesman*, Jan. 7, Feb. 4, 1842.
43. *Patriot*, Feb. 3, 17, 24, 1842; *Hill's Patriot*, Feb. 11, 1842.

All winter radical and conservative Democrats exchanged accusations and called each other names. Democratic newspapers accused Hill of uniting with the Whigs, of selling land to the Concord Railroad at exorbitant prices, and of representing banking and manufacturing interests. He was, they said, the "shuttlecock of corporations" and his followers were nothing less than "rabid, hard-cider-log-cabin, corn shine feds." Hill denied that he favored "privileges" for corporations, but he did seem to be bidding for Whig support. He called on a number of groups, who would normally vote Whig, to back him: large landowners, factory workers, prosperous farmers who sold land to railroads, and stage owners, who were threatened by radical legislation.[44]

On the eve of the election, Franklin Pierce gave up the final year of his term in the United States Senate to return to New Hampshire politics. It is a commentary on politics in the nineteenth century that both Hill in 1836 and Pierce in 1842 preferred the state to the national scene. It is also a commentary on Hill and Pierce, because both found their talents more suited to party battles in Concord than to those in Washington. Neither was a distinguished United States Senator. Pierce arrived dramatically in Concord to endorse Hubbard and to denounce the "bolters." Hill responded with an election extra accusing Pierce of being a "trimmer." Confident of victory, Pierce said that he was unconcerned about the "falsehoods and vulgar abuse" heaped on him by Hill, whom he accused of having "monomania." Hubbard won by a solid majority.[45]

Since corporation policy had been the major issue of the campaign, radical Democrats felt that they had a mandate. As Treadwell and Baker increased their pressure, the Democrats renominated Hubbard in June and called for unlimited liability

44. *Patriot*, Feb. 24, Mar. 3, 10, 1842; *Hill's Patriot*, Jan. 7, Feb. 7, Mar. 4, 1842; [Haverhill] *Democratic Republican*, Feb. 23, Mar. 2, 1842.

45. Hubbard 26,831; Stevens (Whig) 12,234; White 5,869; Hoit (Abolitionist) 2,812. *New Hampshire Manual 1891*, p. 154. Pierce to John McNeil, Mar. 7, 1842, Pierce Papers, NHHS; *Patriot*, Mar. 3, 10, 17, 24, 31, 1842. For Pierce's decision to return to Concord, see Nichols, *Pierce*, pp. 109–111.

for all stockholders. In his inaugural address the same month, the governor opposed any increase in the number of private corporations and demanded unlimited liability. After an inconclusive session in June 1842, the legislature heeded the radical call when it met in November. First, it warmed up with traditional locofoco resolutions against distribution of the federal surplus, tariff protection, and bankruptcy laws. Next, it postponed four bills to extend bank charters. Finally, it passed the Unlimited Liability Act of 1842. The act stated that stockholders of all corporations should be "personally holden to pay the debts and civil liabilities" of such companies. If a corporation failed, each stockholder was to be responsible not simply for debts up to the value of his investment but for all the debts of the corporation. In so doing, the legislature reversed the conservative act of 1837 that had broadly granted limited liability. The step taken in 1842 was particularly radical because limited liability had become an established principle in almost every state in the union.[46]

The railroad act, the liability act, and the depression brought business expansion to a halt. In the four years 1840–1843 the legislature chartered no manufacturing companies, one railroad, and a total of only nine corporations, compared to a total of seventy-six in the preceding four years. The radicals not only took economic issues seriously but transformed their theories into action.[47]

In 1843 Hill tried once more to stop the radical bandwagon. But he found that old conservatives like Abner Greenleaf and Richard Ayer were no match for young radicals like Harry Hibbard and John Parker Hale. Hale, who was running for Congress, fought so hard that Hill dubbed the opposition nothing but "Hales." Even the enigmatic Woodbury issued another radical statement. In January Burke was a "little suspicious"

46. *Patriot,* April 7, 14, 21, June 9, 1842; Henry Hubbard, *Message to Both Branches of the General Court of New Hampshire, June Session, 1842* (Concord, N.H., 1842); *Laws of New Hampshire,* Nov. 1842, pp. 23–28; *Patriot,* Nov. 10, 24, Dec. 1, 1842, Feb. 9, 1843; *Manchester Democrat,* Oct. 18, 1842; *Hill's Patriot,* Dec. 29, 1842; *Revised Statutes, 1842,* p. 286.
47. *Laws of New Hampshire,* 1840–1843, *passim.*

because Woodbury did not "denounce this conservative movement with sufficient decision." In response to a number of letters, Woodbury finally wrote that if corporations were public, "lands of individuals" could be taken "on making due compensation." But railroads were private, not public, because they permitted "only the corporation to put cars & engines" on the tracks. Toward the end the campaign turned into a showdown between Pierce and Hill. Hubbard won reelection in March by a margin so narrow that in Washington President John Tyler's newspaper *The Daily Madisonian* called it a "Hannibal victory." But close or not, Pierce had control of the party and Hill was finished in New Hampshire politics.[48]

Hill now turned to Washington, where he was soon writing for the *Daily Madisonian*. In return for supporting President Tyler since 1841, he had regained his federal pension agency and had won a Post Office printing contract. According to Burke, Hill was "omnipotent in the dispensation of official patronage" in New Hampshire. Tyler even tried to appoint him chief of the Bureau of Provisions and Clothing, but the Senate again rejected him.[49]

48. For the campaign see Hibbard to Hale, May 26, 1842, A. G. Allen to Hale, Mar. 28, 1843, Hale Papers, NHHS; *Patriot*, June 16, July 7, Dec. 8, 1842, Jan. 5, 19, Feb. 9, 1843; *Manchester Democrat*, Jan. 4, 18, 25, 1843; Samuel Cushman to Levi Woodbury, Jan. 17, 23, 1843, Woodbury Papers, LC. For the Woodbury letter see *Hill's Patriot*, Nov. 10, 1842; Burke to Hale, Jan. 19, 1843, Hale Papers, NHHS; Woodbury to Pierce, quoted in *Patriot*, Feb. 23, 1843; Cushman to Woodbury, Jan. 17, 23, Feb. 11, 1843, Woodbury to Butler, Feb. 24, 25, 1843, Woodbury Papers, LC. The vote for governor in 1843 was: Hubbard 23,050, Anthony Colby (Whig) 12,551, John White (Conservative Democrat) 5,497, Hoit (Abolitionist) 3,402. *New Hampshire Manual 1891*, p. 154; *Patriot*, Feb. 2, Mar. 23, 30, 1843; Nichols, *Pierce*, p. 121; *Hill's Patriot*, Jan. 19, Mar. 9, 1843; *Daily Madisonian*, Mar. 21, 1843.

49. Hill's Massachusetts friends David Henshaw and Robert Rantoul also supported Tyler, as did John C. Calhoun. Darling, *Political Changes in Massachusetts*, pp. 301–307; *Hill's Patriot*, Feb. 9, 1843; *Patriot*, Feb. 16, Mar. 30, April 6, 13, July 13, 27, Aug. 3, 1843; *Daily Madisonian*, Mar. 29, April 3, 10, June 14, 1843; Burke to Hale, Jan. 19, 1843, A. Jenkins to Hale, Jan. 29, 1844, Hale Papers, NHHS; Robert McClelland to Van Buren, Feb. 3, 1843, Van Buren Papers, LC. McClelland claimed that Hill had received "a load of patronage" in January 1843.

With Hill out of the way, Democrats tried to bring the party together. Hubbard's inaugural address was conciliatory. Although renewing his position against the right of eminent domain, he conceded that "the acquisition, possession, and protection of property" was "one of the essential ... rights of man." At the Democratic convention, radicals sought harmony by nominating for governor the moderate mill owner John H. Steele. After trying vainly to avoid the convention, Woodbury presided and followed what diehard radicals called an "equivocal ... *milk-and-water noncommittal course.*" No one could surpass Woodbury in avoiding hard and fast positions. With their newfound harmony Democrats easily won the next two elections.[50]

The reunification of the party, the end of the depression, and increased interest in railroads helped end the radical period in New Hampshire. In the fall of 1843, the *Patriot* and Professor Charles Haddock of Dartmouth came out in favor of the proposed Northern Railroad, which would run from Concord to the Connecticut River at Lebanon. The next spring the Lebanon town meeting voted to have the state restore the right of eminent domain, and a railroad meeting in Franklin warned that if the laws were not changed, railroads in other states would soon encircle New Hampshire and cut it off. Petitions in favor of the Northern Railroad poured into the legislature, coming from thirty-six towns and 4,766 persons in June 1844 alone.[51]

Under this sort of pressure, moderate radicals sought a formula whereby they could repeal the Railroad Act of 1840 without completely renouncing their philosophy. Hubbard and Woodbury had already hinted at a way. Both had argued that rail-

---

50. *Patriot*, June 8, 1843. Hill backed John White again in 1844, but White polled less than 2,000 votes. *New Hampshire Manual 1891*, p. 154. Henry Hubbard, *Address to Both Branches of the General Court of New Hampshire, June Session, 1843* (Concord, N.H., 1843); Nichols, *Pierce*, p. 137; article in *Portsmouth Mercury*, n.d., Woodbury Papers, LC. Woodbury wrote in his diary, June 10, 1843: "Had to attend State Convention." "Political Memoranda of Levi Woodbury," Blair Family Papers, LC.

51. *Patriot*, June 29, Oct. 19, 26, Nov. 30, 1843, May 16, June 20, 1844; *Hill's Patriot*, June 6, 27, 1844.

roads should not employ eminent domain because they were "private," not "public." If somehow they could be considered public, then they could be granted the privilege. When President Nathaniel Upham of the Northern boldly asserted in the spring of 1844 that his railroad was indeed public, radicals were ready to listen. The *Patriot* immediately suggested that the state grant the right of eminent domain to any "public" railroad. The newspaper made the concession seem Jacksonian by publishing a letter from a "Poor Man's Son," which said that another railroad would help farmers.[52]

In December 1844, the House reported a bill restoring the use of the right of eminent domain. If a railroad was unable to buy land at reasonable rates, it could be declared a public facility and thereby allowed to take property. A board of three commissioners was to investigate each petition and to report to the governor and council for action. Once the railroad was declared public, the commission was to lay out the line and assess the damages with the aid of the selectmen in each town. The bill gave the state great powers over railroads: the commission (the second in New England) could reduce rates if profits exceeded 10 percent; after twenty years the state could repossess the railroad; no railroad could discontinue service without permission from the legislature; any citizen could run his own cars on the tracks (thus making the tracks uniquely public). Like the New York Free Banking Act of 1838 and the New York Free Corporation Act of 1848, the New Hampshire bill allowed incorporation as a general right, not as a special privilege. At the same time it established a measure of state regulation, even to the point of limiting profits. As the *Sentinel* correctly put it, the bill would bring about a "great change."[53]

52. Woodbury to Josiah Butler, Feb. 24, 25, 1843, Woodbury Papers, LC; Hubbard, *Address to General Court 1843*. Upham's speech elicited a debate in the *Patriot* including a mock petition to the legislature in which a storekeeper demanded the right to take land from his neighbor. *Patriot*, April 4, 25, May 2, 30, 1844.

53. *Patriot*, Dec. 19, 26, 1844; *Sentinel*, Dec. 25, 1844; *Laws of New Hampshire*, Nov. 1844, pp. 83–88.

The bill quickly passed the House 172-59, most nay votes coming from towns that had little to gain from railroads. The real test came in the Senate the day after Christmas. After seven of the twelve senators had voted, the count stood 4-3 against the bill. Since all the remaining votes were Democratic, the party held the future of railroads in New Hampshire in its hands. One after another, Haskins, Cooke, Davis, Swett, and Cross voted aye. Democrats had ended the Railroad War by allowing railroads to take land with the help of the state. Whigs said that Democrats had simply come over to the Whig position; and in Washington Hill crowed that the radicals had "backed down."[54]

The Railroad War was over, for the legislature chartered ten railroads in 1844 and twenty-nine between 1845 and 1850. Since only three railroads had been chartered from 1838 to 1843, the sudden reversal of policy is apparent. In the next two years conventions met to propose a railroad from Manchester to Lawrence, Massachusetts, and others to Chesire County, to Claremont, and to Haverhill. Both conservatives and radicals joined in the expansion. Hill complained that the state was pushing a railroad to Keene faster than one north out of Concord because of Hubbard's influence. Pierce suggested a line from Concord to Portsmouth and worked to secure a mail contract for the Concord Railroad.[55]

Amidst the boom, businessmen and newspapers charged that other radical laws were hampering the economic development of the state by frightening away investors. Old Charles H. Atherton wrote his son Senator Charles G. Atherton that no more railroads would be built in New Hampshire unless the state allowed large stockholders to have extra votes through proxy voting. He said

54. *Patriot*, Dec. 26, 1844, Jan. 2, 1845; *Statesman*, Jan. 10, 1845; *Hill's Patriot*, Jan. 23, 1845. The one Whig senator voted for the bill. The Democrats were 7-4 in favor.

55. *Laws of New Hampshire, passim; Patriot*, Jan. 30, May 8, Nov. 20, 1845; *Hill's Patriot*, May 15, June 19, July 24, 1845, May 7, 1846; [Manchester] *Semi-Weekly American*, Nov. 10, 1845; Charles Peaslee to John Hatch George, Feb. 22, 1846, Charles Peaslee Papers, NHHS.

that the proposed railroads had had little success in raising money in Boston because of "universal disgust" at the rule that each stockholder, whether he held one share or a thousand, had but one vote. There was similar disgust, he added, at the unlimited liability law. One Whig newspaper claimed that if the New Hampshire legislature had not been so rigid, money about to be invested in Lawrence, Massachusetts, would be going into Hooksett, Manchester, and Bow, New Hampshire. Another added that radical laws had allowed Portland, Maine, to get ahead of Portsmouth; it insisted that the Lawrence family had invested in Saco, Maine, where there was no unlimited liability, after the radical victories in New Hampshire. The *Manchester American* became the avowed agent of free enterprise in New Hampshire, asking its Whig readers to support "vigorous action to help manufacturing in the state." The sum of a million dollars became symbolic. The Keene *New Hampshire Sentinel* said that radical laws had driven a million dollars out of the state, while agent Reed at the Amoskeag Mills wrote that the liability law had diverted a million dollars of Boston money from the Amoskeag to Saco.[56]

The influence of Whigs, conservative Democrats, the business interest, returning prosperity, and plain logic combined to change the laws in 1846. After no candidate received the necessary majority to be elected governor in March, Whigs, Independent Democrats, and Abolitionists combined to control the legislature in June and elect Whig Anthony Colby governor. In his inaugural address Colby called on the legislature to establish a limit on liability, and the legislature complied. The new liability law held stockholders liable for debts only up to the value of their own stock after the corporation had paid out all its

<hr/>

56. Charles H. Atherton to Charles G. Atherton, Feb. 12, 26, 1845, C. G. Atherton Papers, NHHS; *Statesman,* Feb. 14, 28, 1845; *Manchester American,* Nov. 22, 1844; Feb. 21, 28, 1845; *Sentinel,* Mar. 19, 1845; *Patriot,* Feb. 29, 1844. The radicals vainly pointed to Boston investments in Keene, Lebanon, and Meredith, New Hampshire. *Ibid.,* Aug. 14, 1845; the *Coos County Democrat,* quoted in the *Semi-Weekly American,* Oct. 30, 1845.

capital. A new proxy-voting law next granted stockholders one vote per share, though limiting anyone's vote to one-eighth of the total number of shares. The *Statesman* said the obvious when it observed that "radicalism" was "dead." Only the arch-radical *Manchester Democrat,* which called the new privileges "most anti-republican," seemed to care.[57]

The legislature responded promptly to the new laws and to the demands of the industrialists. Before the year was out, it had chartered fifty-seven new corporations—more than the combined total for all the years back to 1838—and within the next two years it chartered sixty-six more. The value of the new corporations in 1846 alone was estimated at some $23 million, one-third that of all New Hampshire corporations up to that time. The average annual number of incorporations rose from two in the years 1840–1843 to twenty-six between 1844 and 1850. And railroad mileage, which had increased by only 57 miles between 1840 and 1845, grew by 375 miles in the next five years. By 1850 New Hampshire ranked second in railroad mileage in New England. Railroads reached from Nashua through Concord to the Connecticut River and the White Mountains.[58] Table 9 indicates the extent of the economic change in New Hampshire.

In spite of the corporation boom, traces of the old locofoco spirit continued in New Hampshire. The legislators in 1847 amended the corporation law of 1846 to give the legislature the right to repeal any charter. They also responded to agitation for labor reform. In 1846 they passed a law that prevented children under fifteen from working in factories unless they had had

57. For a study of the election of 1846 and the Democratic Party split over slavery, see Chapter IX. In March, Democrat Jared Williams had 26,740 votes, Colby 17,707, Independent Democrat Nathaniel S. Berry 10,379, scattering 568. The legislature consisted of 124 Democrats, 107 Whigs, 16 Independent Democrats, and 11 Abolitionists. *New Hampshire Manual 1891,* p. 154; *Patriot,* Mar. 19, June 11, 25, 1846; *Hill's Patriot,* Mar. 19, 1846; [Concord] *Independent Democrat,* Mar. 26, June 25, 1846; Sewell, *Hale,* p. 82; *Manchester Democrat,* June 3, July 15, 1846; *Statesman,* June 26, July 23, 1846; *Laws of New Hampshire,* June 1846, pp. 63–64.

58. All figures include renewals of charters. *Laws of New Hampshire, passim; Patriot,* July 23, 1846; Kirkland, *Men, Cities, and Transportation,* I, 284.

Table 9. Acts of Incorporation in New Hampshire, 1840–1850

Year	Number of incorporations[a]	Year	Number of incorporations	Year	Number of incorporations
1840	3	1844	20	1848	38
1841	3	1845	11	1849	8
1842	3	1846	57	1850	21
1843	0	1847	28		

Period	Mill or manufacturing company	Bank	Railroad	Road, bridge, canal, navigation, or aqueduct	Other	Total
1840–1843						
Total	0	1	1	3	4	9
Annual Average	0	0.3	0.3	1	1	2
1844–1850						
Total	73	39	39	17	15	183
Annual Average	10	6	6	2	2	26

Source: *Laws of New Hampshire, passim.*
[a] All figures include charter renewals.

twelve weeks of school in the preceding twelve months. The next year the legislature established ten hours as the normal day's work and said that no one could work more than that unless he signed a special contract. Still another act kept minors under fifteen from exceeding ten hours a day unless their parents gave written consent. Finally, in 1850 and 1852, laws were passed curtailing the use of free passes in railroads and making it illegal to charge more for a short haul than a long haul. All of these laws were among the first of their kind in the United States. But the reform gestures did not hide the fact that the radical war against railroads, banks, and textile mills had ended in 1846.[59]

59. *Manchester Democrat*, Jan. 4, 1843, July 1, 1846; *Semi-Weekly American*, Sept. 11, Nov. 17, 1845; *Laws of New Hampshire*, June 1846, p. 61, June 1847, pp. 465–466; Henry W. Farnam, *Chapters in the History of Social Legislation in the United States to 1860* (Washington, D.C., 1938), pp. 258, 264; *Patriot*, June 10, 17, 24, Sept. 2, 1847, May 24, 1849; Kirkland, *Men, Cities, and Transportation*, I, 272, 275, 283; *Laws of New Hampshire*, June 1850, pp. 429–437, June 1852, p. 1214.

The radical movement caused a disastrous lag in the growth of the New Hampshire economy. The Panic of 1837 slowed economic growth everywhere, but the radical revolt, 1840–1846, prolonged the stagnation in New Hampshire at the very moment when industrialization was moving rapidly ahead elsewhere. Money that might have been invested in New Hampshire went instead into Maine and Massachusetts. Uneasy about the Granite State, Boston financiers in 1844 planned the textile city of Lawrence in Massachusetts just south of the New Hampshire line. With its strong start in the 1820's and 1830's New Hampshire might have become one of the leading industrial states for its size in the union. But after 1840 New Hampshire grew far less rapidly than Massachusetts or Connecticut. Capital invested in manufacturing in Connecticut, for example, increased 233 percent between 1840 and 1860, compared to a 157 percent gain in the Granite State. During the same period the population of Connecticut grew 49 percent, that of New Hampshire only 14 percent. There are other reasons, of course, why Connecticut outstripped New Hampshire, but the locofoco legislation played a part.[60]

The evidence of the radical period, furthermore, suggests that Arthur Schlesinger's interpretation of Jacksonian Democracy is more accurate than that of the entrepreneurial historians. Locofocos were more radical than the consensus school will admit. They cared enough about the issues of eminent domain

---

60. Population figures: 1840: New Hampshire 285,000; Connecticut 310,000; 1870: New Hampshire 318,000; Connecticut 537,000. *Statistical History*, p. 13. Capital invested in manufacturing in Connecticut: 1840—$13,669,139; 1860—$45,590,430. Capital invested in manufacturing in New Hampshire: 1840—$9,252,441; 1860—$23,274,094. In the value of cotton and woolen manufactures alone, New Hampshire pushed ahead of Connecticut between 1840 and 1860, but in the other branches of manufacturing Connecticut made much greater gains than New Hampshire. Value of cotton and woolen manufactures: New Hampshire 1840—$4,938,088; 1860—$16,980,847; Connecticut 1840—$5,210,277; 1860—$13,914,580. United States Census Office, *Compendium of the Sixth Census*, pp. 360, 361, 364; United States Census Office, *Manufactures of the United States in 1860; Compiled from the Original Returns of the Eighth Census* (Washington, D.C., 1865), pp. 49, 52, 329, 330.

and limited liability to split their party. According to Schlesinger, the "tradition of ... Jackson" was a "movement on the part of other sections of society to restrain the power of the business community." For almost a decade radical Jacksonians supported legislation that not only restrained business but helped slow the economic growth of the state.[61]

61. For Schlesinger on locofocoism, radicalism, and industrialization, see Schlesinger, *Age of Jackson,* pp. 190–209, 334–349; for the quotation, *ibid.,* p. 505.

IX

The Slavery War, 1843-1851

During the 1830's New Hampshire Jacksonians had served southern Democrats by scorning Negroes and by attacking abolitionists.
On the issues of race and slavery, John Parker Hale was a typical
Democrat, as his behavior indicated when George Storrs gave antislavery lectures in Dover in 1835. New Hampshire was an unlikely
place and Hale an unlikely person for antislavery agitation.[1]

Yet early in the 1840's the state and Hale began to change. By
1843 there were antislavery societies in more than forty towns,
and the Liberty Party received 3,402 votes in the March election.
Concord alone had three societies and was the home of the abolitionist *Herald of Freedom*. Escaped slaves occasionally made their
way to Concord by way of Boston and then continued on through
the White Mountains to Canada. After Hale was elected to the
House of Representatives in 1843, he became the first New Hampshire Congressman to vote against the gag rule.[2]

1. In this chapter I have drawn on Sewell, *Hale*, chap. III–V. I do not
attempt to supersede Sewell, but I approach the events of 1845 and 1846
somewhat differently in relating them to Jacksonian Democracy. For the
Jacksonians and the antislavery movement, see Chapter VII. For the Dover
incident, see Sewell, *Hale*, p. 32. Sewell covers Hale's early career in *ibid.*, pp.
13–44. See also William E. Chandler, *The Statue of John Parker Hale* (Concord, N.H., 1892).

2. See Petersen, *History of Elections*, p. 143; see also Coolidge and Mansfield,
New Hampshire, p. 709; Ernest L. Sherman, "A Study of the Slavery and Anti-
Slavery Movement in New Hampshire to 1850," unpublished manuscript, Uni-
versity of New Hampshire Library, 1947; Skinner, "Slavery and Abolition in
New Hampshire," pp. 130–131.

Hale's vote against the gag rule in December 1843 led to a brisk party battle in which the split was mostly regional. Democrats from Rockingham, Strafford, and Carroll counties in the east generally supported the Congressman; those farther west opposed him. The *Dover Gazette* and the *Exeter News-Letter* both came out for Hale; the *Patriot* and *Hill's Patriot* in Concord and the *Argus and Spectator* in Newport denounced him. According to William Claggett, "all the radical Democrats" of Portsmouth were behind Hale and "fast coming out against slavery," but other radicals like Henry H. Carroll of the *Patriot* and Edmund Burke, once of the *Argus,* were against him. When Pierce tried to adjourn a Concord meeting in which pro-Hale resolutions were proposed, the crowd yelled "gag, gag," and Pierce shouted back that he was opposed to the "abolition excitement" anyway. But Hale had supporters in Concord, notably Jacob H. Ela, editor of the *New Hampshire Statesman,* and former postmaster Joseph Low. With the east for Hale, the west against him, and Concord divided, and with radicals and conservatives split two ways, trouble loomed for the Democratic Party.[3]

The party was less divided over Texas. When President Tyler submitted his treaty to annex Texas in the spring of 1844, most Democratic leaders were for it. The *Patriot* argued that the United States should take Texas, not in order to spread slavery, but rather to keep Texas away from a European nation. Hill agreed. Senator Woodbury, who voted for the treaty, called Texas vital to the security of the Mississippi Valley and promised that annexation would not lead to war. He said that he opposed slavery but maintained that only slave owners could abolish it. Pierce's resolutions, which passed the legislature in the fall, directed the delegation in Washington to vote for the annexation of Texas; the statement insisted that annexation would add more free than slave states to the Union. With this formula New

3. *Patriot,* Feb. 15, Mar. 21, 1844; *Hill's Patriot,* Jan. 11, Mar. 21, 1844; Sewell, *Hale,* pp. 45–46; William Claggett to Hale, Jan. 3, 1844, John H. Wiggins to Hale, Jan. 5, 1844, G. McDaniel to Hale, Mar. 22, 1844. John Peavey to Hale, Feb. 6, 1844, G. A. Grant to Hale, Mar. 20, 1844, Ezekiel Hand to Hale, Mar. 25, 1844, Hale Papers, NHHS.

Hampshire Democrats could back Woodbury, Tyler, and Polk on annexation without appearing to favor slavery. In this way they could continue their policy of supporting the South.[4]

Hale dutifully presented the resolutions in the House of Representatives, but on Jan. 10, 1845, he asked for suspension of the House rules in order to introduce a proviso on Texas. The proviso said that once annexed, Texas should be divided equally into slave and free territory. Hale won the support of one New Hampshire Congressman, John Reding, for suspension of the rules, but the two others, Moses Norris and Edmund Burke, were opposed. When the House failed to suspend the rules, Hale was convinced that annexation of Texas meant extension of slavery.

Despite the fact that he was running for reelection in March, he decided to disobey the resolutions from Concord and oppose annexation. On January 11 he appealed to the party over the heads of its leaders. In a letter to the state's Democrats he said that the Pilgrims would have despaired had they foreseen the day "when their degenerate sons should . . . extend their boundaries . . . for the purpose of . . . sustaining slavery." He hoped to arouse support.[5]

Friendly letters poured in, mostly from seacoast and lakes regions that had backed him the year before. Jacob Ela predicted that in the election Hale would win Whig and Liberty support as well as some Democratic votes. In the next two months Ela wrote Hale seven times proposing a combination of Whigs, Liberty Party men, and Democrats opposed to annexation. From Exeter, Amos Tuck wrote that the "question of slavery" would be the "dividing point between the parties" that would soon split the nation. Tuck had given up teaching to attend Dartmouth College and become a lawyer. As a radical Democrat he could not

4. *Patriot,* May 2, 30, 1844; *Hill's Patriot,* May 9, 1844; Levi Woodbury, *Letter on the Annexation of Texas* (Washington, D.C., 1844); Benton, *Thirty Years' View,* II, 619; *Laws of New Hampshire,* Nov. 1844, pp. 120–122; Sewell, *Hale,* p. 50.

5. John P. Hale, *Letter to His Constituents on the Proposed Annexation of Texas* (Washington, D.C., 1845); *Patriot,* Jan. 23, 1845; Sewell, *Hale,* pp. 50–53.

resist attacking Isaac Hill, for he added: "Old party catch words are worn out. The party cannot discover the music of that billingsgate vocabulary, established in this state by Isaac and other low bred men." Another Democratic lawyer, John Lord Hayes of Portsmouth, said that only by appealing to the people could they overcome Pierce and "the southern influence" that Pierce was "wielding." Hayes added cautiously: "Don't tell Mr. Pierce about this letter." Both Tuck and Hayes were so angry at the Democratic nomination of southerner James K. Polk for President in 1844 that they were ready to leave the party.[6]

With an election coming up, Pierce had to act promptly. Advice came swiftly from Washington, where Woodbury urged Pierce to ask Democrats if they agreed with Hale or with the legislature on Texas. Perhaps, he added, there should be "a new nomination." Senator Charles G. Atherton felt that Hale should be rebuked and ignored. Burke said that he should be dumped. Determined to drop Hale, Pierce denounced him in the *Patriot*, hinting that he was in collusion with Rufus Choate of Boston and other leading Whigs. As chairman of the central committee, Pierce made plans for a convention in February to review the nominations for Congress.[7]

Pierce then took the fight into Hale country. He "bitterly" attacked the Congressman in his hometown of Dover and next swept on through Portsmouth, Exeter, Nashua, and Manchester. Everywhere he convinced Democrats that Hale should be replaced. The *Dover Gazette*, which had backed Hale in 1844, came out against him and so did the *Gazettes* of Nashua and Portsmouth. Contrary to Ela's expectations, Hale had no early support from Whigs. The Whig *Manchester American* praised him but asked its readers to vote for the regular Whig candidate. Among

---

6. Ela to Pierce, Jan. 15, 1845, and *passim,* Jan.–Mar. 1845, Tuck to Hale, Jan. 15, 1845, Hayes to Hale, Jan. 16, 1845, Hale Papers, NHHS; Amos Tuck, *Autobiographical Memoir* (Exeter, N.H., 1875).

7. Woodbury to Pierce, Jan. 11, 1845, Pierce Papers, NHHS; Charles G. Atherton to Pierce, Jan. 13, 15, 1845, Pierce Papers, LC; Nichols, *Pierce,* p. 133; Sewell, *Hale,* pp. 54–55; *Patriot,* Jan. 16, 1845.

Democrats, only the followers of Tuck in Exeter and Hayes in Portsmouth seemed loyal to the Dover man. Pierce had seized the initiative in the southeast.[8]

Pierce's efforts stimulated attacks on Hale. The *Patriot* and *Hill's Patriot* revived the old Jacksonian charge that he had gone over to the Federalists; the *Argus* accused him of collaboration with Whigs; and the *New Hampshire Sentinel* opposed his stand on Texas. From Washington Hill attacked Hale and from Goffs-town came word that Hubbard also opposed the Congressman. Pierce wrote Woodbury cheerfully that they all were united against Hale.[9]

A number of radical Democrats, however—angry at Pierce for the Railroad Act of December 1844—lined up behind Hale. Ela had counted on them in his optimistic letters regarding the Congressman's political future. Hale soon received similar letters from John Hayes and John Wiggins claiming that locofocos in Portsmouth and Dover were on the Hale bandwagon. Pierce alienated Concord radicals at the caucus to select delegates to the state convention. When radicals were slow in arriving, Pierce hastily called the meeting to order, arranged for the choice of delegates, and within six minutes adjourned the caucus. Five minutes later Albert Baker, the radical leader, arrived to find the meeting over. He cried out that if Hale were to be replaced for disloyalty to the party over Texas, then the party "should throw over also all the traitors on the radical platform who had taken part in the General Railroad Law."[10]

Winter ice and snow made Pierce's task easier than expected at the Democratic Convention on February 12. Democrats in Coos County, who praised Hale for his "correct and manly course,"

8. E. Hurd to Hale, Jan. 22, 1845, Hayes to Hale, Jan. 16, 1845, Hale Papers, NHHS; *Manchester American*, Jan. 24, Mar. 7, 1845; Sewell, *Hale*, pp. 55–56.

9. *Patriot*, Jan. 16, 23, 1845; *Hill's Patriot*, Jan. 23, 1845; *Sentinel*, Feb. 5, 1845; E. Holcombe to Hale, Jan. 22, 1845, David Gilchrist to Hale, Jan. 20, 1845, Hale Papers, NHHS; Pierce to Woodbury, Jan. 20, 1845, Woodbury Papers, LC.

10. Ela to Hale, Jan. 15, 29, Feb. 2, 1845, Hayes to Hale, Jan. 16, 1845, Wiggins to Hale, Feb. 4, 1845, Hale Papers, NHHS. The Baker quotation appears in the letter from Ela to Hale, Feb. 2, 1845.

found it impossible to get to Concord. Many who might have supported Hale, such as the Albert Baker group from Concord, were absent, some because the roads were impossible, others because they had not been elected. At the convention the delegates first unanimously voted to replace Hale with John Woodbury, a Democrat from Salem, who was not related to Levi Woodbury. They then sat back to hear a spirited speech by Pierce in favor of annexing Texas.[11]

Hale's supporters, known as Independent Democrats, optimistically made plans for electing him in March. Ela wrote that the Concord clique was "desperate," and that even if Hale lost in March, he could run for Levi Woodbury's seat in the Senate; while William Claggett said that the "Concord dictators" could "begin to shake." From the north country came word that Coos and Carroll counties were safe for Hale. According to one report, seven-eights of the Democrats, a quarter of the Whigs, and all the Abolitionists in Conway were for Hale.[12]

The heart of the Independent Democratic faction was in Portsmouth and Exeter, where John Hayes and Amos Tuck took the lead. When Pierce visited Portsmouth in January, Hayes stood up for Hale. Hayes had already published a pamphlet defending Hale, in which he maintained that the Congressman was simply following the views of Benton and Van Buren in regard to Texas. At the caucus to pick delegates to the state convention, Hayes tried to deliver another such defense but was shouted down. He then printed his remarks and circulated them in the northern part of the state. In addition to Hayes and Tuck, N. Porter Cram, a farmer, and Professor Joseph Hoyt of Phillips Exeter Academy were important Independent Democrats.[13]

11. *Patriot,* Feb. 13, 1845; Nichols, *Pierce,* p. 135.
12. Ela to Hale, Feb. 7, 28, 1845, Claggett to Hale, Feb. 20, 1845, S. B. Parsons to Hale, Feb. 18, 1845, N. F. Barnes to Hale, Feb. 14, 1845, Hale Papers, NHHS.
13. John L. Hayes, *Remarks Made at a Democratic Meeting in Portsmouth, on the 7th of January 1845, in Defense of the Course of John P. Hale, Member of Congress from New Hampshire, in Relation to the Annexation of Texas* (Portsmouth, N.H., 1845); Hayes to Hale, Feb. 15, 1845, Hale Papers, NHHS; Tuck, *Autobiographical Memoir.*

This inner circle called on Democrats, Abolitionists, and Whigs sympathetic to Hale to meet in Exeter on February 22. The day was cold, the roads blocked with snow; yet several hundred hardy persons met in the Congregational Church in the morning. After Hoyt was elected presiding officer, various speakers rose to heap abuse on Pierce and the clique running the Democratic Party. That afternoon the convention endorsed resolutions rededicating the Democratic Party to "the principles of human equality and universal justice," and agreed to support Hale for Congress.[14]

The convention attracted national attention. The *New York Tribune* commented: "Meetings of Loco Focos who are not prepared to be transformed into the mere instruments of slavery fanaticism have been held in Exeter, . . . and at other points." In Cherry Valley, New York, Democratic politician Jabez Hammond wrote that Hale had become famous. From Baltimore, New York City, Herkimer, New York, and other distant places came requests for Hale to speak, while praise and support flowed in from Erie, Pennsylvania, Bangor, Maine, and New York City. A Hale headquarters soon sprang up in Boston and from nearby Amesbury, Massachusetts, John Greenleaf Whittier penned the poem:

> God Bless New Hampshire! from her granite peaks
> Once more the voice of Stark and Langdon speaks.
> The long-bound vassal of the exulting South
> For very shame her self-forged chain has broken;
> Torn the black seal of slavery from her mouth . . .[15]

In time the Independent Democratic movement would become the Free Soil Party and then the Republican Party. Those taking

14. George Street, *A Memorial Discourse Delivered at Exeter, N.H., 11 Jan. 1880* (Boston, 1880); Charles R. Corning, *Amos Tuck* (Exeter, N.H., 1902); John W. Dearborn, *Sketch of the Life and Character of Hon. Amos Tuck* (Portland, Maine, 1888); Tuck, *Autobiographical Memoir;* Tuck to Hale, Feb. 18, 1845, N. P. Cram to Hale, Jan. 18, 1845, Hale Papers, NHHS; *Patriot,* Feb. 27, 1845; Sewell, *Hale,* pp. 62–63.

15. S. N. Cochrane to Hale, Jan. 19, 1845, J. C. Hammond to Hale, Jan. 28, 1845, Edmund Chadwick to Hale, Jan. 21, 1845, N. R. Lang to Hale, Feb. 8, 1845, James Hill to Hale, Mar. 13, 1845, Asa Davis to Hale, June 6, 1845; Sewell, *Hale,* p. 65; *Patriot,* Mar. 20, April 3, 1845; Horace E. Scudder, ed., *The Complete Poems of John Greenleaf Whittier* (Boston, 1892), p. 293.

part in the movement had various reasons for breaking with the Democratic Party. Some, like Tuck and Hayes, were highly moral men, earnestly opposed to slavery; others felt that they could advance their political careers more rapidly outside the old party; still others were revolting against the Concord Regency. Most independent Democrats came from southeastern New Hampshire or the north country, regions that had often rebelled against Hill. Many had been locofocos. The committed radicals, frustrated as Pierce and the others began to give way on railroads and banks, were ready to adopt the antislavery movement as another crusade. Lukewarm radicals saw the political possibilities in the movement. Independent Democrats were more likely to be rebellious Democrats than devoted antislavery advocates. But they succeeded in splitting a state organization that had been loyal to the South.[16]

The March election of 1845 was the last election in which the New Hampshire voters elected Congressmen on a general ticket. The next time they would be chosen by districts. Both the Whigs and the Democrats printed ballots listing their four candidates for the House of Representatives, and voters selected one ballot or the other at the polls. The Independent Democrats prepared a third ballot with the names of three of the regular Democratic candidates, but with Hale's name in place of John Woodbury. The Abolitionist Party also put up some candidates. There were some false ballots and much confusion. Efforts were made to obtain Whig support for Hale, but none of the Whig candidates for Congress stepped down.

Pierce knew that in a close election Hale might prevent Woodbury from getting a majority and thereby force another election in September. Ela later described to Hale the way Pierce and the

16. Arthur Schlesinger suggests that a large number of Democrats, radical on economic issues, joined the antislavery movement. Some surely did—Hale, Tuck, Hayes, for example—but many others did not—Pierce, Hibbard, Woodbury, for example. Schlesinger, *Age of Jackson*, pp. 430–431, chap. 34. Letters in the Hale Papers at the New Hampshire Historical Society, dated Jan.–May, 1845, came from about thirty towns, half of them in the southeastern part of New Hampshire, principally, Dover, Portsmouth, Exeter. Hale Papers, NHHS. Hayes wrote Hale that the conservatives in the states were against him. Hayes to Hale, Jan. 25, 1845, Hale Papers, NHHS.

Concord Regency tried to secure a majority for Woodbury: "Baker and others stood at the outside door denouncing them [Hale supporters] as they handed out their votes. Allen and Carroll stood at the inside door to see that no man had a vote for you. Pierce stood at the point where the line formed to go up and vote, and Robinson stood close by the place where the ballots were taken. You will see by this what a man had to go through who voted against dictation." In spite of such tactics, Hale received enough votes across the state to hold Woodbury 827 votes short of the majority. Woodbury received 22,314 votes to 14,562 for the Whig candidate and 7,788 for Hale. As the stage driver from Conway told Tuck the day after the election, "there had been a *terrible Hale* Storm" in New Hampshire.[17]

Independent Democrats were elated. According to Ela, "the Dictators" had "received a lesson" they would not "soon forget." In Washington, Hill thought that Hale had done well to prevent Woodbury's election and feared that Hale would soon be elected United States Senator if not Congressman. Encouraged by Hale's showing, the Independent Democrats set up a newspaper in Manchester. In its first issue the *Independent Democrat* described Hale as a "Democrat of the Jefferson school," for New Hampshire Democrats still found it expedient to bow to Thomas Jefferson and the "spirit of '98." By midsummer the *Independent Democrat* had moved from Manchester to Concord, where it could more easily take part in party battles, and had accumulated 657 subscribers, half of them from the seacoast region.[18]

Hale took no direct part in the winter campaign; instead he

17. The Whig was Ichabod Goodwin. Joseph Cilley, an Abolitionist candidate, had 4,493 votes. Moses Norris, Mace Moulton, and James Johnson—all regular Democrats—won the other three seats. 23,141 votes were necessary for election. *Patriot*, Mar. 20, May 22, 1845; Sewell, *Hale*, pp. 66–67; Ela to Hale, Mar. 20, 1845, Tuck to Hale, Mar. 14, 1845, Hale Papers, NHHS. The Ela quotation is in a letter from Ela to Hale, Mar. 18, 1845, Hale Papers, NHHS.

18. Ela to Hale, Mar. 20, 1845, Tuck to Hale, Mar. 14, 1845, D. S. Palmer to Hale, April 13, 1845, R. C. Wetmore to Hale, June 22, July 25, 1845, Hayes to Hale, Mar. 20, 1845, Hale Papers, NHHS; *Patriot*, April 24, 1845; *Hill's Patriot*, May 8, 1845; G. J. Abbot to Hale, Mar. 6, 1845.

remained in Congress. When he returned to New Hampshire in April, he was not an abolitionist, but he was firmly opposed both to slavery and to its extension. In his first speech, at the Exeter Congregational Church on April 21, he accepted Tuck's advice. He stuck to the moral issue and gave a passionate two-hour denunciation of slavery. At the end he stated his belief in the "obligation of Christian morals" and cried that as "long as God occupied the throne of eternity," he would consider slavery a sin. Hayes later described "his imposing person, his sonorous voice, his genial face, his self-abandonment, and his honest sympathy with the masses." Hale was guided by moral and political motives as he sought reelection to Congress. He had changed dramatically from the young Jacksonian who had heckled Storrs in Dover a decade earlier. In May, as roads dried and the temperature climbed, he was stumping the state in earnest, from Portsmouth, to Lancaster, to Colebrook, to Bristol.[19]

Pierce fought to eliminate the threat that Hale posed to the Concord Regency. On June 5 the two former allies met in debate at the Old North Church in Concord. Hale, who spoke first, began by stressing morality and avoiding politics. But Pierce and Carroll were in the front row, and before long Hale was casting "withering glances" in their direction. Crude shouts from the crowd reminded him that office as well as morality was at stake. Soon he was on the attack, charging Pierce and the regulars of disloyalty in abandoning Van Buren for Polk. Southerners were too sure of New Hampshire, he said, too certain that her Congressmen would support slavery. He called on Democrats to break

19. The quotation from Hale's Exeter speech is taken from the [Boston] *Post*, quoted in *The Liberator*, May 9, 1845. See also Sewell, *Hale*, p. 71. Sewell concludes that "Hale's antislavery convictions became stronger, more clearly defined," in the three years following his letter to his constituents in January 1845. Sewell, *Hale*, p. 87. His speeches in the spring of 1845 suggest that he was already committed to opposing slavery. The New Hampshire Independent Democratic movement, however, was more political than antislavery. John Hayes, *A Reminiscence of the Free-Soil Movement in New Hampshire, 1845* (Cambridge, Mass., 1885), pp. 41–42; *Patriot*, May 1, June 5, 1845; *Independent Democrat*, May 1, 8, 1845.

free from southern control and from the party dictation of Pierce and Hill.

In his reply Pierce spoke angrily, for Hale had hit a sore point in denouncing New Hampshire's subserviency to the South. At the start he drew a laugh by parodying Hale's swagger. He denied being for slavery and called the annexation of Texas a national necessity. After criticizing Hale for giving his January letter to the "Federalist" press, he concluded that Hale was misguided and disloyal, an Abolitionist and a Whig.

When the crowd in an uproar called on Hale to defend himself, he did so in an emotional final word. "I expected to be called ambitious," he said, "But, if . . . truth and duty are to be publicly held up to ridicule, . . . it matters little whether we are annexed to Texas or Texas is annexed to us . . . the measure of my ambition will be full, if, . . . when my wife and children shall repair to my grave, . . . they may read on my tombstone, 'He who lies beneath surrendered office, place, and power, rather than bow down and worship slavery.' "[20]

Independent Democrats were convinced that he had won. Hayes said years later that the debate made Pierce President and Hale Senator. James Peverly praised Hale for not returning Pierce's abuse and for brushing off Hill so easily. George C. Fogg congratulated him and reported that Hill himself had admitted that Pierce had failed to "touch Hale's main positions." But Independent Democrats Peverly and Fogg were not likely to tell their leader that he had lost, and Hill was angry at Pierce anyway. The September election would more accurately determine the winner.[21]

The "Hale storm" brought out democracy at its best. Hale appealed to the people; his followers went to the people. Pierce spoke out from platform and press. Partisans wrote hundreds of

20. *Patriot,* June 12, Sept. 11, 1845; *Manchester Democrat,* June 11, 1845; *Independent Democrat,* June 12, 1845; Sewell, *Hale,* pp. 72–74; Chandler, *Statue of Hale,* pp. 45–46.

21. Hayes, *Free-Soil Movement,* pp. 41–42; Peverly to Hale, June 9, 1845, Fogg to Hale, June 17, 1845, Hale Papers, NHHS.

letters. Politicians founded new newspapers and filled the columns of old ones. Citizens met in courthouses, churches, schoolhouses, town halls, and private homes. They signed petitions; they staged debates; and, finally, they voted. Just as during the early Jackson years, popular democracy was part of a way of life in New Hampshire. The *Patriot,* which had mailed out copies of Hill's speeches in 1828, sent out 10,000 copies of Pierce's reply to Hale in 1845. Robert C. Wetmore, editor of the *Independent Democrat,* complained that the Hale people should do more.[22]

All summer long Hale campaigned, speaking almost every day, back and forth across the state. Only a day after the Concord debate, he confronted Congressman Moses Norris, who had twice voted to annex Texas, before 150 people in the village of Pittsfield. At Moultonboro, next to Lake Winnipesaukee, he held a Fourth of July crowd for hours. He wound up the campaign at Bradford, only a few miles from Benjamin Pierce's old tavern, reminding his listeners that Congressmen were calling New Hampshire the "South Carolina of the North." On September 23 Hale incréased his vote to 8,355, but he still ran third behind Woodbury, with 18,010 votes, and Ichabod Goodwin with 10,155. No one was elected. A third election in November still failed to produce a majority. Regular Democrats could not elect the fourth Congressman, but neither could Whigs or Independent Democrats, unless they united.[23]

From the moment Hale sent his letter in January, Whigs, Independent Democrats, and Abolitionists had been aware that alliance might mean victory, but no one was willing to take the first step. Independent Democrats might be against Pierce, but supporting a Whig was something else. The Whig press applauded Hale, but warned its readers to vote Whig. Even the tiny Abolitionist Party insisted on keeping its own identity. But after three

22. Wetmore to Hale, July 25, 1845, Hale Papers, NHHS.
23. In November Woodbury had about 20,000 votes, Goodwin about 12,000, Hale about 10,000. *Patriot,* June 12, Sept. 19, Oct. 2, Dec. 4, 1845; Sewell, *Hale,* p. 75.

unsuccessful elections, the three parties began to edge closer. In January 1846, Independent Democrats and Abolitionists held simultaneous conventions in Concord, and both nominated Nathaniel S. Berry of Hebron for governor. In February Dudley S. Palmer of the Whigs went on a trip to organize Whigs, Independent Democrats, and Liberty Party men against the Democrats. Gradually a covert alliance began to develop. In any given town Whigs and Independent Democrats would support a Whig for one job while agreeing on an Independent Democrat for another. But it was all done secretly for fear that an open movement would backfire and allow Woodbury to win his majority.[24]

All parties campaigned vigorously for the March election. On one trip through Franconia Notch in the White Mountains, Hale "rode all night till 2 in the morning, most of the time in an open sleigh." He would have "suffered much with the cold had it not been for . . . the stage proprietor who kindly took a new Buffalo skin and wrapped" him up in it. Aware of the developing alliance, Pierce fought against what he called the "Federalist" coalition. In March Woodbury failed for the fourth time to get a majority. Nor did any one gain a majority in the vote for governor, as Jared Williams, Democrat, had a plurality over Anthony Colby, Whig, and Nathaniel Berry, Independent Democrat and Abolitionist. Hale was elected to the lower house of the state legislature.[25]

During the spring Hale considered several possible deals. Palmer wanted to send Hale to the United States Senate and elect Colby governor. The Whigs, added Palmer, would go as far on an antislavery resolution as the Abolitionists or the Independent

24. Alliance was difficult. In November the *New Hampshire Gazette* quoted an article from the *Dover Gazette,* warning that if Whigs voted for Hale, enough Independent Democrats would desert him to give the election to Woodbury. *Gazette,* Nov. 11, 1845. *Patriot,* Jan. 22, 1846; D. S. Palmer to Hale, Feb. 2, 1846, Amos Tuck to Hale, Feb. 2, 1846, Hale Papers, NHHS; Sewell, *Hale,* p. 77.

25. Hale to Mrs. Lucy Hale, Feb. 27, 1846, Hale Papers, NHHS; Sewell, *Hale,* p. 78; *Patriot,* Mar. 19, 1846; *Hill's Patriot,* Mar. 19, 1846; *Independent Democrat,* Mar. 26, 1846; *New Hampshire Manual 1891,* p. 154. There were 568 scattering votes.

Democrats. In return the latter must support a law granting limited liability. Several other Whigs hinted that Hale could become Senator if he would promise to favor the protective tariff. Hale made no commitments.[26]

When the legislature convened in June, the allies united sufficiently to elect Hale speaker of the House. But Abolitionists would not vote for Colby for governor, and some Whigs would not agree on Hale for the Senate. The Independent Democrats, who held the balance of power, were making hard demands: They wanted the speaker of the House and secretary of state. On Friday the House and Senate met together and chose Colby over Williams for governor by ten votes. Four days later they elected Hale to the United States Senate to start in December 1847, with 139 votes in the House for Hale to 119 for Democrat Harry Hibbard. The legislature also made Independent Democrats Peverly and Fogg state treasurer and secretary of state.[27]

The outbreak of war with Mexico, which came at about the same time that Whigs and Independent Democrats were seizing power in New Hampshire, widened the gap in the Democratic Party. Late in June, Hale stepped down from the speaker's chair to deliver what Democrats described as a "harangue" against the war. Independent Democrats and Whigs forced the legislature to accept Hale's resolution denouncing the war. The resolution also condemned the annexation of Texas, opposed the extension of slavery into any land acquired from Mexico, and called for the abolition of slavery in the District of Columbia.[28]

The legislative session of 1846 was a disaster for the Democratic Party. The united opposition had elected Colby governor and

26. Palmer to Hale, Mar. 21, 1846, Prentiss to Hale, Mar. 15, 1846, Fogg to Hale, April 29, 1846, Washington Hunt to Hale, June 3, 1846, Hale Papers, NHHS. Democratic efforts to prevent the Whig-Independent Democratic coalition failed. Sewell, *Hale*, p. 80.

27. *Manchester Democrat*, June 3, 24, 1846; *Independent Democrat*, June 4, 1846; *Patriot*, June 11, 1846.

28. *Statesman*, June 26, 1846; *Independent Democrat*, May 21, 1846; *Manchester Democrat*, June 24, 1846; *Patriot*, June 25, 1846, Sewell, *Hale*, pp. 83–84.

Hale United States Senator. It had passed resolutions against slavery and the Mexican War. It had repealed the locofoco anti-corporation laws and had chartered dozens of new businesses. In each case the regular Democrats had lost. As the session came to a close in July, the Concord Regency faced the problem of reuniting the party.

Pierce tried to put the pieces together. At a giant rally held on a crisp October morning in the state house yard, the Democrats tried to reconcile their differences. It was not easy because Independent Democrats were meeting simultaneously at the Old North Church. Hale and 200 of his followers soon crept into the rear of the state house and climbed up to a balcony, where Hale tried to address the Democrats below, only to be shouted down by the crowd. Whenever Pierce spoke, the editor of the *Granite Freeman* shouted "gag, gag," and Governor Colby's son ran about making as much disturbance as possible. It was such a wild assembly that the Whig *Statesman* called it "Jacobin Democracy" at its worst.[29]

The battle in the state house yard led to a parliamentary battle over resolutions. George Barstow, a lawyer in Manchester who was sympathetic toward Hale, called on the Democratic Party to oppose "all wars of conquest," demanded "firm resistance to the further extension of slavery," and denounced the "slave party" in the South. He also proposed that California be annexed without slavery and insisted that slavery be abolished in 'the District of Columbia. Bidding for locofoco support, Barstow proposed that the people be allowed to alter the charters of all corporations. Pierce, Hibbard, and Atherton then spoke against Barstow's resolutions. Barstow kept trying to answer, but the crowd hooted him and his resolutions down. In a move for party harmony, however, the delegates later voted to support Congressman David Wilmot's famous proviso, which opposed slavery in the land to be acquired from Mexico.[30]

29. The description of the rally is in *Patriot,* Oct. 22, 1846. The *Statesman* quotation is in *ibid.,* Oct. 29, 1846.

30. *Ibid.,* Oct. 22, 1846.

Democrats united sufficiently in March 1847 to elect Jared Williams governor and to gain control of the legislature—both by narrow margins. They were able to pass resolutions in favor of the Mexican War in June. But the Congressional delegation was divided three ways. In addition to regular Democrats James Johnson of Bath and Charles Peaslee of Concord, Independent Democrat Amos Tuck and Whig James Wilson were also sent to Washington.[31]

For the next few years Democrats tried to hold a middle ground on slavery. In 1848 the *Patriot* agreed with Lewis Cass that since California and New Mexico were already free under Mexican law, Congress should not bother to legislate there on slavery. In the legislature that December, Democrats pushed through another resolution, justifying the Mexican War. After denouncing Daniel Webster for being too soft on slavery and William H. Seward for being too hard, the *Patriot* came out in support of the Compromise of 1850.[32]

But the precarious balance was almost upset by the election that followed the Compromise. The party in 1850 nominated John Atwood of Manchester for governor to run in March of 1851. Atwood supported the Compromise, but like many Democrats in southeastern New Hampshire he was sympathetic with the Free Soil (Independent Democratic) position. The Democratic consensus was threatened in December 1850 when Free Soilers published a letter from the candidate attacking the Fugitive Slave Act. Pierce called him to Concord to discuss the matter. Atwood worked all day, rode in the cold twenty miles, and arrived exhausted. Pierce immediately produced a letter that he had written himself, in which Atwood retracted his opposition to the Fugitive Slave Act. Atwood signed it and went to bed. On the way back the next morning he decided to retract the retraction

31. *Ibid.*, Mar. 12, 18, 25, April 8, July 15, 1847; Sewell, *Hale,* p. 87; Frank L. Leidtker, "Political Development in New Hampshire from the Revolution to 1850," unpublished thesis, University of New Hampshire, 1952, pp. 122–126.
32. *Patriot,* Oct. 12, Dec. 21, 1848, June 21, 1849, Mar. 14, April 18, May 2, 23, Nov. 7, 1850.

but discovered on arrival in Manchester that the *Patriot* had already published his letter. Now the Free Soil side demanded meetings with Atwood and on December 23 published a letter announcing that he was still opposed to the Fugitive Slave Act. Caught between two forces, on Christmas Day he wrote a letter to Pierce explaining that he had agreed to the retraction only to stop a party split. "Am I to be sacrificed," he cried, "after having staked my all to prevent the ruin of the party?" The answer was yes.

All during January the New Hampshire press was full of the incident. Atwood finally decided that he could accept the Fugitive Slave Act but only in the context of the Compromise and only because the alternative was nullification. During January, thirty-two separate Democratic conventions voted on the controversy; all agreed that there should be no further "agitation" over slavery. On January 30 the *Patriot* condemned Atwood for "renewing the dangerous and senseless agitation" and for making slavery an "issue" and a "test." With this support Pierce called a party convention for Concord in February; by an almost unanimous vote Samuel Dinsmoor, son of old Samuel Dinsmoor, replaced Atwood at the head of the Democratic ticket. Atwood decided to run anyway as a Free Soil candidate.[33]

The Democrats were unable to secure a majority in the March election, for the combined total of Atwood's vote and the Whig vote was almost 31,000 compared to barely 27,000 for Dinsmoor. But the legislature chose Dinsmoor governor in June, and Pierce had succeeded in getting his man elected.[34]

The Slavery War between 1843 and 1851 pointed to the end for the Democratic Party in New Hampshire. Even though Pierce had held his party together, New Hampshire Jacksonians were finding it harder and harder to maintain their old policy of defending slavery. A few years later as President, Pierce would

33. *Ibid.*, Nov. 7, 30, Dec. 26, 1850, Jan. 2, 16, 23, 30, Feb. 6, 13, 20, 27, Mar. 6, 1851.

34. Nichols, *Pierce*, pp. 182–185; *Patriot*, Mar. 27, June 12, 1851; *New Hampshire Manual 1891*, p. 155.

pay the penalty for supporting the slavery interest. During the 1840's the Slavery War had been a complex struggle in which dissident Democrats, frustrated Whigs, and idealistic Abolitionists drew together to challenge the Democratic Party. Although they disagreed on economic and slavery questions, Independent Democrats and Whigs prepared the way for the Republican Party in New Hampshire. The Railroad War had created rifts in the Democratic Party of Franklin Pierce; the Slavery War had widened those rifts. The crisis of the 1850's would bring the party down.

X

Presidential Politics and the
Passing of a Generation, 1843-1851

As New Hampshire Democrats fought the Railroad War and the Slavery War, Levi Woodbury was drawn into presidential politics. A leading Democrat from New England, Woodbury had the geographic background to make him a useful vice-presidential running mate for a southern candidate. Furthermore, he had always been on good terms with southerners. He had served as Secretary of the Navy and as Secretary of the Treasury, and he carried impressive credentials from the party battles of the Jackson and Van Buren years. The combination gained him both presidential and vice-presidential attention in 1844 and 1848. He was within striking distance of the presidency when he died in 1851.

Van Buren kept good track of Woodbury in the two years before the Democratic convention of 1844. Former Secretary of War Joel R. Poinsett wrote in June of 1842 that John C. Calhoun was dangling the vice-presidency in front of Silas Wright and Woodbury. "The Devil" had taken them to a "lofty mountain," Poinsett reported, and had tempted them if they "would fall down and worship John C. Calhoun." Poinsett wrote again in September that Thomas Hart Benton thought that Woodbury might side with Calhoun. Two months later George Bancroft advised that Woodbury "loves himself most" but "despises" Lewis Cass. Toward the end of 1842 Henry D. Gilpin, who had briefly been Attorney General, confided that he had sounded out Woodbury on the presidency, but that "not a muscle" of his "countenance throbbed." As always Woodbury was hard to fathom. When he himself wrote Van Buren in January 1843, he confined his remarks to financial matters.[1]

Backing for Woodbury grew in New Hampshire, where first locofocos and then conservatives in 1843 nominated him for Vice-President. Bancroft accused him of enacting "the part of the ultra-radical to blind the people" and labeled his instincts "selfish," his character "terribly, terribly treacherous." He warned Van Buren that Woodbury sought "to divert the voice of New Hampshire from its natural [Van Buren] tones" and said that parts of New England were already under Woodbury's sway. Bancroft also reported accurately that Woodbury had written the New Hampshire Democratic resolution nominating him for President after an effort to nominate Van Buren collapsed. In his own diary Woodbury confided that he "made speeches" at the convention "to advance [his] wishes as to the Presidential election" and admitted that he had gone against his own "sense of delicacy." He had his eye on the White House.[2]

In the spring and summer of 1843 reports continued to come in to Van Buren about Woodbury. Both Gideon Welles and Gilpin reassured Van Buren that he had little to fear. According to Welles, Woodbury was "as timid" as he was "ambitious," and Gilpin said flatly that Woodbury's move was not successful. But Benjamin V. French reported that in Boston, J. O. Barnes was

1. J. R. Poinsett to Van Buren, June 5, Sept. 13, 1842, Bancroft to Van Buren, Nov. 23, 1842, H. D. Gilpin to Van Buren, Dec. 14, 1842, Woodbury to Van Buren, Jan. 18, 1843, Van Buren Papers, LC.
2. Samuel Cushman to Woodbury, Jan. 23, 1843; clipping from Portsmouth *Mercury*, c. Jan. 1844, Woodbury Papers, LC; *Hill's Patriot*, Jan. 16, 23, 1843; Bancroft to Van Buren, Nov. 23, 1842, Van Buren Papers, LC; Bancroft to Van Buren, May 23, June 6, 12, 22, 1843, Massachusetts Historical Society, *Proceedings*, 42 (1909), 394–408; "Political Memoranda of Levi Woodbury," Blair Family Papers, LC.

working for his brother-in-law Woodbury as well as for Tyler and Calhoun. After Woodbury spoke at one meeting, Hill and David Henshaw attacked Van Buren, while Robert Rantoul and Marcus Morton defended the Little Magician.[3]

Van Buren's good friend Francis Preston Blair was also worried about Woodbury's opposition to Van Buren. In January 1843, he wrote General Jackson that "Mr. Van Buren's Yankee friends Woodbury and Kendall will be very apt to give him the slip like the Yankee Hill unless the New York Star shall be very much in the ascendant when the trial comes before the convention." Jackson replied in July that Van Buren would overcome the opposition. In the end, he said, New Hampshire and Maine would go for Van Buren and carry Massachusetts and Connecticut with them. By the spring of 1844 Van Buren's hesitation on the question of annexing Texas had given Jackson second thoughts and the New Yorkers knew it. Wright wrote Hill asking him to get Jackson to come out strongly for Van Buren. "Set the Old Man right," he pleaded. Hill copied part of Wright's letter and sent it to the Hermitage with the comment: "I judge the New Yorkers don't care so much about getting a President as they do about forcing a candidate." Hill was hardly "setting the Old Man right."[4]

As the convention approached, the Texas issue became Van Buren's undoing. Jackson deserted Van Buren and wrote: "The cry now is no man who will not pledge himself for speedy annexation." As alternatives he suggested Wright, Buchanan, and Woodbury. George Bancroft wailed that Massachusetts Democrats would "adopt any Northern man" who favored the annexa-

3. Gideon Welles to Van Buren, April 29, 1843, H. D. Gilpin to Van Buren, June 15, 1843, Silas Wright to Van Buren, June 19, 1843, Benjamin V. French to Van Buren, Sept. 12, 1843, Van Buren Papers, LC; Van Buren to Bancroft, Oct. 7, 1843, Massachusetts Historical Society, *Proceedings*, 42 (1909), 415; Mark A. DeWolfe Howe, *Life and Letters of George Bancroft* (New York, 1908), I, 210, 246.

4. Blair to Jackson, Jan. 29, 1843, Jackson to Blair, July 14, 1843, Jackson to Van Buren, Nov. 29, 1843, Bassett, *Correspondence of Jackson*, VI, 186, 223, 245–246. For the Wright and Hill quotations, see Buell, *Jackson*, II, 404–405.

tion of Texas, "be it Cass! . . . or Heaven save the mark, Levi Woodbury!!!" At the same time, Azariah Flagg warned Van Buren that Cass and Woodbury were "determined to fish for immortality in the Texas pool." Woodbury had little chance for the presidential nomination, but with his strong northern and southern support he was a likely vice-presidential candidate.[5]

New Hampshire Democrats were prominent as the party gathered in Baltimore. Not only was Woodbury a candidate but Hubbard and Henry Carroll were vice-president and secretary of the convention. On the first two ballots New Hampshire gave its six votes to Van Buren, but on the third ballot two went to Woodbury. Since no Woodbury movement developed, the delegation then split its vote between Van Buren and James Buchanan on ballots four through seven. At adjournment time Lewis Cass with 123 votes, and Van Buren with 99, had the lead; but neither seemed likely to get the necessary two-thirds vote.[6]

During the night, Bancroft, Gideon J. Pillow of Tennessee, and others planned the shift to James K. Polk. Bancroft consulted Carroll and Hubbard because New Hampshire voted second on every ballot and could start a swing. Pillow promised that if New Hampshire and Massachusetts led off he could deliver the votes of Mississippi, Alabama, and Tennessee. "You should have heard the cheers," Bancroft wrote later, as Hubbard and he "announced the whole vote" of New Hampshire and "the majority of Massachusetts" for Polk. At the end of the eighth ballot, Polk with forty-four votes stood third.[7]

Before the ninth ballot began, Hubbard called the convention to order and spoke briefly for Polk and party harmony. When the balloting reached Virginia, Polk had forged ahead. Announcing Virginia's vote for Polk, former Senator William H. Roane, a Cass man, then reached across the stage to shake hands with

5. Jackson to F. P. Blair, May 11, 1844, Bassett, *Correspondence of Jackson*, VI, 286; Bancroft to Van Buren, May 23, 1844, Howe, *Bancroft*, I, 250; Flagg to Van Buren, May 23, 1844, Van Buren Papers, LC.
6. *Patriot*, June 6, 1844.
7. *Ibid.*; Howe, *Bancroft*, I, 252–254.

Hubbard, who had been for Woodbury or Van Buren. The handshake symbolized party unity for Polk. Under the stands the New York delegation decided that all was lost and sent up word that it would go for Polk. He was soon nominated.[8]

In the hours and months that followed Senator Woodbury maneuvered for a new position. After Wright turned down the vice-presidency, Woodbury had his chance. On the first ballot he was second only to John Fairfield of Maine, but on the next, delegates shifted to George Dallas of Pennsylvania, who won the nomination by a landslide. Woodbury helped carry New Hampshire for Polk in the fall and waited to hear what the new President had to offer. Bancroft commented acidly that Woodbury had the "condescension" to think he would be Secretary of State and suggested that he be minister to England. Polk finally appointed him to the Supreme Court.[9]

By defending the commerce power of the states, Woodbury made the Taney Court even more Jacksonian than it had been. In the License Cases (1847) he argued that individual states could restrict the sale of liquor within their boundaries. Although the majority in the Passenger Cases (1849) repudiated New York and Massachusetts laws taxing immigration, Woodbury spoke for the minority in an opinion that went further than that of any other justice in defending state rights. He argued that even though the commerce clause gave the federal government certain powers, it did not deny the authority of the states. He concluded in Jacksonian style that the federal government had become too powerful, that where doubt existed, the concurrent power of the states should be maintained.[10]

8. Benjamin F. Butler to Van Buren, May 31, 1844, John L. O'Sullivan to Van Buren, May 29, 1844, Van Buren Papers, LC; John A. Garraty, *Silas Wright* (New York, 1949), p. 276; *Niles' Register*, 66 (1844), 217.

9. *Patriot*, June 6, 1844; Bancroft to Van Buren, Jan. 22, 1845, Massachusetts Historical Society, *Proceedings*, 43 (1909), 435; C. W. Woodbury to Levi Woodbury, April 21, 1845, Woodbury Papers, LC.

10. Woodbury's opinions in the License Cases (*Thurlow v. Massachusetts, Fletcher v. Rhode Island,* and *Pierce v. New Hampshire*) are to be found in 5 Howard 618–631. His opinions in the Passenger Cases (*Norris v. City of Boston* and *Smith v. Turner*) are in 7 Howard 518–573.

Woodbury also defended the state's right to control corporations even at the risk of violating an original charter. In *West River Bridge v. Dix* (1848) he argued that the state could build a public highway and bridge even though it might interfere with the rights of an existing toll bridge. Using the distinction that he had helped create during the locofoco debates in New Hampshire, Woodbury said that the state could take land by eminent domain whenever the user was to be the public or a public institution. Woodbury was unwilling to resort to the contract clause to defend property. He adhered to his state rights position in *Waring v. Clark* (1847) when he gave the state of Louisiana jurisdiction over the collision of two ships on the Mississippi River even though the accident was in tidewater.[11]

Like many Jacksonians, Woodbury defended the South on the slavery issue. He spoke for the Court in *Jones v. Van Zandt* (1847), in which William H. Seward and Salmon Chase for the plaintiff challenged the Fugitive Slave Act. Slavery, said Woodbury, was a political matter for the voters in each state to decide. As long as it existed, the federal government had the right to enforce the return of fugitive slaves.[12]

In *Luther v. Borden* (1849) Woodbury sided with the rebels in the Dorr Rebellion. Thomas Dorr and his followers had called a revolutionary convention in 1841 to widen suffrage in Rhode Island by amending the state constitution. When this failed, they set up their own unofficial legislature. After the official state government used martial law to quell the uprising, one of Dorr's men sued a member of the original legislature for breaking and entering. Following state rights, Woodbury and the majority decided that the Supreme Court lacked jurisdiction to determine the legitimate legislature. But although the majority stopped there and gave Dorr's side no satisfaction, Woodbury went further, holding that Rhode Island had no right to impose martial law against Dorr.[13]

11. Woodbury, *Writings*, II, 57–69, 106–154, 171–206, 275–284; West River Bridge Case, 6 Howard 539–549; *Waring v. Clark*, 5 Howard 467–503.
12. 5 Howard 223–232.
13. Woodbury, *Writings*, II, 70–105; 7 Howard 48–88.

In Woodbury, Jacksonian Democracy had a champion on the bench. He stood for the public welfare. He preferred state rights to federal rights. Since he insisted on a strict interpretation of the Constitution, he narrowly defined the contract and commerce clauses. Like many Jacksonians, he had more confidence in legislatures than in courts. He would widen democracy but would leave slavery up to the states.

The movement to make Woodbury President revived in the spring of 1848. Starting in Coos County, the boom spread to Concord, where the *Patriot* picked it up; to Boston, where members of the Massachusetts legislature nominated him; to South Carolina, where Congressman Robert B. Rhett was for him; and all the way to Alabama, where former Congressman William L. Yancey wrote that he might back Woodbury. In Maine, Hannibal Hamlin, an antislavery Democrat, called Woodbury "a wheelhorse of the Democracy," and supported his nomination. From the Mississippi Valley came word that Illinois and Missouri would vote for him on the first ballot. When Congressman Howell Cobb of Georgia wrote temptingly that the South would accept a northerner, Woodbury sent Yancey a carefully worded letter leaving the door open to the nomination. Harry Hibbard advised him to play up to Yancey by quietly defending slavery in the territories. On the first day of the Democratic convention, Hibbard reported that Woodbury's stock was rising.[14]

It did not rise high enough. Although New Hampshire voted for Woodbury on each ballot and votes came from South Carolina and Alabama, Woodbury was second to Cass, who was nominated on the fourth ballot. But defeat in November put Cass out of the way, and anyone who could combine the support

14. Patriot, April 6, 13, 1848; C. L. Woodbury to Levi Woodbury, Mar. 8, 1848, Edmund Burke to Woodbury, April 24, 1848, Yancey to Woodbury, Mar. 10, 1848, Fred Clapp to A. H. H. Clapp, April 25, 1848, McLane to Woodbury, April 30, 1848, Cobb to John G. Holland, May 11, 1848, Woodbury to Yancey, May 15, 1848, Hibbard to Woodbury, May 19, May 22, 1848, Woodbury Papers, LC; Charles E. Hamlin, *The Life and Times of Hannibal Hamlin* (Cambridge, Mass., 1899), pp. 179–180.

of Hibbard and Hamlin of the North with that of Yancey and Rhett of the South was in a strong position for 1852.[15]

Charles Peaslee was looking ahead to 1852 when he spoke for Woodbury at the Democratic convention in Concord in June 1851. Citing the loyalty of New Hampshire soldiers at Bunker Hill and Saratoga and the loyalty of New Hampshire Democrats in the disastrous election of 1840, he shouted that the state was due a President. He traced the Justice's career from the Hillsborough Resolves in 1812 to the Bank War and on to the Supreme Court. When Peaslee finished, the convention again nominated Woodbury for President. Other Democrats fell in line. Blair felt that Woodbury's nomination was certain, while Benton, Hamlin, and others were pushing him as a unifier on "the middle ground." Hamlin convinced New Englanders that Woodbury would veto any attempt to extend slavery to the territories. Benton told Hamlin that they needed a newspaper in Washington to reply to the "venomous attacks" on Woodbury in the Whig press but reported that New York was safe and that he was winning the West over to Woodbury.[16]

Woodbury might easily have been the Democratic candidate in 1852, for the party needed a moderate old Jacksonian to regain the White House. Woodbury had always held the middle ground in the party: from the early days when he stood between Van Buren and Calhoun, to the Railroad War when each side claimed him, to the fight over slavery in which he was able to satisfy the large majority of both northerners and southerners. Not a great man, but capable and hard-working, he might have avoided many of the pitfalls that beset Pierce and Buchanan in the White

15. *Patriot*, June 1, 1848.
16. Hildreth M. Allison, "Honorable Levi Woodbury: Presidential Timber," *Historical New Hampshire*, 23 (Autumn 1968), 3–18; Charles H. Peaslee, *Speech at the Democratic State Convention Held at Concord, June 11th, 1851* (n.p., n.d.); *Patriot*, June 19, 1851; Hamlin, *Hamlin*, pp. 252–255; Nathaniel Blair to Colonel Isaac O. Barnes, Feb. 18, 1851, Gustavus Vasa Fox Papers, Naval History Society Collection, New-York Historical Society. Benton reported that he was talking up Woodbury to his "friends in the West, and always with the best effect." Hamlin, *Hamlin*, p. 253.

House. And, as he was well aware, the presidency would have been a fitting climax for a distinguished career. But death ended that dream on September 4, 1851. Benton wrote that it "was a great shock to us personally as well as politically." He knew of no one who had all of Woodbury's qualities. The *Patriot* stole a phrase of Benton's when it commented that the "rock of New England Democracy" was dead.[17]

A few months earlier death had also removed Hill. Though he was plagued increasingly by asthma and catarrh, his last few years were satisfying and nostalgic. In March of 1845 he paid his last visit to Andrew Jackson. After a long, tiring journey—he was ill during the trip—Hill rested for a few days at Nashville before sending a note to Jackson at the Hermitage. When he finally arrived, he found the Old General sitting in an easy chair surrounded by writing materials, the Bible, a hymnal, and several newspapers. Short of breath and very weak, he was nonetheless alert and much interested in political events, particularly the annexation of Texas. Hill spent four pleasant days with Jackson.[18]

After 1845, Hill lived mostly in Washington, but he returned to New Hampshire occasionally when party or business called. He came to Concord in 1846 for the October rally, and in 1847 —his reconciliation with Pierce complete—he gave up publication of *Hill's Patriot*. By 1850 Hill and the *New Hampshire Patriot* had come to an understanding with Webster. When Webster made a short speech on the opening of the Northern Railroad, the *Patriot* commended him for his "plain, common sense remarks," and reminded its readers that he still owned his old New Hampshire farm. In 1850 Hill congratulated Webster on the "great principles" of his seventh of March speech in support of the Compromise, and the Senator graciously replied that Hill's

17. Benton to Isaac O. Barnes, Sept. 29, 1851, Fox Papers, New-York Historical Society; *Patriot*, Sept. 10, 1851.
18. Hill described his visit in a letter to *Hill's Patriot*, which was reprinted in the *Daily Madisonian*, Mar. 29, 1845.

letter was "gratifying." Hill died of asthma on March 22, 1851, in Washington.[19]

A whole generation of politicians died with Hill and Woodbury: Jackson in 1845, Adams in 1848, Calhoun in 1850, Webster and Clay in 1852. In New Hampshire, Morril, Plumer, and Samuel Bell of the opposition died in 1849 and 1850. Democrats Badger, Atherton, Norris and Hubbard followed by 1857. In the summer of 1851—between the deaths of Hill and Woodbury—a fire swept through Main Street in Concord destroying the Eagle Hotel and Coffee House. The demise of the Eagle, where Jackson had stayed in 1833 and where many party meetings had taken place, symbolized the passing of the generation and the end of the Jacksonian era in New Hampshire.

With the old generation gone, Franklin Pierce was in a strong position. In New Hampshire he had ousted Atwood and had made Dinsmoor governor. Nationally he had few enemies, and, like Woodbury before him, occupied the center of the Democratic Party. Antislavery Democrats did not trust him, but he and his followers now opposed the extension of slavery. A doughface like Woodbury, Pierce had cultivated many southern friends. Some politicians compared him with Jackson. He stood four-square for the Union; he had fought in the Mexican War. Like Jackson, he had resigned from the Senate to continue his law career. Franklin Pierce was a faded image of Jackson, but the epithet "Young Hickory" was useful in politics, and in the 1850's faded images were good enough.

After Woodbury's death, his supporters considered Benton, Blair, and Sam Houston for their presidential candidate, but finally settled on General William O. Butler of Kentucky, who had been the Democratic vice-presidential candidate in 1848. Harry Hibbard, Charles Peaslee, and John Hatch George of New Hampshire hoped to persuade Butler to take Pierce as Vice-President. When the Butler movement foundered, Edmund

19. *Patriot*, Sept. 2, 1847, Oct. 24, 1850, Mar. 27, April 3, 1851.

Burke and Benjamin French convinced Pierce to try for the presidential nomination. From all over New Hampshire, Jacksonians worked to help send Pierce to the White House: Burke and Hibbard from the Connecticut River Valley; Peaslee and George of Concord; Atherton of Amherst; and Norris of Pittsfield. New Englanders joined—Caleb Cushing and Benjamin F. Hallett of Massachusetts—and others more distant such as Gideon Pillow of Tennessee. Pierce kept out of sight. When asked about slavery, he simply said that he favored the Compromise of 1850.[20]

At the convention Pierce's managers decided to spread his votes between Cass and Buchanan until a deadlock developed. When after thirty-four ballots southerners despaired of nominating Buchanan, some of them shifted to Pierce. He had 15 votes on the thirty-fifth ballot, 55 on the forty-eighth, and 282 and the nomination on the forty-ninth ballot.[21]

On August 4 the Democratic Party held a large rally at the old Pierce Homestead in Hillsborough. Railroad rates in several states were reduced to get as many there as possible. All day long, 25,000 listened on the side of a hill to Democratic speeches and ate heartily from a giant barbecue. In November 1852, Pierce was elected President over General Winfield Scott. New Hampshire voted 28,884 for Pierce, 15,540 for Scott, and 6,568 for John Parker Hale, who was the Free Soil candidate.[22]

The momentum of Pierce's victory helped Democrats carry New Hampshire in 1853 and 1854, but in 1855 the anti-immigrant Know Nothing movement swept them out of office. Neither before nor after the Civil War could the party regain its dominant position as the state became a Republican stronghold. It was ironic that Jacksonian Democracy came to an end in the state shortly after a presidential election in which two New Hampshire

20. Roy Nichols, *The Democratic Machine, 1850–1854* (New York, 1923), pp. 70, 83, 120–128; Nichols, *Pierce*, pp. 189–199; Hamlin, *Hamlin*, p. 257; Allan Nevins, *Ordeal of the Union* (New York, 1947), II, 17.

21. *Patriot*, June 9, 1852; Nevins, *Ordeal*, II, 20; Nichols, *Pierce*, p. 203.

22. *Patriot*, Aug. 25, 1852; *New Hampshire Manual 1891*, p. 159.

Jacksonians were on the ballot and one was elected. It was not, however, really surprising. The rising controversy over slavery in the territories created a new political situation and brought on a new political party system. Since the old Jacksonian program was not adequate for the new problems, the party failed both in New Hampshire and in Washington.[23]

23. *Patriot,* Sept. 9, 1852, Mar. 16, June 22, Nov. 23, 1853, April 5, 1854, Jan. 17, 24, Feb. 7, April 4, 1855, Nov. 12, 1856; *New Hampshire Manual 1891,* p. 155; Petersen, *History of Elections,* p. 143; Nichols, *Democratic Machine,* pp. 169–170, 201.

Conclusion

The political history of New Hampshire between the War of 1812 and the Mexican War is largely the history of Jacksonian Democracy. From the fight over Dartmouth College, on through the Bank War and the Railroad War, the concept of Jacksonian Democracy gives meaning to the political events. In New Hampshire, as across the nation, Jacksonian Democracy was a complex phenomenon, not just a simple lower-class, democratic movement. Jacksonians in New Hampshire included all types of men, from the urbane lawyer Levi Woodbury to the poor farmers in the town of Jackson, who voted unanimously for the Old Hero. And yet they all stood for democratic economic and political principles. They fought Dartmouth College for the same reason that they opposed the Bank of the United States and the railroads: They believed that they were defending the public against private privilege. At times their rhetoric exceeded the proportions of the issues, but the Jacksonians cared about the issues. No one cared more than Isaac Hill, who was as complex as the movement he personified. Aggressive and acquisitive, he rose from poor boy to affluent entrepreneur as he fought the Jacksonian battles. There were limits to Jacksonian Democracy; Hill, Woodbury, and Franklin Pierce fought for the plain men of the North, but they ignored the plain slaves in the South. When Hill and Woodbury died in 1851, they left Pierce to face a political crisis, in which northerners refused to accept the extension of slavery. As Pierce applied old formulas to new problems, Jacksonian Democracy fell apart in New Hampshire and in the nation.

Appendix

Bibliography

Index

Appendix

Voting Statistics for

the Presidential Election of

1832 in New Hampshire

Table A. Distribution of Votes

Towns	Voting for Clay	Voting for Jackson	Tied	Total
Number	63	142	4	209
Percent	30	68	2	100
	Voting 67–100% for Clay	Voting 51–66% for Clay	Voting 51–66% for Jackson	Voting 67–100% for Jackson
Number	25	38	63	79
Percent	12	18	30	38

Table B. Voting Results Arranged by Elevation. I

Region	Voting for Clay	Voting for Jackson	Tied	Total
Low regions				
number of towns	39	39	3	81
percent of towns	48	48	4	100
High regions				
number of towns	24	103	1	128
percent of towns	19	81	1	100

Region	Voting 67–100% for Clay	Voting 51–66% for Clay	Voting 51–66% for Jackson	Voting 67–100% for Jackson
Low regions				
number of towns	12	27	28	11
percent of towns	15	33	35	14
High regions				
number of towns	13	11	35	68
percent of towns	10	9	28	53

Table C. Voting Results Arranged by Elevation. II

Percentage of:	In low regions	In high regions
All towns	39	61
Clay towns	62	38
Jackson towns	30	70
towns voting 67–100% for Clay	48	52
towns voting 51–66% for Clay	71	29
towns voting 51–66% for Jackson	44	56
towns voting 67–100% for Jackson	14	86

Table D. Voting Results Arranged by Geographic Region and Number of Towns

Region	Voting 67–100% for Clay	Voting 51–66% for Clay	Voting 51–66% for Jackson	Voting 67–100% for Jackson	Total[a]
Low regions					
Southeast lowlands	4	6	10	4	25
Connecticut Valley	5	11	7	0	23
Merrimack Valley	3	10	11	7	33
High regions					
Southeast uplands	1	1	8	9	19
Southwest uplands[b]	12	6	8	26	52
Winnipesaukee region	0	0	1	6	8
Mountain region	0	4	18	27	49

[a]Totals include one tied town in Southeast lowlands, two in Merrimack Valley, and one in Winnipesaukee region.
[b]Including Monadnock section, in which 12 towns voted 67–100% for Clay; 2 voted 51–66% for Clay; 1 voted 51–66% for Jackson; 1 voted 67–100% for Jackson.

Table E. Voting Results Arranged by Agricultural Region. I

Region	Voting for Clay	Voting for Jackson	Tied	Total
Good regions				
number of towns	43	62	2	107
percent of towns	40	58	2	100
Poor regions				
number of towns	20	80	2	102
percent of towns	20	78	2	100

Region	Voting 67–100% for Clay	Voting 51–66% for Clay	Voting 51–66% for Jackson	Voting 67–100% for Jackson
Good regions				
number of towns	14	29	35	27
percent of towns	13	27	33	25
Poor regions				
number of towns	11	9	28	52
percent of towns	11	9	27	51

Source: New Hampshire Agricultural Experiment Station, *Types of Farming Areas in New Hampshire,* Circular 53, 1936–1937.

Table F. Voting Results Arranged by Agricultural Region. II

Percentage of:	In good regions	In poor regions
All towns	51	49
Clay towns	68	32
Jackson towns	44	56
towns voting 67–100% for Clay	56	44
towns voting 51–66% for Clay	76	24
towns voting 51–66% for Jackson	56	44
towns voting 67–100% for Jackson	34	66

Table G. Voting Results Arranged by Acres of Arable Land per 100 Eligible Voters[a]

Size	Voting for Clay	Voting for Jackson	Tied	Total
0–150 acres				
number of towns	38	116	2	156
percent of towns	25	74	1	100
151 and over acres				
number of towns	13	10	2	25
percent of towns	52	40	8	100

	Voting 67–100% for Clay	Voting 51–66% for Clay	Voting 51–66% for Jackson	Voting 67–100% for Jackson
0–150 acres				
number of towns	15	23	50	66
percent of towns	10	15	32	42
151 and over acres				
number of towns	5	8	5	5
percent of towns	20	32	20	20

Source: Farmer, *New Hampshire Register 1829*.

[a]Twenty-eight towns are not included: 3 had no record of arable land; the data would not have been relevant for the 25 manufacturing towns.

Table H. Voting Results Arranged by Tax Rate and by Number of Towns

Tax Rate[a]	Voting 67–100% for Clay	Voting 51–66% for Clay	Voting 51–66% for Jackson	Voting 67–100% for Jackson
Below $3.00	2	3	10	19
$3.00–$3.49	4	9	19	25
$3.50–$3.99	7	10	17	18
$4.00–$4.49	7	6	10	10
$4.50 and over	5	10	4	5

Source: *Laws of New Hampshire*, 10 (1829–1835), 412–418; *Patriot*, April 11, 1831.

[a]Tax rate was a town's apportionment of every $1,000 in taxes to be raised by the state, adjusted per 1,000 population. It was based on assessed value of property.

Table I. Voting Results Arranged by Tax Rate and by
Percentage Vote

Percentage of:	Tax Rate[a]				
	Below $3.00	$3.00– $3.49	$3.50– $3.99	$4.00– $4.49	$4.50 and over
All towns	17	28	26	16	13
Clay towns	8	21	27	21	24
Jackson towns	21	32	26	15	7
towns voting 67– 100% for Clay	8	16	28	28	20
towns voting 51– 66% for Clay	9	24	26	16	24
towns voting 51– 66% for Jackson	17	32	28	17	7
towns voting 67– 100% for Jackson	25	32	23	13	6

[a]Tax rate was a town's apportionment of every $1,000 in taxes to be raised by the state, adjusted per 1,000 population. It was based on assessed value of property.

Table J. Tax Rate of Clay Towns in the Monadnock Section[a]

Location	Tax Rate				
	Below $3.00	$3.00– $3.49	$3.50– $3.99	$4.00 and over	Total
Monadnock section number of towns voting for Clay	0	1	6	7	14
percent of towns voting for Clay	0	7	43	50	100
New Hampshire number of towns voting for Clay	5	13	17	28	63
percent of towns voting for Clay	8	21	27	44	100

[a]See Map 3.

Table K. Voting Results Arranged by Population and Number of Towns, 1830

Population	Voting 67–100% for Clay	Voting 51–66% for Clay	Voting 51–66% for Jackson	Voting 67–100% for Jackson	Total
Under 1,000	10	10	15	40	75[a]
1,000–1,999	9	21	40	32	102[a]
2,000–2,999	6	5	5	7	23
3,000 and over	0	2	3	0	5
Total	25	38	63	79	205

Source: Patriot, April 11, 1831.

[a]Total does not include 4 ties: 2 towns under 1,000 in population, and 2 with population 1,000–1,999.

Table L. Voting Results and Churches Arranged by Counties

County	County vote for Jackson, percent	Total number of churches	Congregational churches		Baptist, Methodist, Universalist, and Shaker churches		Friends, Episcopalian, and Presbyterian churches	
			Number of churches	Percent of all churches in county	Number of churches	Percent of all churches in county	Number of churches	Percent of all churches in county
Coos	78	14	5	36	9	65	0	0
Merrimack	66	51	17	33	30	59	4	8
Grafton	59	58	21	36	36	62	1	2
Strafford	59	68	19	28	44	65	5	7
Hillsborough	58	44	22	50	15	33	7	16
Sullivan	55	31	12	41	16	48	3	11
Rockingham	54	65	27	43	29	43	9	14
Cheshire	37	35	21	60	14	40	0	0
Total	—	366	144	40	193	52	29	8

Source: Farmer, New Hampshire Register 1828, pp. 88–93.

Table M. Jackson Vote and Tax Apportionment

	In tax apportionment Group:[a]									
	1	2	3	4	5	6	7	8	9	10
Number of towns from										
Jackson vote Group 10[b]	0	1	2	2	1	3	3*	4	2	2
Group 9	0	2	0	2	1	4	1*	2	2	6
Group 8	1	1	2	3	3*	1	0	1	5	3
Group 7	2	4	2	1	0	0	4*	3	2	2
Group 6	2	0	2	4	4*	2	1	2	2	1
Group 5	2	2	2	3	2*	3	4	3	1	2
Group 4	2	3	3	3*	1	3	1	1	2	1
Group 3	3	3	2	3*	1	2	1	0	4	1
Group 2	0	1	4	2	3*	3	2	2	1	2
Group 1	8	4*	1	2	1	2	2	0	0	0

[a]Tax apportionment Group 1 consisted of the 20 towns with the lowest tax rate; Group 2 the next lowest, and so on up to Group 10, the highest. Several of the groups have slightly more or less than 20 towns.

[b]Jackson vote Group 1 consisted of the 20 towns with the highest percent of vote for Jackson; Group 2 the next highest, and so on down to Group 10, the lowest. Group 5 had 24 towns, the rest 20.

*Median of the towns in each Jackson vote group. The bulk of the towns from each Jackson group cluster near the comparable tax group. As a result, the median moves diagonally from left to right and from bottom to top, as it should if there is a correlation. Note the deviations.

When both the vote and tax groups were arranged in two units with one-half of the towns in each unit, the results were as follows: Of the towns in Jackson vote Groups 6–10, forty-two were in tax Groups 1–5, fifty-eight were in tax Groups 6–10. Of the towns in Jackson vote Groups 1–5, sixty-one were in tax Groups 1–5, forty-eight in tax Groups 6–10.

——"Speech on the Expurgation of the Journal," *Congressional Globe*, May 27, 1836, 24th Congress, 1st Session (1835–1836), Appendix, pp. 406–417.

——*Speech on the Subject of the Removal of the Deposits from the Bank of the United States in the Senate, Mar. 3-4, 1834*. Washington, D.C., 1834.

——Isaac Hill to Henry Lee, Sept. 16, 1828, Massachusetts Historical Society, *Proceedings*, 43 (1909), 70.

Hoogenboom, Ari, and Herbert Hershkowitz. "Levi Woodbury's 'Intimate Memoranda' of the Jackson Administration," *Pennsylvania Magazine of History and Biography*, 92 (Oct. 1968), 507–515.

Hubbard, Henry. *Address to Both Branches of the General Court of New Hampshire, June Session, 1843*. Concord, N.H., 1843.

——*Message to Both Houses of the General Court of New Hampshire, June Session, 1842*. Concord, N.H., 1842.

Page, John. *Message to the Legislature, June 1840*. Concord, N.H., 1840.

——*Message to Both Houses of the Legislature, June Session, 1839*. Concord, N.H., 1839.

Peaslee, Charles H. *Speech at the Democratic State Convention Held at Concord, June 11th, 1851*. n.p., n.d.

Pierce, Benjamin. "Autobiography." n.p., n.d.

Proceedings at the Dinner to Honorable Isaac Hill, at the Eagle Coffee House, . . . Concord, N.H., August 8, 1832. Concord, N.H., 1832.

Sullivan, George. *Oration Pronounced at Exeter on the Fourth Day of July, 1800, in Commemoration of the Anniversary of American Independence*. Exeter, N.H., 1800.

——*Speech at the Late Rockingham Convention with the Memorial and Resolutions and Report of the Committee of Elections*. Concord, N.H., 1812.

Tuck, Amos. *Autobiographical Memoir of Amos Tuck*. Exeter, N.H., 1875.

Upham, N. G. *Concord Rail-Road vs. Greeley*. Concord, N.H., 1844.

Van Tyne, Claude H. *The Letters of Daniel Webster*. New York: McClure, Phillips, & Co., 1902.

Woodbury, Levi. *Argument . . . before the Hon. Messrs. Henry Hubbard, Leonard Wilcox, and Frederick Vose, . . . in the Case of Isaac Hill Against Cyrus Barton, September 29, 1841*. Concord, N.H., 1841.

——*Letter on the Annexation of Texas*. Washington, D.C., 1844.

Bibliography

I. Manuscripts

Charles G. Atherton Papers, New Hampshire Historical Society.
John Bailey Papers, New-York Historical Society.
Samuel Bell Papers, New Hampshire Historical Society.
Samuel Bell Papers, New-York Historical Society.
Nicholas Biddle Papers, Library of Congress.
Blair Family Papers, Library of Congress.
Blair-Lee Papers, Princeton University Library.
Edmund Burke Papers, Library of Congress.
Edmund Burke Papers, New Hampshire Historical Society.
Henry Clay Papers, Library of Congress.
Azariah Flagg Papers, Manuscript Division, New York Public Library, Astor, Lenox and Tilden Foundations.
George Gilman Fogg Papers, New Hampshire Historical Society.
Gustavus Vasa Fox Papers, Naval History Society Collection, New-York Historical Society.
Duff Green Papers, Library of Congress.
John Parker Hale Papers, New Hampshire Historical Society.
John Parker Hale Papers, Phillips Exeter Academy.
Jonathan Harvey Papers, New Hampshire Historical Society.
Harry Hibbard Papers, New Hampshire Historical Society.
Isaac Hill Papers, New Hampshire Historical Society.
Miscellaneous Isaac Hill Papers, Houghton Library, Harvard University.
Miscellaneous Isaac Hill Papers, Library of Congress.
Miscellaneous Isaac Hill Papers, New York Public Library.
Henry Hubbard Papers, New Hampshire Historical Society.
Andrew Jackson Papers, Library of Congress.

Francis Lieber Papers, the Huntington Library, San Marino, Calif.
Jeremiah Mason Papers, New Hampshire Historical Society.
John McLean Papers, Library of Congress.
Jacob Bailey Moore Papers, Houghton Library, Harvard University.
John R. Parrott Papers, New Hampshire Historical Society.
Charles Peaslee Papers, New Hampshire Historical Society.
Franklin Pierce Papers, Library of Congress.
Franklin Pierce Papers, New Hampshire Historical Society.
William Plumer Papers, Library of Congress.
James M. Rix Papers, New Hampshire Historical Society.
Tristram Shaw Papers, New Hampshire Historical Society.
Roger B. Taney Papers, Library of Congress.
John W. Taylor Papers, New-York Historical Society.
Amos Tuck Papers, New Hampshire Historical Society.
United States Treasury Department, Letters from Banks, 1833–1841. National Archives.
United States Treasury Department, Letters to Banks, 1833–1841. National Archives.
Martin Van Buren Papers, Library of Congress.
Gulian Verplanck Papers, New-York Historical Society.
Daniel Webster Papers, Dartmouth College Archives.
Daniel Webster Papers, Library of Congress.
Daniel Webster Papers, New Hampshire Historical Society.
John M. Weeks Papers, New Hampshire Historical Society.
Gideon Welles Papers, Connecticut Historical Society.
Gideon Welles Papers, Library of Congress.
Levi Woodbury Papers, Library of Congress.
Levi Woodbury Papers, New Hampshire Historical Society.
Miscellaneous Levi Woodbury Papers, New-York Historical Society.
Miscellaneous Levi Woodbury Papers, New York Public Library.

II. Published Writings of New Hampshire Figures

Badger, William. *Message to Both Branches of the Legislature, June 6, 1834.* Concord, N.H., 1834.
——— *Message to Both Branches of the Legislature, June Session, 1835.* Concord, N.H., 1835.
Barton, Cyrus. *Defense against the Attacks of Hon. Isaac Hill.* New Hampshire Patriot Extra, Sept. 7, 1840.
Burke, Edmund. *An Address Delivered before the Democratic Republican Citizens of Lempster, N.H. on the Eighth of January, 1839.* Newport, N.H., 1839.

——— *An Address at a Meeting of the Democratic Republicans Unity, N.H. on the 8th of January, 1838.* Newport, N.H., 1838.
Dinsmoor, Samuel. *Message to the Legislature of New Hampshire, Ju Session, 1831.* Concord, N.H., 1831.
——— *Message to Both Houses of the Legislature, June Session, 183* Concord, N.H., 1832.
——— *Message to Both Branches of the Legislature, November Sessio 1832.* Concord, N.H., 1832.
Hale, John P. *Letter to His Constituents on the Proposed Annexatio of Texas.* Washington, D.C., 1845.
Harper, Joseph M. *Address on the Thirteenth Anniversary of Jackson Victory at New Orleans.* Concord, N.H., 1828.
Harvey, Matthew. *A Message to Both Branches of the Legislature June 4, 1830.* Concord, N.H., 1830.
——— *An Oration Pronounced at Henniker, New-Hampshire, July 4 1811.* Concord, N.H., 1811.
Hayes, John L. *Remarks Made at a Democratic Meeting in Portsmouth on the 7th of January 1845, in Defense of the Course of John P. Hale, Member of Congress from New Hampshire, in Relation to the Annexation of Texas.* Portsmouth, N.H., 1845.
——— *A Reminiscence of the Free-Soil Movement in New Hampshire, 1845.* Cambridge, Mass., 1885.
Hill, Isaac. *Address before the Members of the Merrimack Co. Agricultural Society, October, 1837.* n.p., n.d.
——— *An Address Delivered at Concord, N.H., Jan. 8, 1828, Being the 13th Anniversary of Jackson's Victory at New Orleans.* Concord, N.H., 1828.
——— *An Address Delivered before the Republicans of Portsmouth and Vicinity, July 4, 1828.* Concord, N.H., 1828.
——— *Brief Sketch of the Life, Character and Services of Major General Andrew Jackson.* Concord, N.H., 1828.
——— *Letter from a Farmer in the County of Rockingham to His Brother in the County of Merrimack, in New Hampshire.* Concord, N.H., 1828.
——— *Message to Both Houses of the Legislature, June Session, 1836.* Concord, N.H., 1836.
——— *Message to Both Houses of the Legislature, June Session, 1838.* Concord, N.H., 1838.
——— "Speech on the Bank of the United States," June 8, 1832, *Register of Debates,* 22nd Congress, 1st Session (1831–1832), pp. 1056–1067.
——— *Speech on the Bill to Appropriate . . . the Proceeds of the Sales of the Public Lands . . . .* U.S. Senate, Jan. 22, 1833. n.p., 1833.

_____ *An Oration Pronounced at Lyndeborough, N.H. in Commemoration of the Independence of the United States of America, July 4, 1815.* Amherst, N.H., 1815.

_____ *Speech Delivered at the Democratic Meeting in Jefferson Hall, Portsmouth (N.H.), November 18, 1841.* Alexandria, D.C., 1841.

_____ *A Vindication of Mr. Adams' Oration.* Concord, N.H., 1821.

_____ *Writings, Political, Judicial and Literary; Now First Selected and Arranged by Charles Levi Woodbury.* 3 vols. Boston, 1852.

III. Newspapers
(New Hampshire unless indicated)

[Washington, D.C.] *Daily Madisonian,* 1843–1845.
[Haverhill] *Democratic Republican,* 1828–1845.
Dover Enquirer, 1828–1840.
Dover Gazette, 1825–1840.
Exeter News-Letter, 1831–1839.
[Concord] *Farmer's Monthly Visitor,* 1839.
[Washington, D.C.] *Globe,* 1830–1835.
[Concord] *Herald of Freedom,* 1835.
[Concord] *Hill's New Hampshire Patriot,* 1840–1847.
[Manchester and Concord] *Independent Democrat,* 1845–1846.
The [Boston] *Liberator,* 1834–1835.
Manchester American, 1844–1845.
Manchester Democrat, 1842–1846.
[Newport] *New Hampshire Argus and Spectator,* 1836–1837.
[Portsmouth] *New Hampshire Gazette,* 1819–1845.
[Concord] *New-Hampshire Patriot,* 1809–1855.
[Keene] *New Hampshire Sentinel,* 1825–1846.
[Concord] *New Hampshire Statesman,* 1828–1846.
[Baltimore] *Niles' Weekly Register,* 1816–1846.
[Portsmouth] *Oracle of the Day,* 1800.
Portsmouth Journal, 1827–1834.
[Manchester] *Semi-Weekly American,* 1845.
[Concord] *The Spirit of the Republican Press,* 1829.
[Amherst] *Village Messenger,* 1800.

IV. New Hampshire Registers, Gazeteers, and Maps

Carey, H. C., and I. Lea. *Geographical, Statistical, and Historical Map of New Hampshire.* Philadelphia, 1822.

Charlton, Elmer E. *New Hampshire As It Is.* Claremont, N.H., 1856.

Coolidge, A. J., and J. B. Mansfield. *History and Description of New England. New Hampshire.* Boston, 1860.

Farmer, John. *The New Hampshire Annual Register and United States Calendar, 1828.* Concord, N.H., 1827.

_____ *The New Hampshire Annual Register and United States Calendar, 1829.* Concord, N.H., 1829.

_____ *The New Hampshire Annual Register and U. S. Calendar, 1838.* Concord, N.H., 1838.

_____ and Jacob B. Moore. *A Gazeteer of the State of New Hampshire.* Concord, N.H., 1823.

Finley, Anthony, pub. *A New General Atlas.* Philadelphia, Pa., 1830.

Hayward, John. *A Gazeteer of New Hampshire* . . . . Boston, 1849.

Moore, Jacob B., ed. *The New Hampshire Annual Register and United States Calendar . . . 1839.* Concord, N.H., 1839.

Ranney, Adolphus. *Morse's Railroad and Township Map of Vermont and New Hampshire.* New York, 1856.

Robinson, Lewis. *Map of New Hampshire.* Reading, Vt., 1850.

V. Other Primary Sources: New Hampshire

Address of the Great State Convention of the Friends of the Administration . . . Concord, June 17, 1828 . . . . Concord, N.H., 1828.

The Concord Directory . . . 1830. Concord, N.H., 1830.

Journal of the House of Representatives of the State of New Hampshire.

Laws of New Hampshire. 1820–1852.

Laws of New Hampshire, Vol. X (1829–1835). Concord, N.H., 1922.

A Letter to a New Hampshire Land Owner upon the Constitutionality of Granting the Power of Taking Private Property to Railroad Corporations. n.p., 1840.

Long, Isaac, Jr., pub. *The Laws of the State of New Hampshire . . . 1830.* Hopkinton, N.H., 1830.

McFarland, Henry. *Sixty Years in Concord and Elsewhere: Personal Recollections of Henry McFarland.* Concord, N.H., 1899.

Manual for the General Court, 1891. Concord, N.H., 1891.

Manual for the General Court, 1957. Concord, N.H., 1957.

Moore, Jacob B. "History of Newspapers Published in New Hampshire from 1756 to 1840." *American Quarterly Register,* 13 (1840), 179–181.

New Hampshire Journal. The Wise Sayings of the Honorable Isaac Hill. Concord, N.H., 1828.

New Hampshire Savings Bank. *Say Not the Old Days Were Better.* n.p., n.d.

New Hampshire Superior Court. *Reports.* Vol. LXV. 1817.

Phillips Exeter Academy. *The Charter and Constitution of the Phillips Exeter Academy.* Exeter, N.H., 1953.

The Present State of the Times. Portsmouth, N.H., 1838.

Proceedings and Address of the New Hampshire Republican State Convention of Delegates Friendly to the Election of Andrew Jackson . . . . Concord, N.H., 1828.

The Revised Statutes of the State of New Hampshire, . . . 1842, ... Concord, N.H., 1843.

Rolfe, Abial. *Reminiscences of Concord or Personal Recollections of Seventy Years.* Penacook, N.H., 1901.

Shirley, J. M. *The Dartmouth College Causes and the Supreme Court of the United States.* St. Louis, 1879.

To the Republican Electors of the State of New Hampshire. n.p., 1827.

VI. Other Primary Sources: United States

Adams, Charles Francis, ed. *Memoirs of John Quincy Adams.* 12 vols. Philadelphia, Pa., 1874–1877.

Bassett, John S., ed. *Correspondence of Andrew Jackson.* 7 vols. Washington, D.C.: Carnegie Institution, 1926–1933.

Benton, Thomas H. *Abridgment of the Debates of Congress, from 1789 to 1836 . . . .* New York, 1859.

———— *Thirty Years' View.* 2 vols. New York, 1854.

Congressional Globe. 1833–1846.

De Bow, J. D. B. *Statistical View of the United States . . . Being a Compendium of the Seventh Census . . . .* Washington, D.C., 1854.

Duane, William J. *Narrative and Correspondence Concerning the Removal of the Deposits . . . .* Philadelphia, 1838.

"Edward Everett to John McLean, and John McLean to Edward Everett," Massachusetts Historical Society, *Proceedings,* Third Series, 1 (1907–1908), 363–370.

Goodrich, Samuel G. *Recollections of a Lifetime; or, Men and Things I Have Seen.* Vol. II, New York, 1856.

Hamilton, James A. *Reminiscences of James A. Hamilton.* New York, 1869.

Hamilton, Luther, ed. *Memoirs, Speeches and Writings of Robert Rantoul, Jr.* Boston, 1854.

House of Representatives. *Report on the Bank of the United States,* Report no. 460, 22nd Congress, 1st Session (April 30, 1832).

Howard, B. C. *Reports of Cases Argued and Adjudged in the Supreme Court, 1843–1861.* Vols. V-VII. Philadelphia, 1847–1849.

"Letter from Isaac Munroe to John B. Davis, Nov. 21, 1828," Massachusetts Historical Society, *Proceedings,* 49 (1916), 214–216.

"Letters between George Bancroft and Martin Van Buren, 1842–1845," Massachusetts Historical Society, *Proceedings,* 42 (1909), 381–442.

Mackenzie, William L. *The Life and Times of Martin Van Buren.* Boston: Cooke & Co., 1846.

McGrane, Reginald C., ed. *The Correspondence of Nicholas Biddle Dealing with National Affairs, 1807–1844.* New York: Houghton, 1919.

McLane, Louis. *Documents Relative to the Manufactures in the United States . . . .* Vol. I. Washington, D.C., 1833.

Peters, Richard, Jr. *Reports of Cases Argued and Adjudged in the Supreme Court, 1828-1842.* Vol. XI. Philadelphia, 1838.

Petersen, Svend. *Statistical History of American Presidential Elections.* New York: Ungar, 1962.

Poore, Ben: Perley. *Perley's Reminiscences of Sixty Years in the National Metropolis.* 2 vols. Philadelphia, 1886.

Register of Debates in Congress. 1828–1833.

Richardson, James D., ed. *Messages and Papers of the Presidents 1789–1897.* Washington, D.C., 1896–1899.

Sargent, Nathan. *Public Men and Events.* 2 vols. Philadelphia, 1874.

Scudder, Horace E., ed. *The Complete Poetical Works of John Greenleaf Whittier.* Boston: Houghton Mifflin, 1892.

The Statistical History of the United States from Colonial Times to the Present. Stamford, Conn.: Fairfield Publishers, 1965.

Stickney, William, ed. *Autobiography of Amos Kendall.* Boston, 1872.

Taney, Roger B. "Explanation of His Relations to the United States Bank . . . ." Roger B. Taney Papers, Library of Congress.

United States Census Office. *Abstract of the Returns of the Fifth Census Showing the Number of Free People, the Number of Slaves, ...* House Document 263, 22nd Congress, 1st Session. Washington, D.C., 1832.

———— *Compendium of the Enumeration of the Inhabitants and Statistics as Obtained at the Department of State, from the Returns of the Sixth Census . . . .* Washington, D.C., 1841.

———— *Manufactures of the United States in 1860; Compiled from the Original Returns of the Eighth Census.* Washington, D.C., 1865.

———— *Sixth Census or Enumeration of the Inhabitants of the United States . . . 1840.* Washington, D.C., 1841.

United States Senate. *Executive Journal.* Vol. IV (1829–1837).

Van Buren, Martin. *Autobiography of Martin Van Buren.* Ed. John C. Fitzpatrick. American Historical Association, *Annual Report, 1918.* Vol. II. Washington, D.C., 1919.

Wheaton, Henry. *Reports of Cases Argued and Adjudged in the Supreme Court of the United States, 1816–1827.* Vol. IV. Philadelphia, 1819.

Wise, Henry A. *Seven Decades of the Union.* Philadelphia, 1871.

VII. Secondary Works: New Hampshire

Allison, Hildreth, M. "Honorable Levi Woodbury: Presidential Timber," *Historical New Hampshire,* 23 (Autumn 1968), 3–18.

Bell, Charles H. *Bench and Bar of New Hampshire.* Boston, 1893.

———— *History of the Town of Exeter, New Hampshire.* Exeter, N.H., 1888.

Bell, Irving. "One Hundred Years Ago in New Hampshire," *Historical New Hampshire,* 2 (Sept. 1946), pp. 16–24.

Bouton, Nathaniel. *The History of Concord from Its First Grant in 1725 to the Organization of the City Government in 1853.* Concord, N.H., 1856.

Bradley, Cyrus P. *Biography of Isaac Hill.* Concord, N.H., 1835.

Capowski, Vincent J. "The Era of Good Feelings in New Hampshire: The Gubernatorial Campaigns of Levi Woodbury, 1823–1824," *Historical New Hampshire,* 21 (Winter 1966), 2–30.

———— "The Making of a Jacksonian Democrat: Levi Woodbury, 1789–1831," unpublished dissertation, Fordham University, 1965.

Chandler, William E. *The Statue of John Parker Hale.* Concord, N.H., 1892.

Chapman, George W. *Hon. Harry Hibbard.* Concord, N.H., 1873.

Clark, G. J., ed. *Memoir, Autobiography and Correspondence of Jeremiah Mason,* rev. ed. Kansas City, Mo.: Lawyers' International Publishing Co., 1917.

Cole, Donald B. "The Presidential Election of 1832 in New Hampshire," *Historical New Hampshire,* 21 (Winter 1966), 32–50.

Corning, Charles Robert. *Amos Tuck.* Exeter, N.H.: *News-Letter* Press, 1902.

Dearborn, John W. *Sketch of the Life and Character of Hon. Amos Tuck.* Portland, Me., 1888.

Dedication of a Statue of General Franklin Pierce . . . . Concord, N.H.: Rumford Press, 1914.

Dictionary of American Biography, s.v. Hill, Isaac; Pierce, Franklin; and Woodbury, Levi.

Douglas, Marian. *In the Poverty Year.* New York: Crowell, 1901.

Dunfey, William L. "A Short History of the Democratic Party in New Hampshire," unpublished thesis, University of New Hampshire, 1954.

Frasier, Dudley P. "The Antecedents and Formation of the Republican Party in New Hampshire 1845–1860," seminar paper, Harvard University.

Foster, William L. *Matthew Harvey.* Concord, N.H., 1867.

Gallagher, Edward J. "Luther Roby, Early New Hampshire Publisher," *Historical New Hampshire,* 2 (Sept. 1946), 1–16.

Grant, Philip A. "The Bank Controversy and New Hampshire Politics, 1834–1835," *Historical New Hampshire,* 23 (Autumn 1968), 19–36.

Hadley, Amos. "New Hampshire in the Fourth Decade of the Passing Century," *Proceedings of the New Hampshire Historical Society,* 3 (1895–1896), 14–62.

Hawthorne, Nathaniel. *Life of Franklin Pierce.* Boston, 1852.

Hazlett, Charles A. *Portsmouth in the Year 1824.* Portsmouth, N.H., 1912.

Heald, Charles B. "Thirty-nine of the Sixty-six Governors of New Hampshire Were Freemasons," *The Masonic Craftsman,* Feb. 1948, pp. 23–25.

Hill, Minot. "The Life of Isaac Hill," manuscript, Phillips Exeter Academy, 1958.

Hitchcock, Charles H. *The Geology of New Hampshire.* Vol. I. Concord, N.H., 1874.

Howarth, Margery D. *New Hampshire: A Study of Its Cities and Towns in Relation to Their Physical Background.* Concord, N.H.: New Hampshire State Planning and Development Commission, 1936.

Irelan, John Robert. *The Republic.* Vol. XIV. Chicago, 1888.

Kalijarvi, Thorsten V., and William C. Chamberlin. *The Government of New Hampshire.* Durham, N.H.: University of New Hampshire Press, 1939.

Kaplanoff, Mark D. "Religion and Righteousness: A Study of Federalist Rhetoric in the New Hampshire Election of 1800," *Historical New Hampshire,* 23 (Winter 1968), 3–20.

———— "The Social and Economic Bases of New Hampshire's Political Change 1800–1805," unpublished thesis, Yale University, 1969.

Kinney, Charles B., Jr. *Church and State: the Struggle for Separation in New Hampshire. 1630–1900.* New York: Columbia University Teachers College, 1955.

Leidtker, Frank L. "Political Development in New Hampshire from the Revolution to 1850," unpublished thesis, University of New Hampshire, 1952.

Lord, John K. *A History of Dartmouth College 1815–1909.* 2 vols. Concord, N.H.: Dartmouth College, 1913.

McClintock, John N. *History of New Hampshire.* Boston, 1888.

Metcalf, Henry H. *Franklin Pierce and Edmund Burke: A President and a President-Maker.* Concord, N.H.: Ranney Printing Co., 1930.

Morison, John Hopkins. *Life of Hon. Jeremiah Smith.* Boston, 1845.

Nesmith, George W. "Matthew Harvey," *Memorials of Judges Recently Deceased, Graduates of Dartmouth College. 1880.* Concord, N.H., 1881.

New Hampshire Agricultural Experiment Station. *Types of Farming Areas in New Hampshire.* Circular 53, 1936–1937.

New Hampshire State Planning and Development Commission, *Population of New Hampshire.* Vol. I. Concord, N.H., 1946.

Nichols, Roy. *Franklin Pierce, Young Hickory of the Granite Hills,* rev. ed. Philadelphia: University of Pennsylvania Press, 1958.

Perry, Charles E. "The New Hampshire Press in the Election of 1828," *The Granite Monthly,* 61 (1929), 454–458.

Pike, Robert C. "Memories of Judge Doe," in Elmer E. Doe, *The Descendants of Nicholas Doe.* Orleans, Vt.: E. E. Doe, 1918.

Plumer, William, Jr. *Life of William Plumer.* Boston, 1856.

Rantoul, Robert, Jr. *Eulogy on the Hon. Levi Woodbury.* Portsmouth, N.H., 1852.

Reid, John. "Doe's World," manuscript, University of New Hampshire Library, n.d.

────── *Chief Justice: The Judicial World of Charles Doe.* Cambridge, Mass.: Harvard University Press, 1967.

────── "The Political Affiliations of Charles Doe During the Ordeal of the Union," unpublished thesis, University of New Hampshire, June 1957.

Robinson, Francis E. "Isaac Hill," unpublished thesis, University of New Hampshire, June 1933.

Robinson, Maurice H. *A History of Taxation in New Hampshire.* New York: American Economic Association, 1902.

Saltonstall, William G. *Ports of Piscataqua.* Cambridge, Mass.: Russell, 1941.

Sanborn, Edwin D. *Sanborn's History of New Hampshire, from Its First Discovery to the Year 1830.* Manchester, N.H., 1875.

Sewell, Richard H. *John P. Hale and the Politics of Abolition.* Cambridge, Mass.: Harvard University Press, 1965.

Sherman, Ernest L. "A Study of the Slavery and Anti-slavery Movement in New Hampshire to 1850," manuscript, University of New Hampshire Library, 1947.

Skinner, Harland. "Slavery and Abolition in New Hampshire," unpublished thesis, University of New Hampshire, 1948.

Smith, Jeremiah. *Memoirs of Hon. Charles Doe.* Concord, N.H., 1897.

Smith, Norman W. "The 'Amherst Bubble,' Wild Cat Banking in Early Nineteenth Century New Hampshire," *Historical New Hampshire,* 20 (Spring 1965) , 27–40.

―――― "A History of Commercial Banking in New Hampshire 1792–1843," unpublished dissertation, University of Wisconsin, 1967.

―――― "A Mature Frontier: the New Hampshire Economy, 1790–1850," *Historical New Hampshire,* 24 (Fall 1969), 3–19.

Squires, James Duane. *The Granite State of the United States.* 4 vols. New York: American Historical Company, 1956.

Stackpole, Everett S. *History of New Hampshire.* 4 vols. New York: American Historical Society, 1917.

Stearns, Ezra S., ed. *Genealogical and Family History of the State of New Hampshire.* 4 vols. Chicago: Lewis Publishing Company, 1908.

Street, George. *A Memorial Discourse Delivered at Exeter, N. H., 11 Jan. 1880.* Boston, 1880.

Turner, Lynn. "The Electoral Vote against Monroe in 1820," *Mississippi Valley Historical Review,* 42 (1955), 250–273.

―――― *William Plumer of New Hampshire.* Chapel Hill, N.C.: University of North Carolina Press, 1962.

―――― "William Plumer, Statesman of New Hampshire, 1780–1820," unpublished dissertation, Harvard University, 1943.

Upton, Richard F. *Revolutionary New Hampshire.* Hanover, N.H.: Dartmouth College Publications, 1936.

Walker, Joseph B. *Birth of the Federal Constitution: A History of the New Hampshire Convention for . . . the Federal Constitution . . . .* Boston, 1888.

Wheaton, Philip D. "Levi Woodbury—Jacksonian Financier," unpublished dissertation, University of Maryland, 1955.

Williams, Myron R. *The Story of Phillips Exeter.* Exeter, N.H.: Phillips Exeter Academy, 1957.

Wilson, Harold F. *The Hill Country of Northern New England: Its Social and Economic History, 1790–1930.* New York: Columbia University Press, 1936.

Woodbury, Charles L. "Levi Woodbury," New England Historic Genealogical Society, *Memorial Biographies,* I (1845–1852), 295–327.

VIII. Secondary Works: United States

Aronson, Sidney H. *Status and Kinship in the Higher Civil Service: Standards of Selection in the Administrations of John Adams, Thomas Jefferson, and Andrew Jackson.* Cambridge, Mass.: Harvard University Press, 1964.

Bassett, John S. *The Life of Andrew Jackson.* 2 vols. in one. Garden City, N.Y.: Doubleday, Page, 1911.

Baxter, Maurice G. *Daniel Webster & the Supreme Court.* Amherst, Mass.: University of Massachusetts Press, 1966.

Benson, Lee. *The Concept of Jacksonian Democracy: New York As a Test Case.* Princeton, N.J.: Princeton University Press, 1961.

Beveridge, Albert J. *The Life of John Marshall.* 4 vols. New York: Houghton Mifflin, 1916–1919.

Biographical Directory of the American Congress. Washington, D.C.: U.S. Government Printing Office, 1961.

Bower, Robert T. "Note on 'Did Labor Support Jackson? The Boston Story'," *Political Science Quarterly,* 65 (1950), 441–444.

Bowers, Claude G. *The Party Battles of the Jackson Period.* New York: Houghton Mifflin, 1922.

Brown, Everett S., ed. *The Missouri Compromises and Presidential Politics 1820–1825 from the Letters of William Plumer, Junior.* St. Louis, Mo.: Missouri Historical Society, 1926.

Brown, Richard H. "The Missouri Compromise, Slavery, and the Politics of Jacksonianism," *South Atlantic Quarterly,* 65 (1966), 55–72.

Brown, Roger. *The Republic in Peril: 1812.* New York: Columbia University Press, 1964.

Bryan, Wilhelmus B. *A History of the National Capital.* 2 vols. New York: Macmillan, 1916.

Buell, Augustus C. *History of Andrew Jackson.* 2 vols. New York: Charles Scribner's Sons, 1904.

Callender, Guy S. *Selections from the Economic History of the United States 1765–1860.* Boston: Ginn, 1909.

Catterall, Ralph C. H. *The Second Bank of the United States.* Chicago: University of Chicago Press, 1903.

Chambers, William N. *Old Bullion Benton: Senator from the New West.* Boston: Little, Brown, 1956.

Clark, Victor S. *History of Manufactures in the United States,* Vol. I (1607–1860). New York: Carnegie Institution, 1929.

Cunningham, Noble E. *The Jeffersonian Republicans in Power: Party Operations, 1801–1809.* Chapel Hill, N.C.: University of North Carolina Press, 1963.

Curtis, George T. *Life of Daniel Webster.* 2 vols. New York: D. Appleton, 1870.

Darling, Arthur B. "Jacksonian Democracy in Massachusetts 1824–1848," *American Historical Review,* 29 (1924), 271–287.

—— *Political Changes in Massachusetts, 1824–1848: A Study in Liberal Movements in Politics.* New Haven, Conn.: Yale University Press, 1925.

—— "The Workingman's Party in Massachusetts," *American Historical Review,* 29 (1923), 81–86.

Dodd, Edwin M. *American Business Corporations until 1860 with Special Reference to Massachusetts.* Cambridge, Mass.: Harvard University Press, 1954.

Ellet, Elizabeth F. *Court Circles of the Republic.* Philadelphia, 1869.

Farnam, Henry W. *Chapters in the History of Social Legislation in the United States to 1860.* Washington, D.C.: Carnegie Institution, 1938.

Fischer, David H. *The Revolution in American Conservatism: the Federalist Party in the Era of Jeffersonian Democracy.* New York: Harper & Row, 1965.

Fuess, Claude M. *Daniel Webster.* 2 vols. Boston: Little, Brown, 1930.

Fox, Dixon Ryan. *The Decline of Aristocracy in the Politics of New York 1801–1840.* New York: Columbia University Press, 1919.

Gammon, Samuel R. *The Presidential Campaign of 1832.* Baltimore: Johns Hopkins University Press, 1922.

Garraty, John A. *Silas Wright.* New York: Columbia University Press, 1949.

Gatell, Frank Otto. "Money and Party in Jacksonian America, A Quantitative Look at New York's Men of Quality," *Political Science Quarterly,* 82 (June 1967), 235–252.

—— "Spoils of the Bank War: Political Bias in the Selection of Pet Banks," *American Historical Review,* 70 (Oct. 1964), 35–58.

Govan, Thomas P. *Nicholas Biddle: Nationalist and Public Banker 1786–1844.* Chicago: University of Chicago Press, 1959.

Hamlin, Charles E. *The Life and Times of Hannibal Hamlin.* Cambridge, Mass., 1899.

Hammond, Bray. *Banks and Politics in America from the Revolution to the Civil War*. Princeton, N.J.: Princeton University Press, 1957.

Handlin, Oscar, and Mary Flug Handlin. *Commonwealth: A Study of the Role of Government in the American Economy: Massachusetts, 1774–1861*. New York: New York University Press, 1947.

―――― "The Origins of the American Business Corporation," *Journal of Economic History*, 5 (1945), 1–23.

Hartz, Louis. *Economic Policy and Democratic Thought: Pennsylvania 1776–1860*. Cambridge, Mass.: Harvard University Press, 1948.

Henig, Gerald S. "The Jacksonian Attitude toward Abolitionism in the 1830's," *Tennessee Historical Quarterly*, 28 (Spring 1969), 42–56.

Howe, M. A. DeWolfe. *Life and Letters of George Bancroft*. 2 vols. New York: C. Scribner's Sons, 1908.

Hugins, Walter. *Jacksonian Democracy and the Working Class: A Study of the New York Workingmen's Movement 1829–1837*. Stanford, Calif.: Stanford University Press, 1960.

James, Marquis. *Andrew Jackson: Portrait of a President*. Indianapolis: Bobbs-Merrill, 1937.

Kirkland, Edward C. *Men, Cities, and Transportation: A Study in New England History, 1820–1900*. 2 vols. Cambridge, Mass.: Harvard University Press, 1948.

Knox, John J. *History of Banking in the United States* . . . . New York: Bankers Publishing Co., 1900.

Libby, Orrin G. *The Geographical Distribution of the Vote of the Thirteen States on the Federal Constitution 1787–1788*. Madison, Wis., 1894.

Litwack, Leon. *North of Slavery: The Negro in the Free States, 1790–1860*. Chicago: University of Chicago Press, 1961.

Livermore, Shaw. *The Twilight of Federalism: The Disintegration of the Federalist Party*. Princeton, N.J.: Princeton University Press, 1962.

―――― "Unlimited Liability in Early American Corporations," *Journal of Political Economy*, 43 (1935), 674–686.

Longaker, Richard P. "Was Jackson's Kitchen Cabinet a Cabinet?" *Mississippi Valley Historical Review*, 44 (1957), 94–108.

Marshall, Lynn L. "The Authorship of Jackson's Veto Message," *Mississippi Valley Historical Review*, 50 (Dec. 1963), 466–477.

―――― "The Strange Stillbirth of the Whig Party," *American Historical Review*, 72 (Jan. 1967), 445–468.

271

McCormick, Richard P. "New Perspectives on Jacksonian Politics," *American Historical Review*, 45 (1960), 288–301.

—— *The Second American Party System: Party Formation in the Jacksonian Era*. Chapel Hill, N.C.: University of North Carolina Press, 1966.

McFaul, John M. "The Politics of Jacksonian Finance," unpublished dissertation, University of California at Berkeley, 1963.

Meyers, Marvin. *The Jacksonian Persuasion: Politics and Belief*. Stanford, Calif.: Stanford University Press, 1957.

Moore, Glover. *The Missouri Compromise, 1819–1821*. Lexington, Ky.: University of Kentucky Press, 1953.

Nevins, Allan. *Ordeal of the Union*. Vol. II. New York: Charles Scribner's Sons, 1947.

Nichols, Roy. *The Democratic Machine 1850–1854*. New York: Columbia University Press, 1923.

Ogg, Frederic Austin. *The Reign of Andrew Jackson: A Chronicle of the Frontier in Politics*. New Haven, Conn.: Yale University Press, 1919.

Parks, Joseph H. *Felix Grundy: Champion of Democracy*. University, La.: University of Louisiana Press, 1940.

Parton, James. *Life of Andrew Jackson*. 3 vols. New York: Mason Brothers, 1860.

Pessen, Edward. "Did Labor Support Jackson?: The Boston Story," *Political Science Quarterly*, 64 (1949), 262–274.

Pratt, Julius W. *Expansionists of 1812*. New York: Macmillan Co., 1925.

Remini, Robert V. *Andrew Jackson and the Bank War*. New York: W. W. Norton, 1967.

—— *The Election of Andrew Jackson*. New York: J. B. Lippincott, 1963.

—— *Martin Van Buren and the Making of the Democratic Party*. New York: Columbia University Press, 1959.

Robinson, William A. *Jeffersonian Democracy in New England*. New Haven, Conn.: Yale University Press, 1916.

Scheiber, Harry N. "The Pet Banks in Jacksonian Politics and Finance, 1833–1841," *Journal of Economic History*, 23 (1963), 196–214.

Schlesinger, Arthur M., Jr. *The Age of Jackson*. Boston: Little, Brown, 1945.

Sellers, Charles. *James K. Polk, Continentalist, 1843–1846*. Princeton, N.J.: Princeton University Press, 1966.

———— *James K. Polk, Jacksonian, 1795–1843*. Princeton, N.J.: Princeton University Press, 1957.

Stewart, Randall. "Hawthorne and Politics: Unpublished Letters to William B. Pike," *New England Quarterly*, 5 (1932), 237–263.

Sullivan, William. "Did Labor Support Andrew Jackson?" *Political Science Quarterly*, 62 (1947), 569–580.

Sumner, William G. *Andrew Jackson*. Boston: Houghton Mifflin, 1882.

Swisher, Carl B. *Roger B. Taney*. New York: Macmillan, 1935.

Taylor, George Rogers. *The Transportation Revolution, 1815–1860*. New York: Rinehart, 1951.

Turner, Frederick J. *The United States 1830–1850: The Nation and Its Sections*. New York: Henry Holt, 1935.

Tyler, Lyon G. *The Letters and Times of the Tylers*. 3 vols. Richmond, Va., 1884, 1896.

Van Deusen, Glyndon. *The Jacksonian Era, 1828–1848*. New York: Harper and Brothers, 1959.

Ward, John W. *Andrew Jackson, Symbol for an Age*. New York: Oxford University Press, 1955.

Wellington, Raynor G. *The Political and Sectional Influence of the Public Lands, 1828–1842*. Boston: Riverside Press, 1914.

White, Leonard D. *The Jacksonians: A Study in Administrative History*. New York: Macmillan, 1954.

Wilburn, Jean A. *Biddle's Bank: The Crucial Years*. New York: Columbia University Press, 1967.

Williamson, Chilton. *American Suffrage: From Property to Democracy, 1760–1860*. Princeton, N.J.: Princeton University Press, 1960.

Woodford, Frank B. *Lewis Cass, The Last Jeffersonian*. New Brunswick, N.J.: Rutgers University Press, 1950.

Index

Abolitionism, 171, 175-182
Abolitionist Party, 211, 221, 223, 227-228
Adams, John Quincy, 48, 55, 90, 139; and election of 1824, 57-58; administration of, 60, 63-65, 67; and elections of 1828, 71, 75, 78-79; and Bank War, 121-122
Albany Regency, 86, 162
American Revolution, 44-45, 59-61, 64, 161, 241; Hill and, 4, 28, 44; spirit of, 70-71, 78, 81, 163, 169, 180
Ames, Fisher, 16
Anti-Masons, 138, 174
Antislavery movement, 175-182, 216-233
Atherton, Charles G., 92, 182, 210, 219, 230
Atherton, Charles H., 210
Atwood, John, 231-232
Ayer, Richard H., 52, 113, 206

Badger, William, 30, 162, 172-173, 243
Baker, Albert, 200-201, 205, 220-221
Bancroft, George, 198, 234-238
Banking in N.H., 14, 17-18, 42-43, 102-106, 125-126, 130-133; credit, 102-103, 106-113, 116-117; crisis of 1809, 103-104; list of banks, 104; panic of 1828, 106-108; pet banks, 113, 130-134; debate over legislation 1837-1846, 192-193, 201-202
Bank of the United States, xi; veto of bill to recharter, 3, 123, 127-128; war against, 103, 125-130, 135; war

against in N.H., 111-117, 121-125, 246; removal of deposits from, 119, 128-130; popularity of in N.H., 126; as issue in 1832 election, 137
Bank of the United States, Portsmouth branch: early policies, 104-108; appointment of Mason, 108-109; and election of 1828, 108-109; change in policies, 109-111; removal of pension funds from, 113-114, 124, 131-132
Barnes, J. O., 235
Barstow, George, 230
Bartlett, Ichabod, 37
Bartlett, Joseph, Jr., 25n
Barton, Cyrus, 168, 197-198
Bean, Benning, 56, 163-164
Beck, Gideon, 168
Bell, John (N.H.), 68, 72-73, 81
Bell, John (Tenn.), 67
Bell, Samuel, 31-32, 66, 84, 132, 243; and Dartmouth College case, 36-37; and state politics, 1822-1824, 48-49, 51, 57; and National Republican Party, 62-63; and elections of 1827-1828, 63-65, 68-69, 71-74, 78, 80; and rejection of Hill, 92, 95
Benson, Lee, 46n, 140-141, 159n, 171n, 183-184
Benton, Thomas Hart, 77, 87, 99, 181, 198, 221; and Panama Congress, 65; and Bank War, 123-124; and Democratic politics, 1844-1851, 234, 241-243
Berrien, John M., 66, 96

275

Berry, Nathaniel S., 228
Biddle, Nicholas: and N.H. Bank
War, 106-123; and national Bank
War, 125-126, 129
Blair, Francis Preston, 84, 87, 168, 236,
241, 243; and Bank War, 121, 123
Branch, John, 84-85
Brewer, Moses, 44
Brewster, Colonel Amos, 33
Broadhead, John, 40, 56, 87
Brown, Francis, 33, 36
Buchanan, James, 236, 244
Burges, Tristam, 67
Burke, Edmund, 168, 243-244; as a
radical Democrat, 187, 192, 201,
206-207; opposes antislavery move-
ment, 217-218
Butler, Josiah, 55
Butler, William O., 243

Cadwalader, Thomas, 116-117
Calhoun, John C., 65, 89; and Wood-
bury, 67-68, 83, 92, 94, 96; and cabi-
net appointments, 85; and Van
Buren, 89-91; and abolitionism in
N.H., 180-181; and Democratic pol-
itics, 1842-1844, 234-236
Cambreleng, Churchill C., 126
Canals, 43, 48-50, 59
Capital punishment, 172
Carroll, Henry H., 217, 224-225, 237
Cass, Lewis, 129, 160, 231; and Demo-
cratic politics, 1844-1852, 235, 237,
240, 244
Catterall, Ralph C., 122
Charles River Bridge case, 37-38, 43
Chase, Salmon, 239
Cilley, Joseph, 224n
Claggett, Clifton, 32
Claggett, William, 55, 221
Clapp, Asa, 10
Class conflict. See Social conflicts
Clay, Henry, 3; and N.H. politics
1826-1828, 61-65, 71, 73; attacked by
Hill, 97, 136; economic policies of,
99-100; and Bank War, 122; in elec-
tion of 1832, 136-138
Clinton, DeWitt, 41, 57
Cobb, Howell, 240
Colby, Anthony, 211, 228-229

Common man, 35, 69-71, 125, 137, 169
Compromise of 1850, 231
Concord, N.H., 3, 6, 17-18, 22, 49, 69;
and Portsmouth, 48-50, 58-59, 94;
banking in, 103; Jackson's visit to,
160-161; abolition meeting in, 177;
and railroads, 189-190, 201, 210
Concord Railroad, 188-190, 200-201,
205, 210
Concord Regency, 86, 94, 97, 111, 162;
and Independent Democratic movement, 221-225
Congregationalism, 173, 175-176; and
elections, 20-22, 29-30, 53, 60, 71;
and Toleration Act, 31, 39-40; in
Dartmouth College case, 33-34; and
election of 1832, 151-153, 255
Connecticut politics, 88, 138
Connecticut River valley, 6, 19, 48-49;
and War of 1812, 24-27; and elections of 1816, 1828, 30, 80; banking
in, 103; in election of 1832, 142-144,
250
Conservative Democrats. See Democrats, conservative
Constitution (U.S.): ratification of,
19-20
Continuity. See Political continuity
Corporations in N.H.: chartering of,
171, 182-183; number chartered,
182-183, 194, 206, 212-213; legisla-
tion concerning, 191-194, 201-206,
210-213
Cram, N. Porter, 221
Crawford, William H., 57-58
Cushman, Joseph, 4
Cushman, Samuel, 88, 92, 113
Cutter, Charles W., 61, 81
Cutts, Charles, 25

Dallas, Alexander J., 119
Dallas, George, 238
Dartmouth College, 9-10, 162; attack
on, 31-39, 71, 173, 246
Dartmouth College case, 36-39
Davis, Jefferson, 198
Decatur, John P., 88, 92
Degler, Carl, 186
Democratic convention 1844, 236-237
Democratic Party: and early Republi-

can Party, 16, 19-21, 27, 30, 42, 44-46; emergence of, 27, 35, 47, 60-64; called "Democrats," 42, 170; organization, 1826-1829, 60, 69-71, 74-75, 81, 162-168; political ideas of, 169-170; and social reforms, 170-184; and slavery, 170, 175-182, 216-233; split by locofoco movement, 185-215; change of generations, 197-198. *See also* Jacksonians, Jacksonian Democracy

Democrats, conservative, 186-187; on railroads, 188-191, 197-201, 209-210; on banks and corporations, 191-194, 201-207, 210-213

Democrats, radical: definition of terms, 185-187; on railroads, 188-191, 197-201, 209-210; on banks and corporations, 191-194, 201-207, 210-213; and antislavery movement, 217-220, 223

Dickerson, Mahlon, 66-67

Dinsmoor, Samuel, 161-162, 197; and War of 1812, 24, 27, 47; and politics 1823-1825, 47, 49-50, 53, 55; and election of 1832, 137, 139; and social reform, 171-172

Dinsmoor, Samuel (younger), 232

Doe, Joseph, 106

Donelson, Andrew J., 83-84, 160

Dorr Rebellion, 239

Drown, Dana, 92

Duane, William J., 129

Eagle Hotel and Coffee House, 3, 70, 136, 161, 243

Eastman, Moses, 35

Eastman, Nehemiah, 55

Eaton, John, 96, 114

Ela, Jacob H., 217, 218, 220, 223-224

Election of 1832, 20; campaign in N.H., 136-139; voting results, 139, 248; geography and, 142-144, 154, 249-250; farmland and, 145-146, 154, 251-252; tax rate and, 146-148, 153, 156, 252-253; Mount Monadnock section and, 147, 154, 253; labor vote in, 148-149, 154; population and, 148-151, 154, 254; correlation of economic and political data,

156-158, 256; religion and, 161-163, 255

Elections, presidential; 1804, 1808, 21-22; 1812, 30; 1824, 57-58; 1828, 19-20, 74-80; 1832: *See* Election of 1832; 1840, 196; 1844, 238; 1852, 243-245

Elections, state: 1800-1817, 17-30; 1823-1827, 47-64; 1828-1829, 68-74, 81, 94; 1832, 137; 1837-1841, 191, 194-196; 1842-1843, 203-207; 1844-1845, 208; 1846-1847, 211, 218-231; 1851, 231-232; 1854, 244

Ellis, Powhatan, 67

Embargo Act, 22

Eminent Domain, right of, 199-200, 208-210

Era of Good Feelings, 31, 47

Everett, Edward, 61-62

Exeter Junto, 17

Exeter, N.H., 12, 17, 22, 36, 155-156; election of 1816 in, 30; manufacturing in, 105; abolitionism meeting in, 177; railroads to, 189-190, 198; Independent Democratic meeting in, 222

Fairfield, John, 238

Farmers: and Republican Party, 17, 21, 30, 44-45, 51; and Jacksonian Democracy, 69, 164-166, 169; and Bank War, 108, 117, 123, 131; and election of 1832, 136; and radical Democracy, 186-187; and railroads, 199

Farrington, James, 164

Federalists, 42, 44, 91, 94-95, 174-176; and elections of 1800-1822, 16-23, 29-32; and War of 1812, 24-26; and Dartmouth College case, 31, 33, 34, 36-37; and elections of 1823-1826, 49-54, 60; and elections of 1827-1828, 64-65, 71-73, 77-81; and Bank War, 119, 123, 135; and election of 1832, 137-138, 144

Federal surplus in N.H., 189-191

Flagg, Azariah, 237

Fogg, George C., 226, 229

Folsom, Abigail, 177

Foot, Samuel A., 98-99

Freemasonry, 29, 45, 138. *See also* Anti-Masons
Free Soil Party, 222, 231
French, Benjamin V., 235, 244
Fugitive Slave Act, 231-232

Gag Rule, 182, 216
Garrison, William Lloyd, 176
George, John Hatch, 243
Gibbs, John T., 86
Gilman, John Taylor, 11-12, 78; and elections of 1800-1815, 17-22, 26-29
Gilman, Nicholas, 24
Gilpin, Henry D., 235
Goodrich, Chauncey Allen, 38
Goodwin, Ichabod, 224n, 227
Green, Duff, 83, 89, 91
Green, Thomas, 137
Greenleaf, Abner, 86, 88, 92, 94, 117, 168, 206
Grundy, Felix, 94, 96

Haddock, Charles, 208
Haines, Charles G., 58
Hale, John Parker, 87, 206; early career, 138, 165-166; and social reforms, 173; early opposition to abolitionism, 177, 216; anti-Negro feeling, 178; as radical Democrat, 199; and Independent Democratic movement, 216-233; opposes gag rule, 216-217; proviso and letter on Texas, 218; campaigns for Congress 1845-1846, 218-228; elected to U.S. Senate, 229; presidential candidate, 244-245
Hale, Salma, 60, 69
Hall, Obed., 24
Hallett, Benjamin F., 244
Hamilton, James A., 96, 121, 123
Hamilton, James, Jr., 74
Hamlin, Hannibal, 240, 243
Hammond, Bray, xi, 103, 134
Hammond, Jabez, 222
Hammons, Joseph, 40, 87
Harper, John A., 24
Harper, Joseph M., 133
Hartford Convention, 26
Harvey, John A., 25, 30, 113, 117
Harvey, Jonathan, 30, 66, 87, 91
Harvey, Matthew, 30, 35, 56, 87, 94,

197; and War of 1812, 24, 27; background of, 162; and social reform, 171
Haven, Joseph W., 112-113, 117
Hayes, John Lord, 219-221, 223, 225-226
Hayne, Robert, 94, 97
Henshaw, David, 87, 195, 236
Herald of Freedom, 177, 181-182, 216
Hibbard, Harry, 206, 229-230, 240-241, 243
Hill, Abraham, 3
Hill, George, 168
Hill, Horatio, 168
Hill, Isaac: and N.H. banking, xi, 5, 42-43, 102-106, 193-195; and election of 1832, 1, 136-137, 145; and Jackson, 3, 82, 98, 160-161, 242; early years of, 3-5; and internal improvements, 3, 43, 100, 187, 196; descriptions of, 3-4, 10, 47, 164, 196-197; family, 3, 23, 82; political views of, 3, 28-29, 34-35, 69, 187, 196, 246; and American Revolution, 4, 44; business interests of, 4, 5, 22, 47, 105, 134, 167, 196-197; government contracts of, 5, 32, 47, 61-62, 207; and Woodbury, 11, 28-29, 47-56, 92-95; and early N.H. politics, 23, 27-29; and War of 1812, 24, 27-28; organization of Republican Party, 27-28; and Freemasonry, 29, 45; and Dartmouth College, 33-39; and Toleration Act, 39-40; and Van Buren, 41-42, 60-61, 97; and Missouri debate, 41-42; and South, 41, 57; and social reforms, 44, 171, 173, 188, 196; and elections of 1823-1824, 47-57; organization of Democratic Party by, 61-64, 69-71, 74-81, 165-168; and elections of 1828, 69-71, 74-81; writings by, 75, 78, 167; in Kitchen Cabinet, 83-84; in Treasury Department, 83; and patronage, 83-89, 207n; and New England politics, 88-89, 168; at Jefferson Day dinner, 89; rejection by the Senate, 89-92, 124; in U.S. Senate, 95, 97-98; and land policy, 99; and tariff, 99-100, 105, 196; and Bank War, 105-

124, 127-128, 132-135; and slavery, 176-181, 187, 196; as governor, 1836-1838, 185-196; opposes radical Democrats, 187-192, 194-196, 200-201, 203-207; and railroads, 189-191, 200-201, 204; final years, 207, 236, 242-243; and Independent Democratic movement, 219-220, 224, 226
Hill, Susan, 4, 82
Hill, William, 204
Hillsborough Resolves, 26
Hill's New Hampshire Patriot, 197, 217, 220
Houston, Sam, 243
Hoyt, Jesse, 137
Hoyt, Joseph, 221
Hubbard, Henry, 35, 87, 161, 210, 243; and elections of 1824, 1828, 53, 64; role in Congress, 98; and pet banks, 134; background of, 162-163; and slavery, 176, 179-181; as a radical Democrat, 187, 191, 203, 205, 208; and elections of 1842-1843, 203-207; opposes Independent Democratic movement, 220; at Democratic Convention 1844, 237

Imprisonment for debt, 44, 171
Independent Democratic movement, 216-233; emergence of, 218-223; and elections of 1845-1846, 223-229; becomes Free Soil Party, 231-232
Indian policy, 99
Ingham, Samuel, 85; and Bank War, 108, 112, 114, 118-119, 121-123, 127
Insane, care of, 172
Interior of N.H., 6, 8, 19-21, 48-49; and War of 1812, 24-27; and election of 1828, 73; credit and banking, 103, 105-110, 112, 126. *See also* Mountain region, Uplands region
Internal improvements, 43, 70, 100, 171, 187, 191, 196
Issues, role of, 22, 46, 69-71, 81, 98-101; in Bank War, 102-103, 135; in election of 1832, 137-139; under radical Democrats, 205-206

Jackson, Andrew, 1, 82, 89, 100-101; early N.H. interest in, 27, 42, 60; and elections of 1824-1825, 47; in election of 1828, 64-65, 69-71, 75-80; and Woodbury, 65, 83, 85, 93; and Hill, 83, 92-98, 120, 242; and Bank War, 119-130, 133; in election of 1832, 136-139; visit to N.H., 160-161; last years, 236, 242
Jackson Day celebrations, 69-71
Jacksonian Democracy: interpretations of, xi, 16, 45-46, 80-81, 103, 135, 139-141, 158-159, 183-184, 246; concept of, xi, 169-170, 246; roots of, xi, 45-46; Hill's, 3, 69, 169, 188, 196, 246; in N.H., 14, 169-170; in 1828, 69-71, 81; in election of 1832, 139-159; and social reform, 170-184; Woodbury's, 169, 238-239; and locofoco movement, 214-215; and slavery, 232-233
Jacksonians, N.H.: in Washington, 82, 98-99; vote on BUS recharter, 127; influence on veto of BUS recharter bill, 128; comparison with political opponents, 165-166; social profile of, 164-166; as reformers, 183-184; on slavery, 232-233
Jaudon, Samuel, 120
Jefferson, Thomas, 21, 31-32, 51-52, 70, 170, 224
Jefferson Day dinner, 1830, 89
Jenness, John H., 113
Johnson, James, 224n, 231
Johnson, Richard M., 174, 196
Jones, John Paul, 11, 161

Kelly, John, 87
Kendall, Amos, 10, 168, 236; and party politics, 1829-1830, 83-86, 89, 91; and Hill-Woodbury conflict, 91-96; and Van Buren, 97; and Bank War, 121-130
Kimball, Samuel, 23
King, Rufus, 41
King, William, 48
King, William R., 181
Kitchen Cabinet, 83-84, 124
Kneeland, Abner, 174
Know Nothing movement, 244

Labor legislation, 212-213

Lafayette, Marquis de, 59-60
Land policy, 99
Langdon, John, 9, 17, 21, 23, 27, 35, 71
Lee, Henry, 89
Lewis, William B., 83, 87, 97, 120, 123
The Liberator, 179
Liberty Party, 216, 218
Limited liability, 191-194, 202, 205-206, 211
Locofocos, 185-186. *See also* Democrats, radical
Low, Joseph, 63, 86, 124, 137, 217
Low, William, 86

McCormick, Richard P., xi, 16, 22, 72, 80, 195
McLane, Louis, 85, 129
McLean, John, 61-62, 83, 86, 91
Madison, James, 70
Maine politics, 48, 168
Manufacturing in N.H., 14-15n, 104-105, 109, 132, 183, 186; comparison with other states, 202, 211, 214
Marshall, John, 38-39
Mason, Jeremiah, 22, 31, 32, 95, 104, 119; and Dartmouth College case, 35-36; and Missouri debate, 42; and N.H. politics 1824-1825, 53-55; and election of 1828, 68, 73, 108-109; president of Portsmouth branch, BUS, 108-117, 123-125, 135
Masters, William, 168
Maxcy, Virgil, 96
Maysville Road veto, 3, 100
Mechanics' Bank, 132, 134, 194
Merrimack County Bank, 5, 106, 114, 126, 131-134
Merrimack Valley, 6, 19-20, 48-49; and election of 1816, 30; and election of 1828, 80; manufacturing in, 105; and election of 1832, 142-144, 230
Mexican War, 229-231
Meyers, Marvin, xi
Missouri debate, 41-42
Monk, Maria, 174
Monroe, James, 30, 57
Moore, Jacob Bailey, 49-50, 54-55, 78
Morgan, William, 45
Morril, David L., 32, 243; in elections

of 1824-1826, 52-54, 56, 59-60; opposes Hill, 61, 63-64, 73, 78
Morton, Marcus, 236
Moulton, Mace, 224n
Mountain region of N.H., 19-20, 30
Mount Monadnock section, 19-20, 30; in election of 1832, 144, 147, 154, 253

National Republicans, 19-20, 27, 57; organization 1826-1829, 62-65, 68-69, 71, 77; social profile of, 165-166; and social reform, 175
Negroes in N.H., 179; hostility toward, 178-180
New Hampshire: government, 13, 31-32, 167; economy, 13-15, 214; population, 14, 150
New Hampshire Anti-Slavery Society, 177
New Hampshire Gazette, 50, 60-61, 94, 100, 133, 168, 178, 190, 219
New-Hampshire Patriot, 4-6, 22, 28, 42, 44, 47, 49; and War of 1812, 24, 26; and election of 1816, 29-30; and Dartmouth College case, 34; and internal improvements, 43, 100; and social reform, 44, 172-174; and election of 1823, 49-50; opposes Adams, 60; and election of 1828, 73, 78; and spoils system, 86; and Hill-Woodbury conflict, 94; and Indian policy, 99; and nullification, 100-101; and Bank War, 124, 130; and election of 1832, 136-138; and Jackson, 170; and slavery, 176-178; and railroads, 188-190, 209; on limited liability, 202, 204; and Whigs, 203; and Texan annexation, 217; opposes Independent Democratic movement, 220, 232
New Hampshire Statesman, 49, 77, 99, 136, 175, 188, 202, 217
Newspapers: Federalist, 18; N.H., 35; Republican, 62-63, 77; Democratic, 167-168
New York Free Banking Act, 193, 209
New York Free Corporation Act, 209
New York politics, 58-61, 77-78, 140
Noah, Mordecai, 89, 168

Norris, Moses, 200, 218, 227, 243-244
Noyes Academy, 179-180
Nullification crisis, 9, 100-101

Page, John, 171-172, 196
Palmer, Dudley S., 228
Panama Congress, 65-66
Panic of 1819, 42
Panic of 1837, 133, 194-195, 214
Parrott, John F., 55
Parton, James, 122
Peaslee, Charles, 172, 231, 241, 243
Penhallow, Thomas W., 117
Pet banks, 126, 130-134
Peverly, James, 226-229
Phillips Exeter Academy, 12
Pickering, William, 113
Pierce, Benjamin, 44, 49, 59-60, 66, 163; and Hill, 28, 30; elections of 1827-1829, 63-64, 70-73, 81; death of, 197
Pierce, Franklin: early years of, 53, 59-60, 162-164; and elections of 1828, 69-70, 72, 74, 78, 80; and rejection of Hill, 90-91; and nullification, 101; and pet banks, 131; and social reform, 173; and antislavery movement, 176, 181-182; as a radical Democrat, 187, 191, 197-198, 200-205; opposes Independent Democrats, 216-233; supports annexation of Texas, 217; and presidential election, 243-246
Pillow, Gideon J., 237, 244
Plumer, William, 95, 243; and War of 1812, 23, 26; and politics 1815-1825, 27, 29-31, 48-50, 55, 57; and electoral vote 1820, 57; and elections of 1827-1828, 63, 74, 75, 78; and Bank War, 115-116, 126; and election of 1832, 138
Plumer, William, Jr., 55, 63, 87-88
Poindexter, George, 98
Poinsett, Joel R., 234
Polk, James K., 219, 225
Political continuity, xi; from Republicans to Democrats, 16, 19-21, 27, 30, 42, 44-47; and public interest argument, 34-35, 37-38, 43; in the Dartmouth College case, 34-36; and

Toleration Act, 40-41; and Panic of 1819, 42-43; in elections of 1828, 1832, 72-73, 80-81, 144, 151
Portsmouth, N.H., 11-12, 20; and War of 1812, 25; and elections of 1816, 1823-1824, 30, 48-51, 54; and Concord, 48-50, 58-59, 94; banking in, 102-107
Prentiss, John, 73, 138
Prescott, Abraham, 172

Radical Democrats. See Democrats, radical
Railroads in N.H.: in 1836-1837, 188-191; legislation concerning, 188-189, 199-200, 209-210; number chartered, 188, 201, 206, 213; miles of track laid, 194, 201, 212; in 1839-1844, 197-201; in 1844-1850, 207-210
Randolph, John, 67, 182
Rantoul, Robert, 198, 236
Recession of 1834, 132-133
Reding, John, 218
Regionalism in N.H.: in politics 1800-1812, 17-20, 22; in War of 1812, 24-27; in politics 1822-1825, 47-51, 58-59; in Bank War, 110
Religious toleration, 174-175
Remini, Robert V., 116, 222-223
Renton, Peter, 132, 204
Republican Party (1850's), 222, 244
Republicans, 42; and elections 1800-1812, 17-23; party organization of, 18, 28, 45; and War of 1812, 24-29; and elections 1815-1822, 29-31; and Dartmouth College case, 33-37; program of, 42-46
Rhett, Robert B., 240-241
Richardson, William M., 32, 36-37
Richmond Junto, 166
Ritchie, Thomas, 162, 168
Rix, James Madison, 71, 168
Rix, Nathaniel, 71
Roads, 58, 154-155
Roane, William H., 237
Rockingham Memorial, 25
Rotation in office, 3, 29

Sargent, Nathan, 123-124
Schlesinger, Arthur M., Jr.: and Bank

War, 102, 135; and Jacksonian Democracy, xi, 140, 148-149, 157-159, 183; and locofocos, 185, 214-215; and antislavery movement, 223n
Seacoast region of N.H., 11, 19-20; and War of 1812, 22, 24-27; and election of 1816, 30; banking in, 103-105, 126; manufacturing in, 104-105; and election of 1832, 142-144, 250; and Independent Democratic movement, 223
Seward, William H., 231, 239
Shapley, James, 106-108
Shaw, Tristram, 200
Sheafe, James, 30
Simpson, Henry Y., 87
Slavery, 178-179
Smith, Jeremiah, 22-29, 31, 42, 53, 73, 78; and Dartmouth College case, 35-36
Social conflicts in N.H., 71-72, 77-78, 80-81, 140, 169; over banking, 103, 116-117, 123, 135
Social reforms, 44, 170-184, 214-215
South, interest in, 41, 57-58, 66, 98-101, 175, 216
Spirit of 1798, 71, 101, 169
Spoils system, 85-89. *See also* Isaac Hill, Levi Woodbury
Stagecoaches, 6, 12, 58
Stark, Caleb, 91-92
Stark, John, 44
State rights, 3, 101, 238-240
Steele, John H., 208
Storrs, George, 177, 216, 225
Sullivan, George, 17, 25, 37, 73
Sumner, Benjamin, 43
Sumner, William Graham, 122
Supreme Court (U.S.) cases, 1847-1849, 238-239
Swasey, Samuel, 200-201

Taney, Roger B., 37-38, 43, 84, 90; and Bank War, 123, 126-127, 130; Taney court, 238-239
Tallmadge, James, 41
Tariff, 67-68, 191, 196, 206
Tazewell, Littleton, 67, 90, 92, 97
Temperance movement, 173
Thompson, George, 177

Toleration Act, 39-41, 171
Treadwell, Thomas, 187, 190-191, 200-201
Tuck, Amos, 218, 221, 223-224, 231
Turner, Frederick Jackson, xi, 140, 148-149, 157-159
Tyler, John, 90, 92, 207, 217, 236

Union Boat Company, 49
Upham, Nathaniel, 87, 209
Upham, Timothy, 68, 72-73; replaced as port collector, 86, 88; director of Portsmouth branch of BUS, 111; candidate for governor, 94
Uplands region of N.H., 6, 8, 19-20, 30, 35; and election of 1832, 142-144, 250

Van Buren, Martin, 160, 196-197, 221, 225; and Missouri debate, 41-42; supports Crawford in 1824, 57-58; and N.H. politics, 60-61, 65, 74; and Panama Congress, 65-66; and Woodbury, 67-68, 234-236; and Kitchen Cabinet, 84; and cabinet appointments, 85; and Albany Regency, 86, 163; conflict with Calhoun, 89-91, 96; rejected by Senate, 89-90; and Bank War, 120-121, 123, 126, 129; and Democratic nomination 1844, 234-238
Van Ness, C. P., 74
Vermont politics, 88-89, 168
Verplanck, Gulian, 67, 77
Voting, percentage, 21, 79, 169, 195-196

Waldron, Isaac, 68, 113, 130
Walker, Timothy, 18, 20
War Hawks, 24, 27
War of 1812, xi, 23-29, 44, 47, 50, opposition to, 24-27; spirit of, 70-71, 169
Ward, John W., xi, 169
Washington *Globe*, 87, 122, 137, 168
Webb, James W., 91
Webster, Daniel, 12, 95, 242; and War of 1812, 22, 25-27; elected to Congress, 26; leaves N.H., 31; and Dartmouth College case, 35-39; and

N.H. politics, 1823-1825, 50-51, 55-56; opposes Hill, 62-67; and Panama Congress, 66; and Mason appointment, 108, 112, 114; and Bank War, 108, 115, 119, 122, 124, 135; and election of 1832, 139, and slavery, 231
Webster, Ezekiel, 31, 49-50, 65, 73
Weeks, John, 82, 86-87, 163
Welles, Gideon, 91, 138, 235
Welles, Jonathan, 161
West, interest in, 98-101
Wetmore, Robert C., 227
Wheelock, Eleazar, 32
Wheelock, John, 33-36
Whigs: in elections of 1838, 1840, 194-195, 203; and radical-conservative fight, 186, 192, 201-202, 205, 211; and Independent Democratic movement, 218, 221, 223, 227-229
White, Hugh, 67, 120
White, John H., 203-204
Whittier, John Greenleaf, 177, 222
Wiggin, J. B., 178
Wiggins, John, 220
Williams, Jared, 228-230
Wilmot Proviso, 230
Wilson, James, 195, 231
Wirt, William, 138
Woodbury, Elizabeth, 10, 82
Woodbury, James, 9
Woodbury, John (17th century), 9
Woodbury, John (of Salem), 221-224, 227-228
Woodbury, Levi: early years of, 9-11, 48; character of, 10, 28-29, 93-94, 96;

and War of 1812, 26-27; political beliefs of, 28-29, 31, 35, 51, 169, 238-239; and Republican Party, 28-30; and Freemasonry, 29; on state Superior Court, 32, 36-37; and Dartmouth College case, 33-37; and South, 41, 58, 65-66; and elections of 1823, 1824, 1828, 47-54, 71, 76-78; and Hill, 47-56, 92-95; U.S. Senator, 56, 98, 197; and N.Y. politics, 58; and Panama Congress, 65-66; and formation of Democratic Party, 65-68; and Jackson, 66-67, 160; dinner parties of, 67, 83, 92, 97; and vice-presidency, 67, 94, 234-238; and Calhoun, 67-68, 92, 94, 96; and Van Buren, 67-68, 234-236; and tariff, 67-68; and patronage, 83-88; Secretary of Navy, 84, 96; at Jefferson Day dinner, 89; and land policy, 99; and Bank War, 109-118, 123-133; Secretary of the Treasury, 130; and pet banks, 130-134; and radical Democrats, 187, 191, 203, 206-207; and Independent Treasury, 203; supports Texan annexation, 217; opposes Hale, 219-220; and Democratic politics, 1842-1851, 234-242; on the U.S. Supreme Court, 238-239
Woodbury, Luke, 93
Woodbury, Peter, 9
Woodward, William H., 33, 36-37
Wright, Silas, 176, 234, 236-238

Yancey, William L., 240-241
Young, Daniel, 39-40